"Every one of us has an "Inner Vegas" wanting to bestow upon us a fabulous life. Joe has a proven track record of success stories, and now he is sharing his infinite wealth of knowledge and inspiration so that anyone and everyone can tap into the infinite creative power within, and choose to consciously create a fulfilling and rich life!"

—Charlotte McGinnis, author, *A Golf Course in Miracles*

"A casino in Las Vegas is not the first place that comes to mind when one considers exploring unconditional love, performing experiments in quantum physics, or pursuing spiritual self-exploration. However, *Inner Vegas* interweaves experiences from each of these areas, and more, as Dr. Joe Gallenberger guides the reader along a winding path of personal growth and the manifestation of abundance. I personally participated in several of Joe's "Vegas Adventures" and can testify to the truth of not only the stories told, but the approaches taught, as Joe offers the wisdom and knowledge gained from a lifetime of self-exploration and experiences in realms of the anomalous, psi, and the extraordinary. Buckle your seat belt as you start reading *Inner Vegas*, as the reality of the importance of the journey rather than the map or the destination becomes clear."

—J. Richard Madaus, Ph.D., author, *Think Logically,
Live Intuitively: Seeking the Balance*

"Unexpectedly, Joe Gallenberger begins his story, *Inner Vegas*, with a painful loss, the departure of his brother. Soon after, we find him in Vegas, with an adventurous trip down the road of psychokinesis. I ask you, what better place could one choose to learn about the manipulation of machines and objects than where you can make lots of money? And through that very effort he steers us toward a greater understanding for what it is to be human. And being human, what we should be doing for the good of all. He speaks very clearly about how risk, change, and evolution of our beliefs can and does impact our future. This is an interesting book that fits our times to a tee."

—Joseph W. McMoneagle

"Both practical and inspirational, *Inner Vegas* takes you on a journey of discovery of the true dimensions of human potential. Tracing his own baby steps through the psychic world of PK (psychokinesis) and manifesting, Dr. Gallenberger finds an unlikely ashram at the Las Vegas casinos, where he diligently works to gain insight and mastery of mind over matter. He offers the fruits of his personal search to readers and program participants alike. Many down-to-earth tips and exercises spark each of us to experience the magic of discovering our own latent abilities and talents. Fascinating stories illustrate mind-stretching truths that change the way one thinks about how the world really works. Truly a journey to higher consciousness amid the Vegas lights!"

—Carol Sabick delaHerran, executive director
and president of The Monroe Institute

"This book is for everyone. All of us have to make decisions every day and I often second guess and doubt myself, because I'm worried that I'll do the "wrong" thing. Reading your book was a reminder for me to be open and awake to guidance, and to create and manifest what I desire to have in my life. And it works! When I pay attention to the principles that you teach, I am always surprised at the outcome—it's often even better than what I imagined. You offer practical and easy-to-use tips and techniques to polish the skill of manifestation that is within all of us! And, most of all, you make it fun!"

—Marinda Stopforth, residential facilitator, The Monroe Institute

Inner Vegas brings intuition, logic, and heart together, a magical formula for creating lasting abundance, inner confidence, and a new freedom to expand our horizons. Joe's principles work. I have accompanied him to the Vegas workshops and assisted in teaching his week-long courses for over ten years. As a result, I have witnessed countless 'miracles' of manifesting, healing, and PK that go beyond logic and move into the realm of the magical. *Inner Vegas* is uplifting, relevant and *liberating*.

—Patty Ray Avalon, author of *Inner States—Dawning of Awareness, The Creative Way* and *Positively Ageless with Hemi-Sync*

INNER VEGAS

Creating Miracles, Abundance, and Health

JOSEPH GALLENBERGER, PH.D.

RAINBOW RIDGE
BOOKS

Cover and interior design by Frame 25 Productions
Cover photo © Carsten Reisinger c/o Shutterstock.com

Published by:
Rainbow Ridge Books, LLC
140 Rainbow Ridge Road
Faber, Virginia 22938
434-361-1723

If you are unable to order this book from your local
bookseller, you may order directly from the distributor.

Square One Publishers, Inc.
115 Herricks Road
Garden City Park, NY 11040
Phone: (516) 535-2010
Fax: (516) 535-2014
Toll-free: 877-900-BOOK

Visit the author at:
www.SyncCreation.com
www.InnerVegas.com

Library of Congress Cataloging-in-Publication Data applied for.

ISBN 978-1-937907-10-5

10 9 8 7 6 5

Printed on acid-free recycled paper in Canada

To my brother John,
who is shining his light through adversity.

Acknowledgements

I thank my wife Elena for creating sacred space in our home, adventuring with me, and helping to edit this book. My appreciation is extended to Robert Friedman, president of Rainbow Ridge Books for believing in this project and bringing it to publication. I am filled with gratitude for all the participants who have been to my workshops, inspiring me by their love and by their courage, as they explore the far limits of consciousness.

Contents

PART 1

CHAPTER 1

Royal Flush in Hearts

For the past twenty years I have used psychokinesis to affect the outcome of games of chance such as dice and slots. When I am "on," I can achieve exactly what I envision. It is great fun! After a long day of teaching in Vegas, I went off by myself to unwind. I also had a specific goal in mind—to get a Royal Flush in hearts (Ace, King, Queen, Jack, and Ten of Hearts in one hand) on a video poker machine. I selected this target as a celebration of what I deeply know—that the power of the heart, which is love, is infinite, and can accomplish any goal. I tucked myself into a quiet corner of the casino. Just as I put my money in the machine and got settled in, I was surprised by several members of my class finding me in my hiding place. They asked if I would show them how to play. I had a split second to choose my response. I could say, "Hey guys, I am off duty and just want some alone time" or I could say "Come join me" but resent the intrusion. Instead, I chose to open my heart and said, "Sure, have a seat and I will show you how to play." I quickly shifted from the anticipated pleasure of being alone to appreciating the presence of their company. I welcomed them into the chairs beside me and explained how to play. They were very excited and had lots of questions, as the game is a bit complex. When they settled down, I focused back on my machine and two pulls later was rewarded with my Royal Flush in hearts. This jackpot occurs only once in 160,000 times by chance. My five dollar bet paid me about $4,300. I felt a rush of delight. As I gazed at the machine it seemed to sparkle with magical energy. I yelled, "Got it!" and pointed to the screen. My friends cheered and hugged me, clowning around and laughing, taking my picture with the machine as we waited for the casino supervisor. I glowed with gratitude as the supervisor counted out forty-three one-hundred dollar bills into the palm of my hand. Once again the Universe had a more elegant plan to carry me to my goal than what I had in mind. I had thought that it was necessary to be alone to be able to concentrate on my target. I was shown that the heart is more powerful than any carefully laid out mental plan. I was very happy that others who cared about me were there to share the event, making the experience richer still.

Inner Vegas discusses love and casinos, two topics that don't pair together often. Yet you will see that they can indeed go hand-in-hand and when they do, magic is created. *Inner Vegas* is a story about how to create stellar results in our lives in the areas that matter most: relationships, business, health, and happiness using an approach that I honed in the casinos of Las Vegas. *Inner Vegas* celebrates the miracle of life at its fullest. It invites you into deep levels of communion with the creative aspects of the life force. It encourages you to open to highest heart energy in each sacred moment. *Inner Vegas* can expand your manifestation and wisdom/intuition skills. It can help you actualize your full power and potential—body, mind, and spirit, so that you experience abundance in all ways.

There are many books about manifestation. This one is different in at least three major ways. *Inner Vegas* pulls together knowledge and first-hand experience and then applies this to the science of psychokinesis (PK)—the ability to influence matter with our intent. PK includes interesting abilities such as bending metal with your mind and growing seeds in your hand in five minutes. This book addresses the essential component of enhanced energy, which is often missing in discussions of abundance. And it activates, nurtures, and channels the tremendous power of our open and loving hearts. Learning the art of integrating psychokinesis, enhanced energy, and an open heart will launch you on your way to becoming a master manifester. I think one of the best ways to understand this art is by hearing someone else's story with all its pitfalls and victories. I hope that you will be inspired by my story to become a conscious creator of your highest dreams.

Some of this story occurs in casinos. If you like to play games of chance, and you apply the principles in this book, you may dramatically improve your gaming success. Yet many people when hearing what I do, say, "Oh, I don't gamble." This book can still be very enlightening and helpful to you as well. If you have married, had children, started a business, or even crossed the street sometimes without waiting for a green light, you are a high roller! In Vegas we play with pieces of paper (money) converted into chips and ideally back into money. In the rest of life we routinely risk much more important things including our health and happiness. Risk is good. It is how we learn, grow, and achieve new things. But we are not taught in school about how to risk intelligently, nor what tools to bring to the table to improve our chances of success. Since we each take risks all of the time, wouldn't it be good to learn to do this more skillfully?

Inner Vegas embodies the powerful premise that we are creating our own experience of reality all of the time. And, all members of the human family link together to create reality itself, all of the time. This premise is ancient. It was present in writings of sages from the middle Egyptian dynasties. The concept is also cutting edge new. It permeates modern physics.

We are usually not conscious of creating reality. Therefore this amazing fact, even if glimpsed, remains for most of us, just a thought—a weak belief. My mission is to make this thought compelling for you, to make the premise so real that it transcends belief, so real that you treasure it as a personal knowing. For when you know this deep in your gut, its power is unleashed for you to use for your benefit. When you fully understand and live this idea, your life is transformed.

The ideas articulated here are floating around within our cultural consciousness at this time in many forms. They are present in films, books, retreat centers, classrooms, places of worship, and think tanks. And I believe that when the fact that we create our reality is accepted, adopted, and lived by many people, our world will be transformed. I trust that *Inner Vegas* is in your hands at this moment to help you more consciously and consistently create what you desire.

This concept that we actively create our reality is an intriguing and an unsettling one. It operates in your life whether you believe it or not. But your power to use this concept in your own life will be in direct proportion to the extent that you know it to be true. It is a "faith can move mountains" kind of thing. And if faith can move mountains just think what a solid knowing can do!

The difference between weak belief and solid knowing creates a huge leap in impact and results. Where you are on the belief-to-known continuum dramatically influences your intent and energy. And this governs the degree to which you will be able to influence reality. Some readers may start this book from a place of strong disbelief in the idea that we create our reality. Some people have really not considered the idea before. Other people may lean towards belief, but experience much doubt, followed by people who feel that it is probable, and so on, up the continuum. At the end of the continuum is a place where the idea is deeply known, understood, proved, and becomes a personal truth. My hope is that this book will create new impressions and reactions that move you toward knowing that you create your reality. And through telling my story I will give you several pathways, many of which have nothing to do with casinos, that can take you toward your own solid concrete experience of this concept so that you can create the life of your dreams.

We can move from belief to knowing that we create our reality by activating this concept consciously and seeing the result. Vegas is a very elegant classroom and ideal playground for this type of experiential learning. The feedback during games of chance is almost instantaneous. This allows us to practice hundreds of times, and see, in comparative safety, the result of even slight changes in our approach. This allows for rapid progress from weak belief to powerful knowns. We can do this while risking only small amounts of money. If our new ways of thinking are successful, in addition to the knowledge gained, we can enjoy a financial profit as well.

In life, feedback about creating our reality is often delayed. For example, it may take years to build a business. Feedback also has the potential to be confused by the agendas of others. And feedback can at times be cruel or even fatal. I selected Vegas for this learning because the feedback is clear, quick, and safe. But if gaming is not your thing, we will also discuss safe ways to practice and get feedback in non-gaming settings. And as mentioned, the principles explored here have tremendous application outside the casino.

I want to give you a taste of what is possible when we know that we create our reality and then confidently apply appropriate power and energy to achieving our dreams. I surveyed eighty people who have worked with my home study manifestation course, *SyncCreation®*. You can learn more about this course at *www.synccreation.com*. Seventy-five percent responded, which is a very high percentage for a survey, and all sixty responding reported positive results. These reports may seem like miracles and magic, and they are. But they are the type of miracles that are our birthright as humans, if we know we create our reality and step into our power. Here is a summary of the survey results.

Health and Wellness

- Ten people healed their pets.

- Eight people each healed children.

- Five people gained self-acceptance.

- Three people healed their ADD and no longer required medication.

- Three people manifested increased memory for studies.

- Two people healed organs, preventing surgery.

- Two people received healing of chronic headaches and migraines.

- Two people significantly healed their fibromyalgia.

- Two peopled healed their acne.

- One person healed a grandparent.

- One person gained freedom from sleepwalking.

- One person received increased vision.

Abundance

- Six people manifested abundant travel.

- Five people were given small fortunes.

- Four people received multiple checks for thousands of dollars that arrived unexpectedly.

- Four people manifested specific breeds of pets.

- Three people created the home of their dreams.

- Two people created money to buy homes.

- Two people manifested hot tubs.

- One person created a swimming pool.

- One person discovered jewels they did not know they had.

- One person created free airline tickets.

- One person experienced books they wanted to read show up in unusual ways, such as on a park bench.

- One person manifested a free vehicle.

Professional

- Fifteen people gained important connections for work.

- Ten people negotiated contracts successfully.

- Three people experience the successful launch of new companies.

- Three people gained freedom from unhealthy work environments for much better positions.

- Three people received awards at work.

- Three people created multiple job offers.

- Two people obtained careers that cover living expenses plus health insurance.

- Two people received substantial promotions.

- Two people received an increase in profitable contracts to the point of nearing retirement.

- One person manifested a book offer, an advance, and 3 months in a cabin to write.

Relationships

- Ten people gained friendship.

- Eight people received important connections for love.

- Five people gained companionship.

- Three people received peace regarding difficult divorces.

- Two people created engagements.

- Two people were reunited with lost family members.

- Two people manifested successful adoptions.

- Two people each received freedom from an unhealthy relationship.

- Two people created rewarding relationships with life partners.

- Two people created safe homes for their families.

Get Lucky!

- Fifteen people manifested winning at casino craps tables.

- Eight people manifested winning at casino slot machines.

- Two people won raffles.

- One person won online poker tournaments.

- One person manifested winning at friend's poker nights.

Personal

- Virtually everyone experienced psychokinesis (PK) success.

- Virtually everyone experienced communication with ethereal, heavenly and other-worldly beings; guides; unborn children; and/or loved ones who have passed.

- Twenty people manifested joy in everyday life.

- Eighteen people were able to lucid dream.

- Five people received answers to important life issues that had prevented forward movement.

- One person turned unusable well water into usable well water.

- One person received acceptance to a prestigious school.

The people answering this survey are ordinary people who allowed themselves to become extraordinary. Quite a list, don't you agree? After reading it, what are you inspired to create in your life? Now, do you feel completely confident about how to go about accomplishing this? If not, keep reading, enjoy hearing about my adventure, and along the way you will pick up the tools to create your dreams. You deserve it!

Our reality is a function of our awareness, intent, and energy, as these processes interact with the awareness, intention, and energy of many other beings. This is very dynamic and forms an ecosystem every bit as alive, complex, and awe inspiring as are the patterns of nature on this planet.

Creation is the ecosystem in which you live. Your dominion (not domination) within the system expands exponentially with your understanding of it. For knowing to be complete, you must experience your creation power with both your mind and your heart. You must settle in, quiet down, and stay awhile in the magic land of manifestation. Consciously living your creatorhood is as joyful, challenging, and surprising as anything you have ever done.

This book is going to get personal. I want to reach you at a deep level. Given this, it is fair for the reader to get personal with me. It is fair to have questions such as: "Who is this guy? Should I listen to and trust him? Does he know what he is talking about?" A question I am asked by the bolder members of the audience when teaching about abundance are: "So, are you rich?" I reply to this question, yes I am rich beyond measure. With a lot of help, for which I am deeply grateful, I have co-created:

- wonderful, resilient health.

- a loving, passionate, and friendship-filled relationship with my soul mate.

- three amazing daughters that grace my life.

- extended family relations that delight me.

- friends of highest quality living around the world.

- an absorbing, creative, and meaningful career.

- a lovely home nestled among acres of beautiful forested mountains within a dynamic community of peace and goodwill.

All these delights nurture, support, and inspire me on a path of ever-expanding amazement at the beauty and sacredness of life. And perhaps the most precious blessing is that I have developed a core of happiness and peace within my own soul. This blessing flowered after a long period in the desert of crushing depression. Inner peace allows for the appreciation of all the gifts of life. I remember how it is to be without it. Depression and anxiety dull awareness, intent, and energy. Unfortunately many of us are living with at least some depression and anxiety transmitted to us from the stressful world we live in.

I have deep compassion for all of us, including myself, for the times when we lose our awareness of the magnificent nature of life; when we experience tiredness, struggle, grief, confusion, pain, and powerlessness without the comfort of awareness of the grand plan. I have great respect for the courage it takes to be human. Sometimes I feel that to be given life as a human is like being given a powerful sports car and then being asked to drive it blindfolded (with no awareness of what the future will hold on the road that we choose nor the direction that is best). We constantly need to make decisions based upon incomplete information and then have to live with the consequences that result for ourselves and the people we love. Sometimes what seem like very minor decisions result in very important consequences. There is a recording called, *The Human Holiday*, which describes the human experience in humorous terms. On it the narrator is a realtor who is trying to sell spirits on incarnating. He says, "Are you tired of unending bliss, I have a place you can forget that bliss even exists. Come to planet Earth!"

My gratitude for my own abundance and the welfare of those I love is unbounded. I know much of this is a function of grace and not my own doing. As part of my thanksgiving I want to ignite in those whom I touch, the abundance creating ability that I know is our birthright. Emerson defined success as follows: "To laugh often, to earn the respect and affection of others, to appreciate beauty, to find the best in others, to leave the world a better place by garden patch or social condition, to know even one life breathed easier because you have lived." I hope to be successful by this good definition.

I am writing this book from the heart and will be honest and open. This is because integrity has amazing power. I am writing from the "still learning explorer" position because that is where I truly am at this moment. I am creating this book as I create my life—with a dream and plenty of hope in how it will come out. I bring to this book quite a bit of experience and expertise, but concerning the creation ecosystem there is plenty of mystery remaining to be uncovered.

CHAPTER 2

Background

One of the most frequent questions people ask me once they hear about what I am doing with psychokinesis, energy healing, and manifestation, is: "Is there something special about you, that you can do these things?" Sometimes I think that is a polite way for them to ask, "Are you for real?" or, "Are you from another planet?" What I think is behind these questions is a deep desire to know, "Are these things real? Can anyone do these things, and can I do these things?" These are very legitimate questions, given the subject matter is so divergent with what most of us have been taught about human limitations.

I think that these skills are part of our inborn abilities and that anyone can tap into them. Much of what is required is to unlearn ideas and behaviors that block these abilities. A good analogy is learning to play the piano. With lessons and practice just about anybody can learn to play. I did. But no matter how much time I put into practice and lessons, I probably would have never reached the level of world class concert pianist. The good news is that way before that, the piano can provide much enjoyment and meaning in one's life and also provide joy to others. I think that it is the same for these psychokinesis skills. You don't have to be performing at a world class level to obtain great value from learning these skills. Frankly, I have been working with these skills for two decades and I don't consider myself much further along than an "average pianist" compared to what I think the potential is for these activities. Yet even at this mid-level performance the miracles that are possible are amazing. So the short answer is yes, I am for real, these things are for real, and most people can do these things with proper preparation.

I would like to spend a little time giving my background, so that you get to know me a bit as a person and understand some of the pivotal experiences that have led me down this path. PK, healing, and manifestation are about raising and focusing a very high positive energy. Having strong curiosity, a loving nature, and a deep spiritual connection have made my learning easier. And I think that some of my experiences and the resulting limiting beliefs made my journey more challenging, such as a family history of depression, and my lack of confidence.

I was born in a small town in Wisconsin as the second youngest child in a Catholic family of seven. At that time my father was a linotype operator and my mom was a homemaker. Both my parents came from families of six siblings, so there were lots of aunts and uncles around the house most of the time. One of the biggest social things we did at home was playing cards. I have many fond memories of first watching and then playing canasta, sheepshead (very popular in Wisconsin at that time), and cribbage. We would play for hours at the large dining table as wonderful smells wafted out of the kitchen. There was much laughter, cuddling on laps for the younger children, and munching on freshly baked cookies. The adults would help me hold the eleven cards required in canasta in my small hands, remind me of the rules, and coach my play. I became very familiar with games of chance at an early age and such games were associated with love and laughter. These early experiences with games allowed me to later have very positive expectations in the Vegas gaming environment.

When I was four we moved to the Boston area when my dad was promoted. Although we now lived on the East Coast we made many trips back to the family home in Wisconsin. I can remember traveling by train on the Commodore Vanderbilt. One of the coolest things was ordering from the train-shaped menu and enjoying the steaming breakfast as we rushed along the rails. Less pleasant and more terrifying was a plane trip on a Capital Airlines Viscount prop plane through heavy thunderstorms over the Great Lakes. I remember the stewardess crawling on her knees to pass out air sick bags to almost every passenger.

We moved again when I was six to northern New Jersey when my dad became vice-president in charge of sales for his company, Banta Corporation, a book printing company. We always had tons of free books brought home for our perusal. My dad and mom both loved everything about books from the quality of their bindings to the ideas within. With my parents' encouragement, from the time I was very young I read voraciously on a wide variety of topics. We continued to play cards as a way to establish friendships in the new neighborhood and visit with family when they came east. The games changed to pinochle, hearts, bridge, and poker. Small amounts of money (pennies when the kids were playing) were bet to increase the fun. My mom was concerned that the kids would "get hurt" by losing their money and she would sometimes try to throw the game in our favor. My dad thought it was all in good fun and a good character building experience. It taught me that actions have results, that fear and greed can be expensive, and that sometimes intuition in the form of a clear knowing what card would come next, saved the day.

Starting at about age seven I began having experiences that one could label as mystical, weird, or nonsense, depending upon one's beliefs. In these experiences I would become a point of consciousness at one with all other beings and filled with complete love. These experiences happened spontaneously and always when I was alone. They usually occurred while I was resting on my bed, not at all sleepy but relaxed. The room would fade, shimmer, and become translucent, and then the experience transcended physical reality. While I have described myself within the experience as a point of consciousness, in fact there was no dimension or center, there was just the One. I was "It," just as everyone and everything from the smallest particle to the largest galaxy was "It." All there really seemed to be was massive, hugely intelligent, delicate, and all-powerful love within whatever "me" was left and also throughout the entirety of the One.

While these oneness experiences would happen rarely, they had a hyper-reality to them, seeming more real than our usual reality. Although it might last for only an hour or so each time, they touch me deeply even now, more than fifty years later. It was as if a huge rock was dropped into the center of the pool of my consciousness sending ripples through all of my life. Indeed, it feels as if gentle ripples from these events are there in each day that I live. They are gentle enough that I can completely ignore them for long periods particularly if I let myself become preoccupied about something, but if I quiet down and tune in they are always there.

From my current perspective as a psychologist, I would say that these experiences were not psychotic hallucinations. I would return from these states feeling very solid, fully organized cognitively, and able to function at a normal level in every way. There was no sense of self-importance or grandiosity one sees in paranoid perceptions. Rather there was a quiet humility and calm.

Some neurologists looking for a pathological explanation might have called what I experienced a form of temporal lobe epilepsy called Dostoyevsky epilepsy, which is named after the famous author who experienced similar states. This temporal lobe idea may be significant in that later I found that high frequency synchronous gamma brain wave patterns in the temporal lobes are associated with reports of various psychic phenomena, which scientists call PSI functioning, such as telepathy, out-of-body experiences (OBE), and psychokinesis, all of which are of high interest to me now.

Whatever these experiences were, they were intense. Here is Dostoyevsky's[1] own description of his experience, related by his friend Nikolay Strakhov. "For several moments," he said, "I would experience such joy as would be inconceivable in ordinary life—such joy that no one else could have any notion of. I would feel the most complete harmony in myself and in the whole world and this feeling was so strong and sweet that for a few seconds of such bliss I would give ten or more years of my life, even my whole life perhaps." I would not say that they were worth my whole life, but for me also these type experiences are definitely treasured.

In addition to a half-dozen oneness experiences, I also had about a hundred out-of-body experiences in childhood, where my consciousness would float up and travel to many places around the neighborhood and to distant locales. I sometimes got confirmation that this was more than imagination. What I perceived was going on in locations beyond my home would at times be verified in great detail. For example I observed my brother eating Oreo cookies, reading page 108 on a particular book at his location hundreds of miles away from me. When I called him, he verified that was exactly what he was doing at that time. When visiting places in the OBE state I could often perceive in high detail the enhanced sights,

---

1 Diagnosing Dostoyevsky's epilepsy, 2007 April 16, by Mo http://neurophilosophy. wordpress.com/2007/04/16/diagnosing-dostoyevskys-epilepsy/

sounds, and smells of that location and be telepathically connected to anyone that I encountered. I could communicate with them by just using thought and could feel their emotions as well. There was also an amazing high energy that made everything extraordinarily beautiful.

These OBE's happened most commonly when I was close to but not within the sleep state. I might find myself thinking of riding my bicycle, which I loved to do. I would be fantasizing about zooming down a hill and suddenly the handlebars would lift off the bike with me still holding on to them and I would begin to fly. As I recovered from the surprise I would know that I was out of body again and could direct myself in consciousness to wherever I wanted to go. These experiences resulted in an excited feeling for days, and again I would not judge them to be fantasy or a sign of mental illness.

As a child I never told my parents about my experiences. They felt sacred and private. Given the intense beauty of these experiences and my background, two things happened—when I came back to ordinary reality, I wanted to leave for the heavens again ASAP! I also wanted to understand what was happening to me. There are Eastern religious explanations of this type experience based on the Kundalini awakening model. But given my family background, I interpreted the experiences though a Christian filter. By ten years old I began reading about the Christian mystics, and their powers. I was impressed with their deep love of God and their personal relationship with that energy. They all seemed to develop a boundless compassion for their fellow man as a result of their ecstasy experiences. As the spiritual experiences continued for me, I also found myself bursting with empathy and compassion. I wanted it to be my life's purpose to be of service and to more deeply delve into the Infinite.

By fifth grade I felt disenchanted with physical life. I understand that is a strange statement to make, but it is as true as I know how to speak about my feeling that the spiritual world was more real than the physical. This sense that the physical world is only tenuously real can be part of the perceptual progression that allows us to see that we are creating this reality. Most of my friends, and the adults that I knew as I was growing up, were interested in things that had little interest for me. Given my mystical experiences, and Christian background, I planned to enter a monastery feeling at that time that such a retreat would be the ideal place to explore consciousness within a like-minded and dedicated community.

I visited a monastery run by the Passionist order in Newark, New Jersey. The Passionists followed a mystic named Saint Paul of the Cross, who had lived in Italy from 1694 to 1775. The religious order he founded lived a life that balanced living within the cloister with activities in service of the outside community. The orders strong guiding principles were compassion and sacrifice. The neighborhood surrounding this Passionist monastery was a typical rough and tumble city with the much agitated vibrations and signs of decline in Newark in the 60's. As I entered the monastery door I was hit physically with an amazing change in vibratory or energy state. The inside of the building almost glowed with peace, order, and presence of spirit. I knew that I was home.

St. Paul of the Cross describes his founding of the order[2]: "I began to write this holy rule (for the Passionist Order) on the second of December in the year 1720, and I finished it on the seventh of the same month. And be it known that when I was writing, I went on as quickly as if somebody in a professor's chair were there dictating to me. I felt the words come from my heart." I find this statement interesting in that I often experience the same thing when I write. When I write from the heart, it flows as easily as if someone were dictating to me.

I had to wait until ninth grade to enter a Passionist seminary in Dunkirk, New York, where I was taught deep contemplation. During the first year there I felt the most profound sense of peace that I had experienced until that time. When one stops talking and devotes much time to meditation and prayer, the mind becomes still and the heart opens. We maintained silence except for group prayer and school lessons. The prayers were in Latin and followed what is called the Divine Office which has been sung continuously within monasteries around the world since the sixth century. It consists of reciting or chanting special prayers at several periods throughout the day and night (including sunrise, sunset, bedtime, and getting up at 3 a.m. to chant).

I think the Latin and all that chanting were very instrumental in

---

2 "Life of St. Paul of the Cross," II, v, Oratorian Series

inducing transcendental states. I even began to dream in Latin! But from what I know now, I think that joining our energies together as a community of a hundred monks linking with thousands of others at prayer around the world, was perhaps the most powerful part of this whole experience. It is true that "where two or three are gathered together" in love, that the transcendent easily manifests. This became one of my first experiences with the incredible power of group intent.

But then my plans changed, or were changed for me by guidance. The short version is that in the second year (sophomore high school) I had a radical shift in how I felt at the seminary. I became very lonely for close one-to-one contact with people. Such contact was prohibited in the monastery. And also I discovered that the vow of obedience to one's superiors was odious to my independent temperament. To top it off it did not feel right (and perhaps even impossible) to suppress the rising sexual energy of adolescence that I was experiencing.

I found the monastery very confining and left. Yet I was distressed at being back in "this mean old world" and unsure about what to do with my life. Back at home I became angry, rebellious, and depressed. The exception to this was whenever I found someone to exchange loving energy with. There was an ancient man in the neighborhood that no one visited. He had been a brilliant architect. I loved the man's stories, his memory filled home—and his eighteen cats. He proudly possessed an immaculate 1926 silver Cadillac. He never drove it. It remained a shiny secret in his garage that he let me explore. The car was definitely the only thing spotless about the man. After supper on hot summer evenings, the gentleman and I would take off on bicycles and go all the way to town, the old man spinning a shaky path on his old Schwinn. We would return, hot from hill climbing with half a dozen flavors of ice cream to feed the cats. We would re-enter his musty house and feed the cats first. There was plenty of yowling as the ice cream was dished out, then a concert of quiet lapping. After our feast, I would listen with rapt attention to his stories about the Roaring Twenties, the Great Depression, and the World Wars.

I spent my teens experiencing very strong emotional ups and downs and enjoying friendships and dating. I took back up with my two best friends from grade school—we were nearly inseparable and got into our fair share of trouble. We would lie to our parents about going to the movies in a nearby town and then head instead by bus to Greenwich Village or 42nd Street in New York City and have adventures. My first puppy-loves provided a sweet oasis from the depression and anger. During these years my dad, sometimes accompanied by my mom would vacation in Las Vegas. They would always come home looking refreshed. I bet just getting away from their five kids was a high point! They would talk about the shows and my dad would either say that they won at the tables, or the code for not doing so well, "we had a great time."

I finished high school in 1968 and applied to Catholic University in Washington, D.C. because of the quality of their psychology program and the school's affordability, and not the fact that it was a Catholic organization. By then I had given up on institutional Christianity as too distorted and corrupted by power. But I kept a deep desire to connect with spirit and a strong faith that we live in an intelligently designed universe. At Catholic University I studied western psychology and eastern religions. I pursued my out-of-body travels on the side. I learned to be able to go out of body at will and achieve fairly good control of the experience.

By then I had gone into therapy for my depression and found it very helpful. It triggered a strong passion to understand how we work psychologically and firmed up my plan to become a psychotherapist myself. For the first time ever in school I was actually interested in nearly all of my courses.

Campus life in Washington, D.C. was intense, with drugs, returning veterans from Vietnam telling us what was really going on there, and the antiwar movement. The government tightened its hold on our Capital, as demonstration after demonstration threatened to disrupt the business of government. I drew number 237 in the draft lottery and did not have to go to Nam. In the dorm we played a lot of cards, mostly the game called hearts, to avoid working on the assignments we did not want to do. The games also were a way to escape from all the pressures we were feeling. I also learned to play a decent game of poker and became interested in understanding the nature and relationship between chance, intuition, synchronicity, and grace.

I had always been drawn to spending time in the woods. The physical and psychic quiet of the forest helped balance and ground my energy, and connect me with spirit. While in D.C. I bought a Honda 350 motorcycle.

I would take the bike many weekends up into the Shenandoah Mountains and camp by myself along the Skyline Drive.

When I was 21, on the way to school a few days after Thanksgiving of my senior year, I had a motorcycle accident. I heard a loud snap as the car crushed my leg between its bumper and the motorcycle, and then I went flying in the air. As I landed there was an explosion of pain that was so total that it had a terrible beauty, sort of like a nuclear explosion. Then complete peace—I was floating about twenty feet above my body, clear and calm in consciousness, while I could see my body in the street flopping around in pain. I could see the cars coming as the light changed on the busy six-lane road. I felt complete detachment from the scene below, just mildly interested as three lanes of traffic approached my body lying there.

My attention then focused on a being of light who appeared and telepathically told me I was going back into my body. That didn't seem like a good idea to me at all, given that I could see that my helmet, with my head still inside it, was crushed like an egg and my left knee was about where my hip should be. The being was compassionate but strong-willed and back I went into my body, and into a nightmare of intense pain and anxiety. I spent four months in skeletal traction, six months in a body cast and eighteen months in a long leg brace. It was my first big lesson about needing to rely on other people (in this case for my most basic needs) and this scared me. I fancied myself an independent person and liked to do everything for myself. In reality we are all profoundly interdependent on one another, and I was forced to accept this fact at a core level.

During recovery I had a lot of time on my hands and read several books a week. I studied Egyptian hermetics, a system of meditation and magic, and practiced my OBE skills. A Catholic University professor, Father Sumoko came to my hospital room and tutored me in Eastern religions so that I could complete my course work and graduate on time. He brought stacks of his personal books for me to read as well. I suspect he was sent by angels to keep me sane during this long period of confinement.

Father Sumoko was one of the most dedicated and challenging teachers I have ever experienced. He was a Jesuit who had lived in India for twenty years. He started my first class in Philosophy freshman year by coming in the first day and saying, "Two-thousand word essay by tomorrow on "Why we are here. No questions, see you tomorrow." The new freshmen, including me, went berserk with anxiety, firing questions at him such as, "Who do you mean by we?" and, "Where do you mean by here?" But he just walked out of the room. We began to think hard that very first night. During the semester he took each of his students out individually for dinner and showed genuine interest in their ideas and plans.

The severe knock on the head and the resultant OBE or near-death experience during my motorcycle accident could be part of a triggering of psychic potential, as there are many reports of such trauma preceding an increased activation of psychic ability. In my work I have seen many people who do well with psychokinesis having had such experiences. But I have seen many who have never had such traumatic experiences also do well.

I had always been physically active in football, track, swimming, etc. The restricted motion of the body cast (I could not even kick myself for the accident) forced me to confront my inner self, and the reality of the body, and to depend on others—all areas that needed work. I played the piano for many years and always loved music. While in the body cast I found that I could remember entire symphonies, and play them note by note within my mind.

The hardest part was my dependence on others for the simplest bodily functions and for kindness. Often the most unexpected people would be the kindest. The hospital janitor was more likely to be kind than the doctors. I began to understand the tremendous quiet power in kindness. I finished this initiation a much different person. The anger was gone. I also promised my mom never to ride a motorcycle again! Before the accident happened I thought when riding, that I would either be fine or dead. I learned there is a vast land in between these two states that is hell to visit. I graduated college on crutches recuperating at my parents' home.

Though the incapacitation was useful, it was highly unpleasant and resulted in my adopting two important affirmations from which to create my reality that have served me well when I remember them. As you will see sometimes I still forget them to my detriment. The affirmations are: "Small lessons please, I will pay attention" and, "I am willing to learn through abundance and joy."

I still wanted to help others and understand myself better. After working for two years in Washington, D.C. as a psychiatric specialist in a mental hospital, I went back to school at the University of Memphis and obtained a Ph.D. in Clinical Psychology. Things were fairly quiet during this period except a lot of hard work on the degree. Clinical Psychology is a rigorous program of five years of post-graduate study. Besides learning about human personality and development, and methods of treating mental illness, one was expected to become well-versed in the scientific method, and research design and analysis. I tell you this because later these science skills would come in handy to objectively assess what I was experiencing in Las Vegas.

I met my first wife, Charleene, during graduate school. She also achieved her Ph.D. in psychology. We completed our internships at the Pittsburgh VA hospital and then moved to North Carolina in 1979. There, I first worked as Director of Psychological Services for the community mental health center and in 1981, began a traditional therapy practice. My wife and I bought a home and settled into family life. My first marriage lasted twenty years. We adopted a beautiful baby girl when she was one day old. Raising her further opened my heart. I particularly loved teaching her about the magic of the woods and the world.

This North Carolina place with eight acres, sitting on what is reputed to be an ancient Cherokee power spot and energy vortex has been my home and haven for the past 33 years. It sits atop a mountain knoll with views out the back overlooking a twenty-mile-wide valley into the Blue Ridge Mountains, and out front is a 4,000-foot peak. There are over 200 waterfalls in the area and much mature and diverse woodland with thousands of acres of state and national forest. Our property has towering old trees and you can go for a walk in any direction and be sheltered within them in minutes. The first time my wife, Elena, walked here alone she felt a strong presence behind her. When she turned, she had the impression of a huge Cherokee warrior holding an axe and conveying the message that she would always be protected on this land.

Throughout the years of raising three wonderful girls and with all the travel that I now do, I have been so grateful that I can call this place of peace and beauty home.

CHAPTER 3

Brother Peter

I'd like to take a break from my history by telling you another slot machine manifestation story from Vegas. A friend, "Bill," my wife Elena, and I were playing slots at Palace Station Casino in Las Vegas. We liked the Station because it was designed to appeal to locals. It was modest but clean, had decent rooms and food, and the slot machines seemed to pay off more often than at the fancy Strip casinos. We went down to a bank of Video Poker machines and Elena and I sat together with Bill playing a machine right behind us. As we started Bill quickly got a Four of a Kind (four of the same card, such as four Jacks). This hand occurs only once in 423 times by chance. Within ten minutes or so we had thirteen Four of a Kind's between the three of us, which is pretty phenomenal. Bill had the most. It was great fun!

On our next trip out we went to the same machines. Bill again got a Four of a Kind quickly. He and I have a friendly competition going over the years on the video poker machines. We are genuinely happy for each other when either of us hits big and often help each other, at times sharing the winnings. On this occasion, after he tapped me on the shoulder with his first Four of a Kind, I felt a strong desire to get something better although I remained in the mood of light-hearted fun. I immediately got four aces and a four. They presented as if the aces were your fingers and the four the thumb. This occurs only once in 13,536 times by chance. The machine paid me $1,000 on a $2.50 bet. Now it got really strange—moments later my wife got the identical hand on the machine beside mine—four aces together with a four, presented as if the aces were your fingers and the four the thumb. She was also paid $1,000. The odds of this happening are hard to figure but look to be one in millions. All three of us were really excited about this. Once again we had proof that what we were learning about creating reality really works.

In my thirties and forties, my psychology practice and home-life kept me busy and fulfilled. Yet I still had curiosity about non-physical realms. In the late 1980s my older brother Peter came to live with us. We set him up in an apartment in the top floor of my therapy practice building. He was down on his luck after a bad car accident, several business failures, and now the ending of a relationship. He stayed with us for a few years and it was wonderful to get to know him more deeply. He had saved my butt many times as I was growing up. And we both had the bond of being the least traditional and most rebellious in our family. We again played poker together as we had done when we had lived in New Jersey. He was an excellent player.

As he moved in, Peter was just finishing the book, *Far Journeys* by Robert Monroe, and he shared it with me. At that time Robert Monroe was the leading expert in out-of-body travel and technology-assisted meditation. Peter and I shared our OBE experiences and it reignited my passion for the subject. This led me eventually to the Monroe Institute (TMI) in rural Virginia. TMI is kind of a Holy Grail place for the study of consciousness. Over 30,000 people have attended TMI's residential programs over the past 35 years. Folks from a large variety of backgrounds attend from all over the world. People from the highest levels of government and industry, Hollywood stars, scientists from all fields, medical personnel, homemakers, and students are attracted by their common interest in consciousness exploration. I recall one young man who came from Japan and worked in the kitchens of New York City for years to learn English and to gather the money to attend the Institute.

Robert Monroe developed a stereo sound technology that helps people easily achieve altered states of awareness. This unique sound technology, called Hemi-Sync®, enhances the effectiveness of meditation by easing brain-wave patterns into a synchronous state. The Institute has an extensive website at *www.MonroeInstitute.org*. It describes their activities which include residential programs, community programs, home study materials, a professional division, a consciousness research division, and a healing circle group from which anyone can request healing without charge.

I attended the Institute's introductory Gateway Voyage® program and found it to be one of the most profound weeks of my life, opening many doors of energy and perception. There, I experienced many out of body states, deep oneness states reminiscent of my childhood experiences, and a state of flowing unconditional love. It was wonderful to be there with so many people who were successful, intelligent, and also had psychic experiences such as OBE. One of the things that I liked best was there was no dogma that you were required to believe. Catholic priests, Buddhist monks, atheists, and agnostics all can attend comfortably. Because of the gamut of professions and diverse cultures represented within a typical group, there is a very dynamic exchange of ideas and perceptions during the social times in the residential programs.

Gateway also opened the door to rapid manifestation for me. I won $10,000 in stereo equipment the week I returned home. This was the perfect prize for me since music is a great passion for me but I would never have been able to justify such a purchase at that time. A week later I won $100 in a radio contest. When I wanted a stamp, there would be one on the ground. When I wanted money, a twenty-dollar bill appeared neatly folded at my feet. I began attending the Institute's graduate programs and soon after became a trainer—another manifestation, given the ample supply of applicants. The ecstasy states I experienced during childhood returned as I applied the meditation techniques that I learned at Gateway. After Gateway my decades-long depression faded and then simply vanished. It has never returned—hallelujah! TMI was a lifesaver for me, as it is for many who attend its programs.

My brother Pete was excited to see all the impact that Gateway had on me, but in his depression, declined to go himself. After living with us for about two years and not being able to find work in my small town, he headed to Las Vegas where he had some connections. Vegas was booming at the time, but Peter still struggled to find work. He had the black mark of bankruptcy on his record and in Vegas most employers required a clean credit history to help guard against temptations toward theft, with all the casino money floating around. I visited him in Vegas a few times and while he put up a good front, I could tell he was under tremendous strain. Peter's plight generated some burning questions for me. He was loved deeply by family and friends. How could someone that I knew to be handsome, creative, hard-working, intelligent, and ethical have such difficulty manifesting the basic blessings of steady work? Why did life often go more easily for others who seemed to have lesser gifts and character than he did? How does manifestation work? These questions still direct much of what I do more than twenty years later. One of many things that I learned from Peter's life was that it was not sufficient to be a good man, for he was a very good man. One also has to feel abundant, and to feel deserving of good, for abundance to flow to you.

In 1991 I was in Monroe Institute's first Lifeline program as a participant. The program was designed to use meditation-induced altered states of consciousness to connect with and help people with the death and dying process, including communicating with them on the other side once they had passed over. This turned out to be fascinating process and Lifeline continues to be a popular program today.

As part of the evaluation of that first program all participants were brain-mapped. A 24-lead EEG neuromapper was attached to one's head so that brain-wave patterns during meditation could be analyzed. My analysis came out unusual. Most people have a resting occipital (back of the head) alpha wave pattern, which is associated with fairly narrow-field attention. I have a resting temporal (side of the head) gamma pattern which is associated with wide field attention and which can look like Attention Deficit Disorder (ADD) because one is aware of so much of the stuff that is usually just background, that one is easily distracted.

Temporal gamma activity is also associated with psychic abilities that involve increased sensitivity, such as telepathy and energy healing. It also appeared that I had learned to dampen my sensitivities in order to live within the chaotic vibes of the world. The scientists at TMI suggested that this dampening might be difficult to overcome as it was so entrenched. While I was the first to be mapped with this gamma pattern at the Monroe Institute, since then they have discovered others with this pattern as well. And while this pattern can be associated with psychic phenomena, other people have great psychic ability without showing this pattern. And once again I want to mention that most people can activate their psychic ability if given proper training.

At this point I had experienced the OBE's mentioned and a good bit of telepathic and clairvoyant activity, but no psychokinesis with one exception. During my first Monroe program, Gateway, a fellow partici-pant complained of headache. I had a strong feeling at that moment that if I touched his head I could remove his headache. I asked his permission, and then put my hands on his head for about 30 seconds and his headache went away instantly.

One week after the first Lifeline in July, 1991 my beloved brother and best friend, Peter, committed suicide. This devastated me and my family. I was the first relative to be contacted by the Las Vegas police. The most difficult phone call I have ever had to make was to call and tell my parents this heart-breaking news.

I was able to use my new TMI and Lifeline skills to help deal with Pete's death. My book, *Brothers Forever, an Unexpected Journey after Death* describes my journey through this experience of grieving. The book was written in an attempt to help me and others go through grieving of any loss in a conscious and enlightened way. The book also probes into the unknown by using very deep states of meditation to discover what hap-pens to loved ones immediately after their death. The book then follows my brother's afterlife experiences for a period of five years.

For about six months I cried every day. I spent two years in the deep-est grief. I was motivated to struggle along mainly to help my family with this event and particularly my daughter who was six at the time and found her sense of security shattered. He was a favorite person in her life too, always willing to play with her and cuddle. Pete's death caused me to address many of the issues raised in this current book about how we create our reality. I agonized over how such a good man could experience such a bleak and frustrating life. This painful life was not imposed upon him by circumstances such as war or famine.

From *Brothers Forever*:

"His life suggests that earthly rewards don't necessarily come to the good. Abundance comes to those who feel entitled to it, and take risks to allow their potency to grow. Goodness is of great value, and it is its own reward. But it is essential to feel deserv-ing at a deep level, for abundance in the form of love, money, meaningfulness, or grace to be fully received. Free will demands this. We are free to reject any or all benefit that could come to us. I raise my daughter to do good deeds *and* to feel worthy of all blessings.

"Life also demands surrender—letting go of fears and attachments. To live well, we must die each day to what is no longer useful, living, and vital in our lives . . . rebirthing each morning to the infinity of possibilities. Few people practice and are good at these mini-deaths. My brother surrendered his life with a gunshot rather than surrendering his deadening thoughts and behaviors. How many more of us slowly and quietly lose what makes us feel most alive, rather than give up an attitude or behavior that is no longer productive?

"One of the biggest challenges for me with Pete's death was that I could feel my heart closing off to avoid further hurt from the loss of anyone in the future. This protective closing off is often experienced by people after a great loss, and can be felt as a dullness, or deadening, or lack of engagement with life. I still had plenty of people who counted on me to be present including my wife, daughter and my patients. I decided that for me this closing off was not an option. I finally came up with an image that guided me out of this deadening:

"Myths are a powerful influence on our perception and experience. Our cultural myth of a broken heart, while speaking accurately of our pain, does a great disservice to our true nature, and underestimates the resilience of the human spirit. My model is that at the deepest level of reality there exists completeness and perfection. From this model, an image emerged to save me from bitterness and fear. The image came in that second winter after Pete's death, while I was struggling with my own hardness and broken heart. The image was of water. That liquid was my answer to my dilemma about openness and protection. If I viewed my heart, my feeling center, as a container filled with water, a great ocean—always complete in itself, yielding easily, full alone, full when embracing some person, full again when the person was removed—if I could do this then I would indeed be open and non-resisting, yet unable to be devastated by the leaving of a love."

This image has worked well for me many times since, through the loss of my mother, my father, and others close to me. Now, when a person comes into my life, they are fully embraced like a hand is embraced when put into water. If they leave, my water heart perhaps loses a drop or two but goes back to complete. It no longer breaks. My myth of an ocean heart—strong and complete, yet yielding and embracing, reflects our ever-renewing nature and allows healing.

CHAPTER 4

Psychokinesis

Time slowly passed and we gradually recovered some sense of normalcy in the family. I began to spend about ten weeks a year as a trainer at the Monroe Institute. During this time I had the pleasure of getting to know Bob Monroe better. Bob was grieving his wife's Nancy's passing as I was grieving Peter. At times we would sit together and talk, watching the birds soar over the beautiful lands surrounding the Institute. When I first met Bob, he was in his late sixties and casually dressed in shorts on a humid Virginia summer night. I noticed scratches on both legs where he made a lap for his cats to knead and settle down to rest, as he worked on a book that he was writing. That told me of a gentleness, and compassion that was at his core.

Robert Monroe had a strong interest in manifestation. He regularly "found" money as a child, in pockets that had been empty, and under rotten boards he was called to peek under. He created a wonderfully varied and interesting life, including stints as a hobo, pilot, radio tycoon, author, and the excellent manifestation of bringing the Monroe Institute into enduring reality. At the Institute he developed what is called the Human Plus® system which uses altered states of consciousness to increase self-mastery and healing. From these successful exercises Monroe's Hemi-Sync® 2000 program was developed.

I then had the privilege of helping Bob evolve this program into a new one called Life Span 2000. This program pushed the limits of human potential in many ways. Within the program we taught participants all fifty of the Human Plus commands to gain mastery over health, emotions, thoughts, physical strength, etc. After several days of meditation, we had a test night designed to be fun and challenging, where folks would practice their new skills. It was called "gaming night" and every time a participant would use one of their newly acquired commands they received an extra chip. No money was exchanged.

Poker was too complicated for some, so we also started a simple game of dice. As I led the dice game, I found my hands getting very hot, my heart center opening wide and then I was able to roll exactly the pattern I envisioned on the dice. After I did this awhile, several participants were able to do the same. We had very high energy, feelings of unity and love, and instant and certain knowing of what number would be rolled. This phenomenon repeated in subsequent Life Span programs. I found that this psychokinesis energy was the same energy I felt when using energy healing, including the hot hands and open heart. During Gateway I had discovered that I had the ability to be a conduit of healing energy, I could touch someone lightly with the intention to ease their headache, and their pain would vanish. This had much in common with the oneness states I had experienced but while focusing on here-now physical reality rather than "flying away somewhere in bliss."

As my grief for Peter was waning, I could access joy through the beauty of nature, art, loving relationships, and deep meditative states. Psychokinesis (in this case being able to affect the outcome in dice) was another way to experience joy while still being focused on the physical world. The psychokinesis experience felt like a wonderful magic space and I wanted to experience it again and understand it better. It also fascinated me because finally I felt that there was a way to study this energy. Psychokinesis with dice was amenable to research because the statistical properties of rolling dice were well known and should follow the exact laws of probability.

As a result of the Life Span experience I started to study psychokinesis (PK)—the ability to affect matter using only the mind. It seemed to me that this PK energy was the same as the energy found in miracle healings, and in strong manifestation. But when doing healing work one never knew whether the illness would have gone away all by itself, whether the sufferer did it, or whether the healer did it, and if it didn't go away perhaps there was a higher reason for the illness to remain. At the time, from a scientific point of view I felt energy healing was just too sloppy a phenomenon to study. In fact there now have been a multitude of studies of energy healing and the results that are very suggestive that such healing is a fact.

From my point of view then, PK on objects would be easier to study than physical healing in that you could more easily eliminate outside (non-psychic) factors causing the event. Examples of psychokinesis, also called telekinesis, include using just your energy and no physical means to control results of dice throws, illuminating light bulbs, growing seeds in your hand in just a few minutes, and bending heavy metal and brittle plastic. It is also the force I use on slot machines.

I received a small grant from a private individual to go to Princeton University's Princeton Engineering Anomalous Research laboratory (PEAR lab). At PEAR scientists had been studying PK for a long time under very strict scientific standards. For example, they had done one study with 12.5 million trials and achieved highly significant results suggesting the PK was a real event. I was very excited for this opportunity. PEAR was highly respected internationally in psychokinesis circles. I spent the days before my trip raising my energy and visualizing success through deep meditation.

When I arrived at Princeton, I had to search around a bit—the lab was located in the basement of the engineering department. I walked into a very interesting space and was welcomed warmly. There were weird looking devices scattered throughout the lab. The staff was very excited to show me all the things that they were working on. One prominent wall had what looked like a huge peg board in the shape of an upward-pointing triangle enclosed in Plexiglass. At the top of the triangle was a large hopper filled with steel balls. They explained to me that in this experiment, when the balls were released, hitting all the pegs as they proceeded to the bottom, the balls should distribute in a normal curve, meaning most of them would fall toward the center and few toward the outside edges. The PK subject would try with his or her mind to influence the falling balls, so that they would distribute more to one side than to the other. How the balls distribute can be counted and the results over many trials combined to assess the reality and strength of PK. If the balls consistently fell more to the left and the intention was to have them fall more to the left, then that was good evidence that PK was operating. The staff demonstrated the experiment to me by releasing the balls. Wow! The balls made a gigantic clatter as they fell and settled to the bottom.

Many other experiments in the lab included what are called random event generators or REG's. The generators are quantum mechanical devices that basically choose either a one or a zero, thousands of times a second. They do this by referencing random atomic action to "decide" which of the two options to pick. Basically it is like flipping a coin thousands of times a second. The results in the coin flip over thousands of flips, if the coin is perfectly balanced should by very close to fifty percent heads and percent tails. The random event generators do the same process but electronically, and the results also should be roughly fifty percent ones and fifty percent zeros by chance, as each option has an equal chance of occurring.

Random event generators allow a very precise and scientific study of psychokinesis. Each time you flip a coin the chances are 1 in 2 that it comes up heads. If you start flipping a coin, and the first two times it comes up heads, that will occur once in every four times by chance. If the first five flips all come up heads, this would be unusual but not a miracle because it will occur naturally once in every 32 times you tried to do so. If the coin came up heads ten times in a row, now things are getting pretty spooky because that would occur only once in 1,024 times by chance. Well you are on a roll and you flip the coin twenty times and it comes up all twenty times as heads. Now we are in miracle territory as this would occur only once in 1,048,576 times by chance.

Random event generators and coin flips operate by the laws of probability that govern chance. Understanding probabilities will help you later understand my experiences with PK in the casinos. So to expand a bit further, if you take a coin and intend to throw only heads and you flip ten times and get five heads, that would be exactly what would be expected by the laws of probability (fifty percent heads and fifty percent tails). If you got seven out of ten rolls as heads (seventy percent heads), this would occur by chance about eleven percent of the times you tried. As you add more attempts which in experiments are called trials, the laws of probability will tend strongly to push the results toward fifty percent heads and fifty percent tails. So if you achieved seventy percent heads out of 100 rolls, this would occur only 0.0023 percent of the time by chance. This points to the fact that as the number of events increase in a chance out-come, it quickly becomes likely that the laws of probability will operate strongly to direct the results to exactly what the laws of probability dictate.

In the Princeton experiments when they are running thousands of chance determinations per second, resulting in millions of events, any deviation from chance will be highly noticeable and scientifically signifi-cant. This indicates that the events are being influenced by something that is causing the events to deviate from chance. And if the only some-thing that can influence the events is mental power, then psychokinesis is proven beyond any reasonable scientific doubt.

Now we can put the Royal Flush in Hearts that I mentioned early in the book in perspective. When I said that it would occur only once in 160,000 by chance, it is like flipping a balanced coin seventeen times in a row, having the goal it come up heads and it coming up heads every time. When my wife and I got identical hands on the poker machines side by side (four aces with a four), it was equivalent of flipping a coin and having it come up heads over twenty times in a row. And to make matters even more interesting, slot machines contain random event generators just like the experiments at Princeton did! [3]

At Princeton, the researchers hooked up the random event generators to many different feedback devices so that the subject would know how they were doing. For example, one could hook up the generator so that for every time it picked a series of zeros, a drum beat would sound. Then you would ask the subject to try to get the drum to beat using only their mind. If they were successful you might hear a steady increase in beats as the subject caused the generator to pick more zeros than ones, defying the laws of chance and proving PK. The researchers had designed many ingenious experiments with different feedback devices, searching for the type of feedback that encouraged the person attempting PK toward best performance. Some of the feedback was auditory such as the drum beat; other feedback was some type of visual display.

---

3 Actually slot machines use what are called pseudo random event generators that use a mathematical formula to randomly select different hands (the cards that will appear on the screen) hundreds of time per second versus the atomic action that drives real random event generators.

The random event generator experiment that I did at Princeton was called Art Reg. For this they used a very elegant feedback device. A computer using a random number generator selects pixels from a picture of a pyramid whenever the random event generator picks the number zero. And on the same screen, at the same time, the computer presents pixels from a picture of a cat whenever the random event generator selects the number one. So what you see on the screen is a mush created by combining pixels from the two different pictures. My job was to somehow affect the random event generator with my mind so that it selected more ones (cat picture pixels). If I could do so, the picture would more and more clearly become a cat.

As I mentioned I had meditated and raised energy for a few days before coming to the lab. I sat down and relaxed in front of the screen and then willed the picture of the cat to emerge—nothing happened, just what looked like a mushy static on the screen. I then stood up and got all excited, building energy and looking at the screen, putting my hand out in a beckoning motion and saying "Here, Kitty, Kitty." The cat picture began to slowly emerge from the mush. The clearer the picture got the more excited I became, and there it was—a clear picture of the cat, with the pyramid completely vanished! The experimenters told me that I had achieved results that were 30,000 to one by chance.

In the three hours I was at Princeton, I tried several other experiments such as the drum beat with only chance results. But my biggest result was with what I called the fountain experiment. The researchers had set up a water fountain in the lab. It shot a narrow column of bubbling water into the air for about two feet, before the water column would break and the water would return to the pool at the bottom. The fountain was attractively laid out against a deep blue background with narrow spot lights shining on it from many directions so that the water stood out clearly and sparkled brightly. The fountain was behind a pane of glass, so that it could not be affected by direct touch and breezes in the air. They explained that the water in the column changed height by random hydrodynamic law. So the up and down dancing of the column height that you see in a fountain changes height randomly if the water remains under steady pressure.

My job in this experiment was to use only my mental energy to make the column of water stay high for ten minutes, then leave it alone for ten minutes as the control or comparison period, then make it low for ten minutes. The researchers asked if I would like to give it a try. I said, "You bet!" I sat down before the fountain and thought for a moment about how I was going to do this. I decided on using techniques from the Monroe Institute meditations where one is taught to focus and direct energy. Sitting about two feet way from the fountain for the high condition, I extended my hands, palms facing each other and imagined that I was supporting the column of water with my "energy hands" so that it would go high and higher. As I continued streaming energy in this manner, the computer measuring the column height recorded the result. It was very hard to tell visually if I was getting anywhere and the column height continued to jump around. But I pretended that I was having great success. Then I took a ten-minute break, which was the control period.

I finished the experiment trying to achieve the low condition. For this I imagined that I was holding an energy sword in my right hand, much like the light sabers in the Star Wars movies. I generated and sent a lot of energy into my "sword." From several feet away from the glass, I began to make fast slicing motions, as if I were slicing the column of water in half repeatedly with my energy sword. Again the computer recorded the results. The results were very strongly indicative of PK at the tens of thousands to one by chance. Then the computers crashed in the lab. We joked that they may have crashed because of all the energy flying around the lab. After we finished, the staff took me to a great backyard party to celebrate where I had a wonderful time meeting many members of the Princeton community.

The Princeton lab staff was terrific. They were curious and excited, relaxed, and encouraging. They were excellent at reducing any sense of pressure. Psychokinesis performance does not respond well to any pressure. If asked to perform in front of friends, let alone on TV, I decline. For me the pressure to perform and the fear of failure would be too great, and I would go into ego, straining to do well. When that happens for me, the energy stops flowing. This almost never works with PK—one just has to intend it and then relax and let it happen. This is true of many natural human abilities. We can see this even in something as simple as going to sleep. Here, on a normal night, you feel tired and intend to go to sleep. Then you just settle down, relax, and not think about it, and sleep comes.

However, if you have only four hours to sleep before getting up for a trip, what happens? The pressure to go to sleep is too great and sleep does not come. Instead you spent the night looking at the clock and saying, "I have to get to sleep quickly now, I only have two hours left before I have to get up." Imagine falling asleep on command on TV with millions of people watching. This is what it would be like to expect someone to perform PK on TV.

The research being done in psychokinesis and clairvoyance have potential to radically alter our beliefs about consciousness and therefore improve our world. This quote is taken from the PEAR website on the spiritual implications of their experiments in psychokinesis and other psychic phenomena[4]:

> "Beyond its revolutionary technological applications and scientific impact, the evidence of an active role of consciousness in the establishment of physical reality holds profound implications for our view of ourselves, our relationships to others, and to the cosmos in which we exist. These, in turn, must inevitably impact our values, our priorities, our sense of responsibility, and our style of life. Our ability to acquire, or to generate tangible, measurable information independent of distance or time challenges the foundation of any reductionist brain-based model of consciousness that may be invoked. The lack of notable correlations in the data with standard learning curves or other recognizable cognitive patterns, combined with the repeatable and distinct gender-related differences, suggest that these abilities may stem from a more fundamental source than heretofore suspected.
>
> "Certainly, there is little doubt that integration of these changes in our understanding of ourselves can lead to a substantially superior human ethic, wherein the long-estranged siblings of science and spirit, of analysis and aesthetics, of intellect and intuition, and of many other subjective and objective aspects of human experience can be productively reunited."

---

4 http://www.princeton.edu/~pear/

My Princeton experience proved to the scientist in me that PK was real and that I could do it. Just to be clear, PEAR did not certify me as psychic. They did not do that for anyone that I know of. But the results were very clear to me. I was able, to a statistically significant degree (that would not occur by chance), to change the outcome of what are usually random events, using just my mind and energy. And it appeared from the results of other experiments that many and perhaps most people can do the same thing.

If water fountains and random event generators could be affected, what else might also be true? I had heard stories of metal and spoon bending, growing seeds in your hand, changing the results with dice (of which I'd had some personal experience in Life Span). I had some experience with telepathy (knowing what someone else was thinking or when someone was going to call on the telephone). I think that most people have had these types of telepathic experiences, though much of traditional science would attribute these to coincidence. I had dismissed spoon bending as a sleight of hand magician's trick without ever investigating the facts myself. Now there are many You Tube videos on these type phenomena, but of course film can be faked.

As I began my search to understand psychic phenomena better, I found that in science such events were often referred to as PSI functioning, meaning functions and events that occurred without adequate explanation by traditional Newtonian physics. I found that other reputable universities and laboratories had confirmed and expanded Princeton's results. Duke University has studied dice rolling, telepathy and other PSI functioning. I met Dean Radin, Ph.D. at University of Nevada and saw his lab. I read his book *The Conscious Universe* which is an excellent summary of what had been proven in the PSI or psychic fields in terms of PK, telepathy, and clairvoyance. Dean Radin currently works at The Institute for Noetic Sciences. He is intelligent, knowledgeable, and sophisticated in his science skills. There was nothing flaky about these people.

Perhaps the most rigorously studied of all PSI function is clairsentience or, as it is called when done under strict scientific protocol, Remote Viewing or Remote Sensing (RV). Using Remote Viewing a person can obtain detailed information about any event, place, or person without limits as to time or distance. It is the skill that has been applied to finding lost persons, mineral and gas deposits, and in secret government psychic spying programs by many countries, including the former Soviet Union and the United States.

I had also met Joe McMoneagle at the Monroe Institute during my Gateway. He is a retired Army Chief Warrant Officer, awarded a Legion of Merit for his Intelligence work as a remote viewer. He often speaks to Gateway groups as part of the program. Joe was remote viewer number 001 in the U.S. government's twenty-year-long secret Stargate program, designed to use remote viewing to gather intelligence on the Soviets and other critical incidents such as the Iran hostage situation. The U.S. Remote Viewing team had great success, as described in Joe's books, *Mind Trek* and *Remote Viewing Secrets*. His experiences, as well as many scientific laboratory experiments in Remote Sensing suggest that we can access any information psychically with no limits as to time or place. Joe has appeared on television many times, successfully demonstrating his ability to find people and locations with only a photograph or name in a sealed envelope into which he cannot see which is used as a target to focus his intention.

Researchers at PEAR and other places have found out many things about psychokinesis and developed quantum physics based theoretical models on how PSI might work. Some of the experiments have been very ambitious. For example, an ongoing experiment called the Global Consciousness Project monitors random number generators in locations around the world and detects significant changes from random when large numbers of people focus on one thing, such as the 9/11 terrorist attacks, Obama's presidential acceptance speech, the tsunami in Japan, etc. It points to the fact that human consciousness affects the random quantum field of possibilities. Here is a description from the Global Consciousness Project's website[5]:

"Coherent consciousness creates order in the world. Subtle Interactions link us with each other and the Earth."

"When human consciousness becomes coherent and synchronized, the behavior of random systems may change.

---

5 http://noosphere.princeton.edu/

Quantum event based random number generators (RNGs) produce completely unpredictable sequences of zeroes and ones. But when a great event synchronizes the feelings of millions of people, our network of RNGs becomes subtly structured. The probability is less than one in a billion that the effect is due to chance. The evidence suggests an emerging noosphere, or the unifying field of consciousness described by sages in all cultures.

"The Global Consciousness Project is an international, multidisciplinary collaboration of scientists and engineers. We collect data continuously from a global network of physical random number generators located in 70 host sites around the world. The data are transmitted to a central archive which now contains more than 12 years of random data in parallel sequences of synchronized 200-bit trials every second.

"Our purpose is to examine subtle correlations that reflect the presence and activity of consciousness in the world. We predict structure in what should be random data, associated with major global events. The data overall show a highly significant departure from expectation, confirming our prediction . . . . Subtle but real effects of consciousness are important scientifically, but their real power is more direct. They encourage us to make essential, healthy changes in the great systems that dominate our world. Large scale group consciousness has effects in the physical world. Knowing this, we can intentionally work toward a brighter, more conscious future."

The PEAR lab at Princeton closed after nearly thirty years of operation, feeling that they had proven beyond any scientific doubt that PK was real and therefore that their primary mission was completed. I have included this scientific look at psychokinesis because I want you to have the opportunity to go into my description of what I experienced in Las Vegas with dice and slot machines with some basis for feeling that what I describe may be real.

There are many debunkers of the PSI phenomena that I have referenced but most of the debunker's material that I have examined is done by people who have never even looked at the data, and come up with explanations that boil down to, "I don't think it is possible—therefore it doesn't occur," or, "It has to be fraud." This is much like the consensus world view at one time that the world was flat. The facts are that Nobel Prize- winning laureates in mathematics have looked at the Princeton data and pronounced it as valid.

There is something called the *experimenter effect* that is well known in science but often ignored, which basically states that if the experimenter believes he or she will obtain positive results then the results will be positive. If they believe the results will be negative, the results are negative. This happens even in more conventional research, for example, into the effectiveness of drugs. The experimenter effect makes sense if you believe that our consciousness affects reality, but of course can produce negative results when debunkers try to replicate results.

Most of us have an intuitive feel that there is something important and sacred about consciousness, that we are more than a mix of a few chemicals in a random universe, and that we can indeed have flashes of extraordinary perception at least occasionally. I feel that we should look at things that are hard to explain with an objective eye, yet honor our own deep sense of truth. Albert Einstein said, "The intuitive mind is a sacred gift and the rational mind is a faithful servant. We have created a society that honors the servant and has forgotten the gift." You, of course are invited and encouraged to examine the facts and stories for yourself and come to your own conclusion about PSI.

I want to extend my gratitude to those who have worked at PEAR and other places like it. They have given me the confidence and clarity to pursue my own adventure into whether consciousness creates reality. They did so by speaking to the scientist in me and helping me to see the facts. They gave me an opportunity to try the experiments myself which moved my belief into a powerful known. They did so with utmost integrity—if experimental results were negative they reported this as such. And they applied their considerable intelligence with great courage, to study such things as psychokinesis within the scientific model and by doing so put their professional careers on the line.

As a tribute to these fine scientists, I have included PEAR's final press release as an Appendix.

CHAPTER 5

Early Vegas

My Princeton experience proved to the scientist in me that I was not deluding myself about what had happened with dice during the Life Span programs at TMI. PK was real. Further, during the experiences at Monroe with dice and at the lab in Princeton, I was given a taste of the type of energy and focus need to achieve these effects in the physical world. As I mentioned earlier, to me it seemed to be the same energy and mental set that I had experienced at TMI in my Gateway when I touched the person and their headache went away. It seemed to occur if you were very relaxed, and had a strong, loving, and connected feeling with the world and those around you. Then you set a clear intent, and followed this intent by letting go—trusting the energy to flow toward your intent. It seemed to me that being able to heal myself or another using only this energy was a miraculous thing to do. Given that the PK work seemed to contain the same ingredients as energy healing, I felt that practicing PK (with the ability to measure the results objectively) would be a great way to also explore energy healing, and perhaps develop confidence and control in this area as well.

After Gateway, while still in its wonderful energy I entered a contest sponsored by *CD Review* magazine and was the one chosen out of 77,000 entrants to win the grand prize of $10,000 in stereo equipment and the entire Telarc Music CD collection which contained hundreds of CD's of well-recorded classical music which I dearly love. So it looked likely that the same set of energy, intention, and focus that was helpful in PK could enhance our ability to manifest in our lives what we really wished for.

If energy healing, manifestation, and PK all used the same energy and processes, then becoming better at PK should make one more insightful, consistent, and powerful in all three of these areas. This really ignited my passion! I thought that it would be a wonderful thing to be able to do PSI and perhaps teach others to do PSI as well. It had potential to help anyone, and perhaps even people in situations like my brother Peter who were spiraling down into lower energy, fearful expectations, and worse outcomes. They might be able to change their manifestation patterns to positive and healthy ones. Working thirty years as a psychotherapist had shown me that even with best of intentions, it was difficult and challenging for people to change destructive patterns through just talk and even action, if their energy was depressed and fearful, if their thoughts were limiting what they felt was possible, or if they felt that were not deserving.

Given it seemed that PK, energy healing, and manifestation were variants of the same energy, I wondered just how much these skills could be brought under conscious control, developed, and consistently repeated. One thing I knew was that I needed a place to practice under objective conditions. It was not practical to go up to the Princeton lab frequently, nor would the scientists there want me to. I had to find a place to practice where I knew for certain that the target was random (not influenced by cheating, or physical manipulation). And to find a place where expected chance results were well understood and established statistically, so I could tell if I was able to create unexplained change or patterns. I figured that this study may take years. So the question became how and where could I devote the time to pursuing a black belt in PK? The answer was suggested by the dice game at Life Span—Las Vegas! There, the dice are guaranteed to be neutral and random, or the casino would be rapidly out of business. There, the laws of probability were very well understood, to the point that one knew exactly what the odds were by chance of any number or series of numbers being thrown. And there, if I were successful at causing the dice to roll in a non-random or patterned way, I could perhaps recoup at least part of my travel and learning costs.

The idea of using Las Vegas as my PK laboratory didn't just pop into my head. I was already familiar with Vegas, having gone there to play about once every two years with my three brothers, sister, and Dad. My mom was not very into it, so she usually stayed home. When vacationing there we would have a great family outing, relax, see the shows, and have a warm sunny break from the winter weather in the Northeast, where my family lived at the time. We usually stayed at the Sahara or Bob Stupak's Vegas World (now called the Stratosphere) because of the specials they would offer tourists on rooms, meals, and free gaming chips. On those trips I played mostly Blackjack and some slots.

Scanning back over those many years, I did have a few very unusual experiences that suggest PSI in action. One time I remember going to wait for my brother Peter by the entrance to a casino restaurant, intending to go to dinner with him. It was around Christmas time. As I was waiting for him to show, I sat down at a video poker machine next to the restaurant entrance. I was at a dollar machine, meaning that with maximum coins in, so that you could have a chance at the big jackpot, you paid $5 a pull to see five cards in draw poker. I usually played 25-cent machines at the time, but I had a good feeling about this machine, so I took a leap of faith. I put $100 in the machine and before long, I hit four of a kind for a $200 jackpot. This was in the day where the machines paid out in actual coin tokens, so 200 coins came spitting out into the metal receptacle, called the hopper, with great clatter.

As the change person came by, I asked for a rack which is a plastic box in which you can stack 100 coins on edge. Being in a very good mood, I tipped her generously when she returned with the rack. I filled the rack and put it on top of the machine, representing the money that I started with. I continued playing with my profits at that same machine. I began to feel more rapport with the machine, talking to it and thanking it for the payouts. I also began to get strong feelings right before it would pay and feelings about whether or not to continue to play. Repeatedly, just close to where I would be out of coins in the hopper another four a kind would show, I would request another rack and put another 100 coins on top of the machine, and tip the change person. She asked if she could do anything for me. I mentioned that I was hungry (having been ready for dinner when I came to meet my brother, and now it being an hour later). She returned with her own dinner sandwich and gave it to me with a drink of water.

After another rack was requested, she returned with it and rubbed my shoulders. When I finished I had eight racks of 100 dollar-coins each stacked on top of the machine. I went to cash these back into money and tipped the change person $100. Walking away I realized that the cashier had overpaid me $100. I went back to the cashier. She became tearful in gratitude for my return. She then explained that they would have taken the $100 out of her pay, if she came up short, which would have prevented her from buying toys for her kids for Christmas. After wishing her a Merry Christmas, I turned and found my brother there, ready to go to dinner. Seeing the big grin on my face, he asked, "What?" I just shook my head, still buzzing from the energy of the experience and said to him, "I am so glad that you were late for dinner!"

Another experience occurred in Puerto Rico. I was vacationing there with my brother John and my girl friend at the time. The pace at these beach resort casinos is more leisurely than in Vegas and is based upon the old European genteel model of gaming. As the casinos didn't even open until 3 p.m., you had plenty of time during the day to just relax and enjoy the ocean. John and I had been playing blackjack each afternoon at the El San Juan casino for two dollars a hand. We were setting a very relaxed pace and using the time at the tables to talk and visit. On our fourth afternoon there, we were following our same routine at the table, sitting together at its center with four other players, two on each side of us. All of a sudden I got a chill, turned to my brother and whispered that I was having a déjà vu and that I knew what the next cards were that were going to be dealt. He said softly and kiddingly, "Bullshit!" I then proceeded to whisper to him each card before it was dealt to each of the six players for two hands running with no mistakes. He look as shocked as was I and asked me, "What are you going to do?" I replied, "Bet my ass off!" I raised my bet and then out of a six deck shoe (six decks of 52 cards all shuffled together) got four blackjacks in a row, won the next two hands and got a few more blackjacks. The crew and pit bosses were upset but paid me. I bought gifts for the folks back home with the winnings.

I have had about two dozen déjà vu experiences in my life. Most of the time, they occurred with a sense of me having been in the exact situation before. Sometimes I had the sense that I had dreamed this before, and then know the next two or three sentences that somebody would say in conversation. Because I kept a dream journal, occasionally I would be able to go back to my journal and verify that indeed, several years before, I had recorded the exact situation of the déjà vu in my dream journal. Often the déjà vu happened a few days before some major unexpected event would occur in my life. If the event was positive there was often positive or neutral emotion with the preceding déjà vu. If the event was negative, the feelings during the preceding déjà vu would be negative, such as feelings of dread or foreboding.

My strongest déjà vu lasted over a period of a week, during which I knew much of what would happen or be said next, for hours at a time during those days. This was accompanied by strong foreboding feelings. Such an extended déjà vu had not happened to me before or since. The strong déjà vu happened right before my motorcycle accident when I was twenty-one. Even though I woke up that sunny morning in a good mood and got on my bike without any thought of crashing, part of me evidently knew what was coming. And with my severe injuries and extended recovery, it was definitely a major event.

As I have mentioned, in my early days in Vegas I played mostly black-jack and slots. But I did accumulate some interesting experiences with dice in those years, well before deciding to use Vegas as my classroom for PK. I was able to do okay at blackjack, and while it was a challenging and interesting game, I did not enjoy sitting for long periods of time at the blackjack table. I sat during much of my ten-hour work day at home as a therapist. To do well at blackjack seemed to consist of much patience and hard concentration work, accompanied by rare flashes of intuition or insight. It is a game where each player plays their own cards against the house, and it therefore can be a very lonely game unless a rare type of table magic happens and you end up being friendly with the other players. At times blackjack can even turn a bit hostile, when you take a card by intuition, that by strict playing guidelines you should not. Then you might win but the next player can feel that you have "stolen their card" by your "stupid but lucky play."

The blackjack tables are usually quite quiet and when seated there, once in a while I would hear tremendous cheering from the dice tables located nearby. On occasion that cheering seemed to go on for a half hour or so. When I would look over there, I could see people standing there grinning, slapping each other on the back, and generally looking like they were having a fabulous time. This intrigued me, but when I would cruise by the game (called craps) it seemed very intimidating—complex and fast moving with an undecipherable felt diagram within the table. People would be making what seemed to be huge variety of intricate bets, all at the same time. These bets differed from one player to the next, then the dice would roll and there would be intense reactions, sometimes with some people cheering while others groaned.

Finally one day when blackjack seemed particularly boring, I got up the nerve to try this game of dice called craps. The rest of this memory is mostly a blur but I do remember asking for help in learning the game from the crew and them kindly assisting me with some simple bets. The dice came to for me to roll and the crew guided me. I should pick a pair of dice that I wanted out of the six die before me. I could only hold them in one hand. I had to roll them all the way down to the other end of the table. I had to have a pass line bet. Once I established a point, I had to roll that point number before a seven in order to win.

Then I remember going into a zone, much like the peak flow state some sports players experience when at top of their form. There was so much cheering that after awhile my brother John stopped playing at his blackjack table and came to see what all the hoopla was about. When he saw that I was rolling the dice (I had been rolling throughout the entire time people were cheering), he stayed back a bit, as to not disturb me, and began to count how many times I rolled the dice successfully. He counted another twenty-seven numbers in a row before I finally seven'ed out and lost the dice. Sevening out means that you get a seven when you don't want one. People usually roll a seven at the wrong time about every five or six rolls because the chances of a seven are one every six. When they roll a seven at the wrong time, it ends their turn and most bets are lost.

Most times a person rolls for only about five minutes before they hit a wrong number and lose the dice. You remember from the coin toss that it is exponentially more difficult to flip ten heads in a row than it is to flip seven heads in a row. In dice, to roll longer than the first five minutes becomes exponentially more difficult. There is also the possibility that in such a long roll that the money made becomes exponentially greater than in a short roll. Longer rolls are statistically more and more unlikely by chance, the longer the roll progresses. In this session I successfully rolled for about an hour. I don't remember how much money I made, but it was a bunch considering my small bets and I do remember the other players giving me a long clapping ovation and tipping me with their chips.

My monster roll was a classic case of "beginner's luck." I put that in quotes because, knowing what I know now, I don't think that it is luck. Beginners can stumble upon PK by bringing to a new experience many things that are helpful for PK. Beginners don't know what they are doing so the ego is often not as active. They often get caught up in the newness and excitement of the game and the well wishes of the other players. That raises their energy and off they go into a wonderland of rolling, blessedly ignorant of how well they are doing until it is over. It is a very different thing to do well on a consistent basis once you know more about what can go wrong.

Needless to say that after experiencing that first long roll, I knew that I really liked the game of craps! I was fascinated by the process and deeply enjoyed the positive energy and excitement of such a roll. After that first roll, whenever I was in Vegas, I would go to the blackjack tables and in over an hour of play raise a few hundred dollars. Then I would go to the dice table seeking to repeat my magic roll and usually lose my money within fifteen minutes. After a few times of this I largely put the dice aside and went back to the blackjack that I knew.

There were two exceptions to this that stand out for me and suggest PK was operating before I ever knew what it was. In the first event I was with my brother John. After several days in Vegas playing blackjack together, he suggested that he would like to play dice together before we went home. We had about an hour before we needed to go to the airport. We went to an empty table and stood about two feet from each other at one end, so he could guide my play, as he knew more about the game than I did at the time.

We were just starting when a "don't better" jostled us and stood right between us, even though the rest of the large table was empty. Don't betters in craps are folks who bet against the numbers that all the other players are wanting to come in. For example if most of the players want a nine, they will bet that the nine will not be thrown. Most don't players are very respectful and stay away from the other players at the table and quietly make their don't bets. But sometimes a don't player will try to use psychological gambits including intimidation to throw the other players off and break their concentration or good fortune. When everybody else loses the don't player wins.

When this man jostled between us, my brother and I looked at each other and thought "jerk." At first I resented the intrusion but then had the idea to encourage this player to leave by using the "Force" like in Star Wars. I felt my energy become stronger. From my heart I focused on wanting this time to play alone with my brother to celebrate our trip together and to end the trip on a good note. I picked up the dice.

On the first roll and all rolls before a point is established, seven and eleven win instantly. I put my $5 bet down on the pass line. A pass line bet wins instantly on a seven or eleven, and loses instantly on a two, three or twelve (these three numbers are called craps). Any other number thrown (4,5,6,8,9,10) becomes the point, and then the point has to made a second time before a seven is thrown for the player to win.

The "don't" better said something snide and put $100 down on don't pass, meaning he was betting against my brother's and my success. I immediately threw a seven and I won my $5 and he lost $100. We bet the same again. I rolled another seven. In fact, I rolled a series of three sevens and two elevens in a row, each time winning for myself and my brother, giving us each a $25 win and costing the don't bettor $500 in about five minutes. He then gave up in disgust and walked away. My brother and I proceeded to have a very pleasant hour at the dice table all by ourselves.

My brother John is interesting to me in this context because many of my early PSI events in casinos and even some of my OBE proofs were in his presence. It was as if he were my lucky charm.

The second dice event that I will remember for a long time occurred on my birthday. I was staying at the Sahara hotel as I had done many times before and had become known to the crews and they were familiar to me. It was about three in the afternoon and I went down to play craps with the attitude that it was time to get a slice of birthday cake just for me. I found an empty table with the boxman Gene sitting in his position at the center of the table. The boxman usually wears a suit and is in charge of that individual dice game. He supervises the other three persons on the crew, which are the two dealers and a stickman. The language in Vegas at the time was still very male-oriented in the game of dice. The boxman initiates the game, checks the dice to be sure that they are the casino's own dice and not loaded ones put into the game on the sly by someone attempting to cheat. All the casino's chips that are in play at that dice table are arranged right before him. He makes sure that all bets are paid accurately and settles any disputes. There is also a supervisor of the entire dice pit which may have several dice tables within it arranged in a circle. Then there is the casino shift manager in charge of the entire casino that shift, and above him or her is a casino manager. From the boxman on up, players not so affectionately call all the supervisory levels, "suits."

I took the place directly opposite Gene and immediately next to the stickman. The stickman's job is to call what number comes up on the dice after the player rolls it. The stickman also accepts bets that are placed in the center of the dice table. Each baseman is in charge of one half of the table and accepts bets from the players on their side.

Gene and I exchanged pleasantries. I mentioned that it was my birthday and he said, "Well, step right up and make yourself a birthday gift!" I put down $50 to play with. Gene had watched me play many times and knew that I was capable of good rolls but that I always kept my betting very cautious and conservative. I began a good roll, making my targets easily. Every few minutes Gene would cajole and encourage me to raise my bets, saying things like, "You are doing great. You are now playing with the casino's money, where is your courage, take a chance would you?" I went into the zone and just kept rolling. Although I had started at an empty table, it now became packed with other players; the action was fast and furious. My run continued. Gene brought in two extra basemen to help handle all the action—something I never had seen done, nor have seen since. But I barely noticed this, nor all the chaos and cheering. I just kept being in the zone and raising my bets whenever Gene told me to. Usually a dice crew consists of four members. At any given time, three are working (two basemen and one stickman) and one member is on a fifteen-minute break. Every fifteen minutes they change positions and a different crew member cycles onto a break. The boxman takes a break about every half hour but this time Gene just stayed at his post, through many crew changes.

When I finally got tired and seven'ed out by throwing a seven at the wrong time, I had held the dice for over 90 minutes. The table exploded in cheers which brought me out of my trance enough to notice the huge pile of chips before me. I was surging with too much adrenaline to even handle my chips easily. The crew stacked them for me. Exchanging smaller denominates for larger ones, and finally giving me the count. I had made well over $3,800 on my roll after starting with a $5 bet. Many players added tips for me to this, as I had made them lots of money too. It was an excellent birthday present and truly a magic thing to experience!

PART 2

CHAPTER 6

Preparation

Now that I had experienced PK events at the dice game during the Life Span program at TMI and in the Princeton lab, I was ready to learn how consistent and powerful PK could become. As mentioned in the last chapter, Las Vegas seemed to me to be an ideal place to study and practice PK. I discussed this "crazy" idea with Bob Monroe. His eyes twinkled and with a broad smile he said that he thought it would be a very interesting enterprise and asked me to keep him informed of my progress. I presented it to my wife, Charleene, and she was willing to support my idea as long as I kept careful track of the finances and kept my trips to Vegas to no more than once a month. Supporting this idea was a challenge for her and a sign of her trust in me. She had been raised in a fundamental Christian family where any gambling, even recreational card playing was considered wrong. So she was very suspicious of and inexperienced with gaming. This was in high contrast to my family playing all kinds of card games with much fun while I was growing up. With Bob Monroe's encouragement, my wife's support, great excitement, and some apprehension, Las Vegas became my PK classroom.

I decided that I would focus on dice rather than slot machines. I figured that the game of craps would provide instant feedback as to how I was doing. And over thousands of throws, the power of repetition would help with the fact that my learning approach was going to be largely trial and error. This would hopefully lead to trial and success. I could not find any "how-to PK" books on the subject. The type of beginner's luck and rare experiences that I have described in earlier occasional Vegas trips showed what was possible, but I really had very little understanding about what I was doing. I wanted to learn just how PK operated, including all the aspects that might enhance or hinder performance. And I wanted to become consistently able to achieve PK. Achieving understanding and consistency in what I was doing was a whole new endeavor.

Because PK phenomena are related to energy healing and manifestation, I also wanted to understand how to achieve healings and manifesting in rough-and-tumble situations. So far I had raised the needed energy and focus for PK in conducive settings. Monroe Institute and the Princeton lab, where most of my experience had occurred, were both very sheltered retreats where it was easy to concentrate. I suspected that it might be a good deal more challenging to do this in Vegas, but I welcomed this challenge. I wanted to be able to manifest whenever and wherever it was needed—even when there was stress, noise, and distraction around me. Then my skill would be robust and useful in real-world situations. If I was going to go through all this work, I did not want any abilities that I developed to be limited to retreat settings. If I could do PK in Vegas consistently, then I felt it likely that I could do it anywhere.

The study of PK in Vegas became a personal yoga for me. The journey was at times lonely and arduous, and it required great discipline. Right from the start both the promise and the difficulty were apparent. I found out quickly that for this to work, I would have to be willing to shift many emotional patterns that were second nature, and detach from many of the beliefs of family and culture. The journey definitely shattered many of my conventional belief systems. This yoga challenged me to confront my fears of risk and loss. It taught me that the most powerful human energy is an open heart, and that there are no limits to what humans can accomplish when their intelligence, energy, and compassion are allowed to flower. We are truly made to be miracle workers.

But to reach this potential, there are dues to pay. To thrive on the PK playground, one must be willing to surrender much of what the ego feels is necessary to hold onto to protect itself. For me, this journey meant taking a ride on an emotional roller coaster that lasted for years. When I went to Vegas for a trip I would struggle to achieve high energy states and when in the states feel tremendous energy and bliss. Then I would return home and have to come down back into normal life. The return to normal reality in contrast to what I was feeling and perceiving in Vegas was quite depressing initially. It would take weeks at home to rebalance my mood and energy, and integrate what I had learned that trip. While the journey definitely did not take the form of a straight and clearly marked path, there was never any question for me of quitting. The setbacks and uneasiness at charting this new territory were outshone by experiences along the way that were inspiring and encouraging. And many of the experiences can only be classified as mind-blowing. So for me the emotional roller coaster was worth it. And the ride settled down considerably as I learned better how to keep my energy higher at home as well.

Before going to Vegas to study PK I decided to keep a detailed journal of my trips to help in my learning and in order to have some way of honestly evaluating my progress. My journal came in handy by helping me avoid falling into the same traps and repeatedly making the same mistakes. And I was often tempted to make these mistakes. For example, I learned the hard way not to gamble when tired. It was tempting to do so because, after months away from Vegas, I would be eager to get out there and get started again. Because of the three-hour time difference from my home, and the energy required to get ready for the trip and travel, I would arrive impatient to start but tired. My journal ruthlessly recorded the results of "pushing it." When I would gamble immediately upon arrival I would lose. Even during the day after arrival I would likely not do well. I began to devote the entire first day after travel for rest and building energy, avoiding the casino entirely during that day.

My journal also became a great place to record insights on what did work. I used it to write down insights gleaned from explorations of ancient spiritual traditions, deep meditation techniques, psychology, and brain science. I even bravely attempted to understand what quantum physics suggested about what was happening. With the help of my journal, through recording my trial and error results, and precisely what I was doing before and during success and failure, I gradually began to develop a pattern of behaviors and attitudes that worked with some consistency.

I would like to give you a taste of what the journey was like. As I have mentioned, I am still very much in the process of learning and do not claim to be an expert or to have arrived at the final destination with this journey. I am still committed to looking at emotional and belief patterns that if surrendered, transformed, or expanded, can give me a clearer glimpse of what our true potential really is. Robert Monroe's most famous quote is: "The greatest illusion is that mankind has limitations." The way I might put this, being where I am along the journey at this time is: "We indeed can be free of all limits and be of great light and great love."

As I prepared for my first PK trip to Vegas I decided to use two different psychological technologies to build energy and shed limiting beliefs. The first is designed to work mainly with one's unconscious mind. Much like hypnosis, it had potential to dissolve entrenched patterns of behavior and belief. I began listening to Hypnoperipheral Processing tapes (HPP) by Lloyd Glauberman. These particular HPP tapes were supposed to help your unconscious mind align with the goal of peak performance. They accomplished this by using stereo headphones to tell one story in your right ear and another completely different story in your left ear at the same time.

The blending of these two stories sounded very confusing. You might try to mentally block out the story in one ear so you could follow the story in the other ear but invariably something would get your attention from the other story and you would become distracted into the other story. Then every once in a while, words immediately following each other but from the alternating stories would make a meaningful sentence, such as "Love" (in the right ear) "Your" (in the left ear) "Self" (in the right ear) "More" (in the left ear). This sentence, "Love yourself more," would stand out strongly from all the background "nonsense." Then you were again so distracted by the nonsense that the conscious mind could not argue with the statement. In this manner the statement seemed to penetrate deep into your unconscious mind by tricking your left brain to "let go." The HPP tapes were a very weird experience but somehow relaxing and empowering at the same time.

In addition to the HPP tapes, before going to Vegas I also meditated by a method I was much more familiar with, the Monroe Institute's Hemi-Sync system. By then I had years of experience with this system and had become a trainer of their residential programs in Virginia. I would go up there about ten times a year, each time to train one of their week-long programs. Perhaps Bob Monroe's most brilliant invention was this Hemi-Sync system. Hemi-Sync stands for the term hemispheric synchronization which refers to synchronizing the two hemispheres of the brain. In this system, stereo headphones are employed to provide each ear with a slightly different steady tone. This causes what is termed a binaural beat which is heard as a warbling tone in the center of the head. This tone does not really exist outside the brain. Rather it is created by the brain when exposed to two slightly different tones, one in each ear.

The interesting thing is that when this binaural beat happens, the person's brain waves tend to synchronize between the right and left hemisphere of the brain. This facilitates more communication between the brain hemispheres, resulting in a more whole brain focused-learning state, compared to our usual state of consciousness. In some ways it is like helping our brain power move from a scattered radiation similar to a light bulb, to focusing it more like a laser.

Sound waves are measured in cycles per second. Human beings can usually hear sounds in the range of 20 cycles per second to 20,000 cycles per second. Our brain waves can also be measured in cycles per second and usually span from a very slow 1 cycle per second to a fairly rapid 50 cycles per second or higher. Bob Monroe discovered that binaural beats tend to move the brain-wave patterns to the speed of the difference between the two tones (one in each ear). So if the difference between the two tones is 4 cycles per second, the brain tends to begin to also go into a 4 cycle per second rhythm. If another difference is presented over the headphones such as 10 cycles per second, then the brain tends to go into 10 cycles per second pattern.

The cool thing about this is that we know that different cycles per second in brain-wave patterns tend to correlate with the different states of consciousness. For example the 4 cycles per second pattern is called the delta range and tends to be present when we are deeply asleep. Many other brain-wave patterns have been identified such as 4-7 cycles, called the theta range which is often present in deep meditative states. Cycles of 7-14 are called the alpha range and are present in lighter meditation states and day dreaming, and 14-25 cycles, called the beta range, occurs during awake states. There is a state called gamma that involves brain wave frequencies of 25-50 cycles per second. Gamma states are particularly significant to my journey in that they seem to be associated with psychic phenomena such as energy healing and PK. There are higher brain waves called epsilon which at this time have just begun to attract researchers' attention.

With Hemi-Sync one can also combine different patterns together at the same time, such as delta and beta patterns. Such a pattern can result in a state where the body is deeply asleep (delta) and the mind still awake and aware (beta) at the same time. In this state many people are surprised to be awake, yet hearing themselves snore! Such a state is excellent for many things including very deep relaxation, pain control, accelerated healing, and receiving intuition.

Many states of consciousness have been mapped, each having particular qualities and uses to it. In the Monroe system different patterns of binaural beats and their most common resulting patterns of consciousness are called "Focus levels." These focus levels are then designated by numbers. In the Monroe system Focus 1 is ordinary awake consciousness. Focus 3 relates to the increased synchronization of brain hemispheres or whole brain activation. Focus 10 is the body asleep-mind awake state already mentioned. Focus 12 is called a state of expanded awareness and an activation of the ability to perceive information beyond what is available through the physical senses. Focus 12 can be thought of as activating our sixth sense or our psychic senses. By the time a person's brain waves have shifted from Focus 1, our usual consciousness to Focus 12, there are profound differences in how we process information and get answers to questions. This can come in very handy.

I would like to give you an example of Focus 12 type problem solving. My mother suffered from Alzheimer's disease. Struggling with the aftermath of my brother Peter's suicide, she was looping over and over through depression and agonizing thoughts. Her constant fretting and distress was wearing out my dad who was her caretaker. He could not stand to see his beloved wife of over sixty years so unhappy.

In ordinary consciousness even with my background as a psychologist I could not see a good way to help her. Medications for depression and anxiety would dampen her already impaired mental function. She did not have enough short-term memory available for psychotherapy to work well. Taking her to new places or introducing new people was disorienting and frightening to her. I took this problem into a Focus 12 meditation and once in Focus 12 I asked, "What was the best solution?" I immediately received a message: "Be in joy." This message didn't come in an angel voice or anything, it just seemed to be my own voice, the same as any other time I might think to myself about something. But it came with a deep feeling of joy attached to it. When I returned to normal Focus 1 consciousness I thought about this message. I concluded that this just might work. I knew that my mother was very focused on her children's happiness. If we were happy she was happy. I made a VCR tape of happy family events, kittens playing, birthday parties, etc. I sent this to her. My dad put it on the TV. She was entranced and immediately improved in mood and calmness. She could watch it over and over, and each time it would be new to her given her diminished short-term memory. It really helped my dad to feel there was something he could do to lessen her pain.

I use this example not to brag about having a good idea but to illustrate the power of shifting our consciousness. I would have never come up with such a solution from my everyday consciousness. It was too simple. I was looking for a complex solution to a complex problem, while being burdened with a sense of futility. I hoped that now as I started to prepare for PK in Vegas, that having an elegant and effective way to shift consciousness, such as Hemi-Sync would help me raise energy and find solutions to the challenges that lay ahead. One of things that I love about Hemi-Sync is that it works without the need to adopt any religious or philosophical dogma. Over these twenty years I have seen atheists, Buddhist monks, fundamental Christians, agnostics, Republicans, Democrats, and Independents, rich and poor, all able to benefit from the technology. In teaching at the Monroe Institute I have opportunity to meet people from every continent and from a huge variety of professions, all feeling that their beliefs, their cultures, and they themselves were respected at TMI.

So Hemi-Sync would be one of my primary tools for my exploration. In the Monroe System, the higher focus level exercises (Focus 15 through 49) were designed to explore even deeper levels of consciousness. These levels facilitate a transcending of the usual limits of time-space thinking and open up one's potential to be in touch with non-physical energies and dimensions. Focus 10 would help me relax and restore energy and Focus 12 would help with expanding creative solutions and receiving intuitions. And the higher focus levels would come in handy with PK, because PK seems to transcend the usual rules of time-space.

Hemi-Sync exercises are efficient and practical. They are mostly about a half-hour long and can be easily used from a compact disc or loaded onto an iPod and be carried around. All you needed to do was to relax in a chair or bed, put on the headphones and listen. There was no need to spend years studying some esoteric system. I had the privilege to meet some advanced meditation practitioners from the Far East in one of my groups at Monroe. They came down on the fourth day of a program beaming and said, "You Americans are so efficient. You can take people deeply into their own consciousness potential in days, where it might take us many years to learn such skills in our system."

CHAPTER 7

First PK Trip

My flight was booked, my schedule cleared, and it was now a week before my first PK Vegas Trip. This was in May of 1994. I intensified my use of the HPP peak performance tapes. I also began to use the Monroe Institute's Free Flow Focus 12 exercise. In this exercise the binaural beats and verbal guidance take you to Focus 12 (expanded awareness) and once there, the verbal guidance fades, leaving you supported by the binaural beats to "cruise" and do whatever you want to do. During the free flow I began imagining being at the dice table, becoming comfortable there, feeling very good, confident, and relaxed yet energetic. Then I imagined picking up the dice and throwing them so that three dots appeared on the top of each of the two die. This would equal six which was my favorite number at the time. I saw myself betting the six and doing very well for a long time, sustaining my energy and focus despite whatever was going on around me. I imagined that my ego was quiet and that I was just feeling playful and enjoying myself. Then I sent this imaginary scene great light, feeling abundant and blessed, and said to myself, "So be it!"

This type of mental rehearsal is called patterning in the Monroe system. The goal is to make it as real in the mind as possible by engaging all of the senses. Some systems call this visualization. It is the main secret, referred to in the movie, *The Secret*, popular a few years back that dealt with manifesting your dreams. Visualization has been used successfully in sports to enhance performance and to help players get into the zone. Studies had found that doing several hours of visualizing meditation can help performance more than spending the same amount of time actually practicing the sport on the field. Some professional football teams take this even further by using sensory deprivation tanks for the meditation time. Then, when all the senses have quieted, a movie is shown of the perfect kick, pass, or whatever activity is the target for better performance. Visualization is a very powerful technique for focusing one's energy and belief in the direction desired. But I do not feel it is sufficient by itself to produce reliable results. The word "visualization" is a bit misleading because it is more than visual. The process is made much more powerful by engaging all of the senses and also feelings on an imaginal level, so that you are involved in the scene as deeply as possible. The goal is to have your body, mind, emotions, and spirit be fully engaged in the process. Bob Monroe called this work, "Patterning" because he felt that what you were attempting to bring into being or to manifest was often a complex pattern, rather than just a thing.

There is a story that appeared in *Chicken Soup for the Soul* by Jack Canfield and Mark Hansen that struck me strongly about the power of this process. As I remember it, there was a prisoner of war confined continually day and night for weeks on end to a small box. To keep his sanity, he imagined playing golf on the course back in his home town and having a wonderful round, shooting par. He would flesh in all the details in his imagination, the freshness of the grass, how good it felt to move his body. He would see each shot clearly, and it landing where he wished. Each day during his confinement he would play the entire course again in his mind. When he was finally released and returned to the freedom of home, he was physically debilitated. Yet the first time he went to play golf on the course he had played so many times in his imagination, he had a wonderful round and shot par, exactly as he had imagined it.

Equipped with my meditation tools, my memories of PK at Monroe and Princeton, and butterflies in my stomach, I boarded the plane for Vegas. I was staying at the Sahara hotel, one of the original casinos on the Strip. It was a property that I was familiar with. I knew the crews there, and knew many of the wait staff and bellmen well enough to follow how their children were doing. When we would talk, they would be interested in events in my family as well. I felt very at home there. I knew where everything was located and the restaurant menus by heart. On the second day, when I felt my energy had caught up a bit from the jet lag, I targeted the evening for my first PK dice attempt.

In the afternoon I took a nap, then a long shower. In the shower I focused upon letting the water cleanse away any tiredness and apprehension. I thanked my body in advance for all the energy I was going to ask from it. I affirmed the beauty and wonder of being in a physical body. I felt that this shower meditation would be helpful for what is called grounding. Grounding means to be very connected with the physical world and to be in the present moment. There is much power in being in the now. We often are not focused in the present moment. We leave the present and become ungrounded when we dwell on the past or worry about the future. We also lose our grounding when we go into our heads and lose track of our bodies, such as times when we are obsessing about something. Another very powerful block to good grounding is to feel unhappy with being in a physical body or with how things are going in our physical lives. This can show up as dissatisfaction or fear about the state of the world with its violence and unfairness, or about ourselves with our perceived faults.

Being grounded is very important any time when we want to be in our maximum power. Unless we are fully here, how can we expect to effect the here-now situation? When athletes or artists are in the zone they often report being so deeply in the present moment, that they lose track of time, or that time stands still.

I am emphasizing grounding here because I feel that it is very important to manifesting what you want to create. I have known many good people who, with best of intentions, cannot seem to get it together in one important area of their lives or another, be it finances, health, career, or relationships. Often what is missing is that they are not grounded. They have plenty of mental activity (wishing and hoping) but do not ground their intentions into action or results. It can be easy to become habitually ungrounded. Trauma can do this by causing us to reenact the past and worry about the future. If life is very stressful in the present, there is a natural tendency to want to escape. Alcohol, drugs, and even television or surfing the net can provide temporary relief from stress. But they also can each easily become a means of perpetual escape. And the more we escape, the more painful our present situation tends to become, motivating even stronger attempts to escape.

When I teach meditation classes at TMI people have a whole week to disconnect from day-to-day-stress. They are taken care of in terms of meals, are in a beautiful setting, and reach states of deep bliss during the exercises. They often begin to feel very good. At the end of the week, we shift gears and say, "Now it is time to ground." We mean in this case that it is time for participants to prepare to reenter their normal lives, with all the attendant problems and challenges. When we remind them that they are about to reenter their normal lives, they groan loudly and jokingly rebel against the thought. This is unfortunate because in fact being grounded can be a very happy, vibrant, and energizing state. I developed a defini-tion for my home study course on manifestation called SyncCreation. It is a lofty definition. But I have found it very useful in my Vegas work, in healing, and in manifesting in general. It is an ideal, which if practiced regularly, becomes a wonderfully magical way to live. "Being grounded means bringing your spirit fully into your body, suffusing your body with energy and light, and allowing your body and emotions to speak freely to you without repression. It involves strongly connecting with the earth and allowing its sacred energy into you—so that you are fully spirit and flesh at the same time. It means being vitally present in the present moment."

Some naturally grounding activities are things that get you in touch with your physical body, engage your senses, and encourage attention to the present moment. They span the gamut from gardening, dancing, pet-ting an animal, holding a new-born baby, chopping wood, and swim-ming, etc. You know that you are grounded if you feel lively, vibrant, powerful, and very aware of your surroundings. You can actually practice grounding and get better at it, so that it becomes more habitual, much like becoming aware of your posture and then improving it until good posture becomes habit and feels natural.

After resting and then grounding in the shower on my first Vegas trip, I lay down to meditate with Hemi-Sync. I refreshed my visualization of rolling sixes, this time imagining doing so well that the other players the table asked me to continue rolling. I heard them saying, "Pass the dice back to him, he is so good." I imagined black one-hundred-dollar chips increasing before me. I also began building a very high energy state by using my intention to pull in great energy with every breath. To make this tangible, I imagined the energy as unlimited happiness, then great light, and then great love. I finished the meditation by asking for the highest assistance from spirit in accomplishing my intention.

It was show time. I went down to the dice table. I worked to keep my energy high by noticing anything beautiful on my trip down to the casino. I stepped outside for a moment to connect with the mountains in the distance. I paid attention to people who were smiling or expressing affection for each other. I affirmed that good sources of guidance and support were all around me. I was clearly in an altered state of consciousness—the lights were sparkling, the music playing in the casino seemed particularly engaging. I felt relaxed but charged, focused, and feeling joy. I started with a small bet on the six. Chance expectations in dice would be for six to be rolled thirteen percent of the time and for it to come up as what is called hard six (a three on each of the dice equaling six) only once in 36 rolls. I silently extended gratitude toward the table (almost like saying grace before a meal) and well-wished all there. I reminded myself gently to release any fear and that this is joyous play.

The following description is approximate. Being in the zone makes it hard to keep exact track of events. During this session I controlled the dice for approximately two hours. I achieved a great run of sixes throwing a six on approximately sixty percent of all rolls with about forty percent of these being hard six, 3-3). I alternated between two tables during this time. I kept my energy flowing well and remained relaxed and unhurried. Fellow players said several times, "Let's give him the dice back, he is so good," which was how I had imaged it during my patterning.

I finished with four sixes in a row (0.03 percent chance) and quit. Then I went to a poker machine to sit down and relax. On my first pull on that machine I immediately got 4 sixes natural. It was a delightful surprise that my PK pattern for dice transferred over to the slot machine without my intending it. My energy soared once again and I thought, "Well, I am a good king of light" and on my second pull I got 4 Kings natural. These two amazing hands were followed by fifteen minutes of sixes and kings coming up in all combinations. Finally I felt complete. I went upstairs to my room and recorded the experience in my journal. I was very happy that all my preparation had paid off, that I had received solid confirmation that PK was real, and that I could do it by intention in Vegas. The state of mind and energy that I had enjoyed felt wonderful. It felt like a very healing space, good for body mind, and spirit. It was great fun to make the other players so happy and to receive financial abundance. After an hour I realized just how tired I was. I must have moved a lot of energy. It felt like I had run electricity through my body. I took a long nap and then went to dinner and a show to celebrate. The next day went well and then I went home.

I returned to Vegas in August of 1994 for my second trip. I was learning a lot. Much of the learning was in the form of trying different things. I would note my self-talk and feelings, and how they differed between sessions at the table that went well and sessions that went poorly. This was a bit like trying to pin the tail on a vigorously squirming donkey! What was at work was a very quixotic and magical flow. It was very difficult to quantify this living flow into a set pattern for success. I had thought that I could just come to Vegas and see what worked, and then just keep doing what worked. It turned out to not be that simple. Once my ego saw that I could do it, it basically said to me, "Okay, I got it. I will take over now!"

By this second trip I had a deepening appreciation of the magic of the whole experience and its resistance to being dissected. I discovered quickly that my learning in Vegas was likely to occur in a non-sequential, non-linear way. It would be very different than learning mathematics. George Ritzer is a sociologist concerned with the over-rationalization and efficiency of our culture—what he calls "McDonaldization." Paraphrasing his thoughts, "Efficiency leaves no room for enchantment. Anything that is magical is apt to be meandering and inefficient. Enchanted systems are often complex and highly convoluted, having no obvious means to an end. Since the magical can not be calculated, it is ignored and often eliminated."

While PK is more of a magical than a methodical system, some principles of science still do apply. One of these principles can be seen very clearly while playing at the dice table. In psychology there is a principle called operant conditioning. Operant conditioning is a method of learning that occurs through rewards and punishments. In this conditioning, an association is made between a behavior and a consequence for that behavior. It states that if you reward a behavior, that tends to increase the frequency and intensity of that behavior. Also if you punish a behavior, that tends to suppress or lessen that behavior. We know that the closer the reward or punishment is to the behavior, the faster the conditioning. The type of learning that happens through conditioning results in very deep, stable, and automatic responses. It is gut learning and once learned is hard to unlearn. We train a puppy by saying "Sit," and then when the puppy sits, immediately rewarding it with a treat. This is operant conditioning. After this learning is entrenched we could be somewhere with the dog being very tempted to run around to explore a new situation, but if we say "Sit," the dog will probably sit. We don't even to have to reward this behavior any longer except perhaps with an occasional "Good Dog" and it will persist.

Learning to throw dice using PK is a considerably more complex behavior than learning to sit. Yet, even without us understanding exactly what we are doing, the dice table will tend to quickly reward us for certain behaviors, thoughts, and feelings, and punish other behaviors just as quickly. At the tables, if I am happy, trusting, in high energy, and focused, I usually get paid at once. Intuition, discernment, awareness, emotional balance, letting go, and decisive action are often rewarded immediately. Also, I am fined instantly for attitudes that I want to extinguish. If I am greedy, fearful, unfocused, or irritated, the casino gladly takes my chips. Impatience, moving out of the present moment, fear of taking risks, confusion, anger about loss, and many other undesired behaviors are punished swiftly. I am being psychologically conditioned (rewarded and punished) in the direction that I want to go in learning to use PK with the dice consistently.

It also became apparent that at the dice table I was instantly rewarded with money for the behaviors and attitudes that I want to manifest in my life. Indeed the same qualities useful for PK dice are useful in relationships, in business, in manifestation, and in healing. Dice play conditions us very well in qualities and behaviors that are highly useful for an exciting and abundant life, as well as for spiritual advancement. It was wonderful to know that what I was attempting to learn would have such positive impact on many areas of my life.

This sounds pretty straightforward but in reality it is not that easy. There are two main reasons of this. The first we might call "The Myth of a Single Cause." As humans we tend to simplify explanations. For example, if Bob gets a bonus and buys a car, Bob might respond when we ask him why he bought a car, "I got a bonus." And we are satisfied with his answer. In fact there were probably many factors converging at once that caused the car buying. He might have been having trouble with his old car, there may be no other big bills such as college tuition for his children pending, he may be turning forty and having a mid-life urge for something new, his wife may have encouraged him, and the salesperson presenting that particular car to Bob may have been an excellent salesperson, etc. To make matters even more complex many of the reasons may not even be conscious to Bob, such as seeing a car ad several months ago, responding to the smell of a new car, and a touch of envy at the fellow down the block who put in a new pool.

In a similar fashion, for PK in dice to occur, many factors known and unknown have to converge to cause the PK. And many factors conscious and unconscious tend to work against it occurring. So it will not work to overly simplify and say, "Oh, I am feeling happy, so PK will occur. This is also true for other ways in which we affect reality. It is not sufficient to say, "Oh, just visualize what you want and it will manifest" or, "Trust and you shall be healed." My goal then in learning to do PK consistently was to identify as many of the causes and hindrances, both conscious and unconscious, which influence whether PK will occur.

The second reason that getting PK to work is not straightforward is that same operant conditioning we have been talking about. I was not a clean slate like a new puppy. I had already been conditioned by more than 40 years of life-experience and training. There were many things that I had to unlearn to do PK well. In these areas I was more like the adult cat who has scratched the same chair for years to mark its territory. Changing this behavior or any other entrenched behavior is a real challenge. There are many things that we have learned and repeated thousands of times which inhibit our expression of our full human potential, including expression of PK. We have learned limiting beliefs such as "nothing good comes easy." We have learned impaired emotional patterns such as feeling performance anxiety. Some of the toughest patterns to change are behaviors that are linked with strong beliefs and deep feelings. An example of this might be to behave in an awkward and shy manner, because of a belief that we are being judged and because of feelings self-conscious embarrassment. Behaving awkwardly only increases chances of failure yet can be very difficult to change.

In my early Vegas PK trips my journal reflected a growing list of things external to me that I thought were enhancing or detracting from performance. The list included things such as:

- What time of day was best for playing?

- What table and position at the table was best?

- Which day of the trip worked well?

- Which food and clothing worked best?

This list kept changing, which was crazy-making. Short and sweet, the good news is that over the long haul I found that none of it mattered very much. Actually it was very good news because in my transition from blissfully ignorant beginner's luck to serious student, this line of inquiry was leading me to the conclusion that for PK to work well for me I had to be wearing a red shirt, having just eaten vegetable soup with a chocolate malt, on the full moon, on a Tuesday. And if a person was smoking a cigar within fifty feet of me or the drink lady bumped my arm, it was all over. I can now easily see how gambling superstitions get started and become self-perpetuating.

In these first trips my journal also reflects a growing list of internal factors that did prove over time to matter. On the positive side the list included things like:

- Relaxation and preparation time were very important.

- Feel confident and abundant before and while playing.

- Open to intuition and have the courage to act upon it.

- If it is not going well, take long break and reset energy.

- Be grounded and expanded in energy at the same time.

- Clear your mind and emotions of anything from the past and be in the present moment.

- Practice manifestation more in daily life, even small things like finding parking spaces. Get a run of small successes going.

- Be generous with everyone and with your money, time, and attention.

- Look for positive energy at the table or create it yourself.

- Allow your intended purpose have delightfully unexpected results.

So as my trips continued I would read my reports of previous adventures and remind myself to implement these positive factors. Some times I would need to remind myself a hundred times about the same thing. But gradually these positive inner attitudes became easier to remember and live.

There was also a long list of internal factors that began to clearly emerge as PK killers. This list included things such as the following:

- Self-consciousness.

- Judging myself or others harshly.

- Feeling responsible for other people.

- Worrying about what others may think of me.

- Feeling that I have to do everything myself.

- Feeling that it is me versus them.

- Feeling that there is a limit to how much good can happen.

- Impatience and pushing too hard.

- Trying to be perfect.

- Reacting negatively to loss.

I would also see warnings about these things in my previous journal reports and would attempt to avoid them. But this was a difficult task. I was swimming against the tide of my forty years of conditioning in these matters. At the time I regularly and automatically used many of these negative behaviors on a daily basis and particularly when I felt threatened in any way. They were my coping strategies and even while they did not work very well, it felt like they allowed me to survive.

As an example of how they challenged me in Vegas was that after I had rolled well a few times, when I would approach the table, the crew would announce (to me it seemed that they shouted to the other players loudly), "Here comes Mister Lucky, bet big now, he is a super hot roller!" This would immediately put me into self-consciousness and fear of failure, and I would often lose quickly. I would then keenly notice the other players' disappointment, and fantasized about the dealers' disapproval. The next time I went to the tables the dealers didn't even have to greet me as "Mr. Lucky" to throw me off my game. All I needed to do was fear that they would say it and I would put a big crimp on my energy before I even started to play. I could have used their Mister Lucky statement as encouragement to bolster my confidence, but that was not how I was built. My training was that if someone praised you, you should act modestly and deflect the attention immediately.

Just to show you how sticky to the ego two words can be, I am going to go a bit deeper with "Mr. Lucky." In my family I was the youngest of four boys. By the time I came along my parents were considerably more affluent and considerably mellower about rules such as curfew. My memory of events is that my brothers would tease me constantly about being the lucky one, whereas they were the hard-working ones who had experienced much stricter parenting. This would often come up when I was petitioning my parents for some favor that I really wanted. And my brothers' teasing threatened my being granted the favor because it increased my parents' reluctance to grant my request. My parents wanted to be fair to all their children. So when they heard, "You never let us do that when we were his age," it gave them pause. I would rebel against this description, saying to my brothers and to myself with vehemence, "I am not lucky." I probably even stamped my feet for emphasis. I would also respond by showing them how hard I worked at everything from school work to chores. Now here I was forty years later being called Mr. Lucky, just when I wanted to be lucky as I started a PK run at the tables. As they say, this really screwed with my Chi! And the bigger issue of working hard had to be addressed continually during learning PK. I definitely had a tendency to make this playful, trusting, and joyous activity into hard work. Just to be clear, I do indeed feel very fortunate and have tremendous gratitude for my blessings and would have to say that I am l lucky. But there is an inner child part of me that is not comfortable when someone else calls me lucky. And that inner child part feels that hard work should be admired much more than luck.

I do not think that I am alone in this belief. When Americans are surveyed they believe most success is based upon hard work. But in fact even the luck of what month you were born dramatically affects your chances of success in school and sports. This is because it can place you with kids who are quite a bit older or younger than you are when you start school. Because of an age difference of almost a year between the youngest and oldest child in the kindergarten classes, you may be either very advanced compared to peers in physical and mental development when you start school, or very behind, depending on what birth month is the cut off for your starting class. Studies show that those who excel in professional sports, for example, tend to be born in certain months that give them a leg up in being chosen for sports teams in grade school due to their age advantage and consequently more advanced physical development of even a few months over their class mates.

When we have done really well at something, do we not prefer to be told that we have worked hard and deserve it, versus that we are lucky? We like this illusion that hard work is all that is needed, because then things feel more under our control and we can feel okay that we are doing better than someone else because we deserve it because of our hard work. Yet there is much that is outside of our control that affects us deeply such as who our parents are, what are their resources including social network, schools, parenting skills, etc.

Yes, we should be inspired by people rising from disadvantaged circumstances and applaud dedication to a goal. Yet it is good to have the humility to understand that luck may also have something to do with success or failure as well. This will deepen our compassion toward ourselves and others when things go poorly and increase our gratitude when things go well. And as we shall see, perhaps as we get old enough to influence our circumstances, we might even be able to increase our luck. If we acknowledge the role of luck in our lives then we can perhaps understand what it is and cultivate good luck's presence in our lives. And if we over-value hard work as a moral pinnacle, then, as we create our reality, we probably will create a lot of hard work for ourselves!

CHAPTER 8

Dragons and Miracles

Despite struggling with the dragons of my past conditioning, as my trips continued I had some amazing experiences. On a November 1994 trip, my intuition flowered into a clear knowing of what number would be rolled next on the dice. I also began to visually perceive what looked like lines of force between me and the dice, and me and the casino's chips. It felt like a description from the Carlos Castenada books about being able to see the usually invisible lines of non-physical energy that connect physical things together. For two hours this knowing of numbers and perceiving lines of force continued as I rolled very well. I wrote in my journal that the trip was very confirming for me. The trip was a maturing process. I was gentle with myself and enjoyed each circumstance that I encountered. I was more observant and more grounded. I kept better control over my priorities of love, light, play, kindness, and generosity. I enjoyed better relations with casino personnel. What I think was happening was that with more experience, the mechanics of the game were becoming second nature. I now knew the rules of this complex game, how to throw the dice without them leaving the table, and how to bet and manage money. It was as if, earlier on I was struggling to remember and find the notes on a piano, and now was far enough along that the notes of the game were automatic and I could start making PK music with them.

My December 1994 trip reinforced my lesson about responsibility for others. I had met a professional poker player at the Monroe Institute. He had played for over twenty years successfully, raising his large family on the income he generated from poker. When he heard what I was doing he made me an offer that I could not refuse. He would pay all my expenses and then front me the money to gamble. He would absorb all my losses and split any winnings with me fifty-fifty. He even bought us cool matching felt Stetson style hats. I still wear mine to this day. This deal should have made me totally relaxed by taking any fear of loss out of the equation. But that is not what happened. I found myself, despite all the meditation and preparation, anxious each time I went to the table to not lose his money. It turned out that I felt more responsibility for someone else's money than my own.

We struggled through the few days and did end up a bit ahead. But when he left and I was on my own, I felt an amazing sense of relief. I immediately went to the tables by myself and had a wonderful two-hour PK experience. I sung, "Whistle while you work" to myself throughout the session, and just relaxed and had fun. By end of this series, I was able to roll exactly what I wanted immediately and also knew what I would roll. I felt very light in my energy and even began to hear what sounded to me like an angelic choir in the background during the second hour of my time there. During this choir experience I felt very loved by and connected with helpers from the spirit world. The roll stopped when I thought "seven" and it was time to catch my plane. As I left the table, I noticed that flowers and even the neon glowed with unusual beauty.

This lesson about responsibility for others was one I would learn very slowly. I stopped playing with members of my family except my brother John because the sense of responsibility for them was just too great to overcome. I seldom made a bet for another person after this trip, even though many people when they hear that I am going to Vegas ask me to do so. You can run but you can't hide forever. Deeper levels of this lesson about responsibility continued to surface. The ultimate challenge was when I began to teach others what I had learned at the dice table.

The reason feeling overly responsible for someone else is so negative to PK and manifestation is that it takes away joy and replaces it with duty and pressure. It tends to increase self-consciousness and the temptation to try too hard. PK and manifestation have an easier time developing when there is a child-like trust in the flow of circumstances and energy. Any pushing collapses this trust. This was a hard lesson for me because I was programmed by family and profession to feel and be responsible at all times, particularly when someone else's welfare was at stake. From taking care of my younger sister to caring for my psychotherapy patients, responsibility was a key way that I received praise and the rewards of being useful in my life. I felt good about myself when being responsible, and felt selfish when I was not. Responsibility, then, was one of my harder PK-killing dragons to slay. From my point of view everyone has their personal dragons, and to them they are formidable. They are never silly to that person though to another they may seem stupid. A person may feel another's fear of heights is silly, yet cringe at the thought of being confined in a small space. For another they may cheerfully go spelunking in the smallest caves yet may fear flying.

In March of 1995 I took a trip that illustrates the struggle with my dragons very well. I was making several changes this trip. First I was moving up in style and I planned also this trip to increase the size of my bets. I flew out first class and stayed at the Desert Inn, which in those days was one of the classiest places on the strip. The Desert Inn was small by today's mega casino standards. Whereas today there are properties with 4,000 rooms, The DI had only 400 rooms. But they were beautifully appointed with waterfall baths and beautiful beds. Some of the high roller suites, overlooking the golf course were over 3,000 square feet in size, quite a bit bigger than the average house at the time. The elegantly decorated casino was very quiet, as the slot machine noises were turned way down and the place was heavily carpeted with high ceilings. There were huge sparkling crystal chandeliers overhanging the dice tables where I could imagine all my spiritual helpers liked to hang out and bless the tables below.

There were signs right from the beginning of this trip that things were not flowing well. I had a room change hassle during check in. Usually when I have prepared my energy at home for the trip, things flowed beautifully on the way to Vegas. I started my first gaming that trip by raising my basic $5 bet to $25. In retrospect this was not a great idea. Going up by five times my normal bet took me into fear and out of the zone. I lost $800 very fast. By the end of Friday I was down $1000 with no wins. By end of Saturday I was down $1,200, with one good run at the Sands with good vibes at the table and after a walk in the sun. By Sunday night I was down further despite another win at the Sands. Monday I managed to break even, finishing the evening with a good run at the Sahara. Finally on

Tuesday I settled down and did more emotional cleansing and preparation work. This included forgiving myself for the losses, letting go of judgment of myself and others, and connecting with God Source for pure clean energy. With these changes I had some nice runs.

I learned a lot this trip the hard way. My journal records that learning to have no judgment or concern with other's opinions is essential. It advises not to rush or push the development of energy. I ended with a good day and morning but still down $2,000, my first loss in eight trips. I think part of the problem was that by staying at the Desert Inn with its higher prices, I allowed myself to feel pressured to gamble high enough to justify the casino giving me free rooms and meals. So I saw a pattern of losing at the Desert Inn and winning at the Sands, Sahara, and other places I played that trip where I was not worried about that.

When the casino pays for your room and meals this is called "comps." Often the casino will give you back about fifteen percent of your statistically expected losses whether you actually lose or not. They may also give back some of your actual losses, by adjusting your room bill. Giving comps encourages players to gamble more and also to return to the same casino again where they will be treated like VIP's. It can be quite intoxicating to be picked up by personal limo, registered in a special lounge, given a beautiful suite on the top floor with fruit baskets and flowers and special notes welcoming you personally to the room. And then to eat for free at the casino's finest restaurants and at the best tables, and have the best seats for shows, with no waiting in line, etc. This is highly appealing to the ego. But as we are seeing, being in ego is not conducive to PK, or even to good judgment while playing in a regular manner. But if you can conquer the ego challenge, then all these treats plus winning money at the same time makes for a wonderful trip!

Pushing past your comfort zone to impress the casino into giving you free stuff to make you feel special is called "playing for comps." The most destructive aspect of this behavior can be that you use all these things to begin to feel superior to other people. This pulls you strongly into ego and separates you from the "we are all one" feeling that makes PK and life flow beautifully. It can be tempting to play for comps in many areas of life. The comp may be that others admire you, or you get that special seat on an airplane, or a bonus and corner office at work. But if you let your ego get into this, you can be easily manipulated and also become disconnected from true sources of good energy such as the beauty of nature, the warmth of family and friends, and the humility needed to feel oneness with the simplest of things.

My June 1995 trip was special in that it was the first time that I went to Vegas directly from teaching meditation for a week at the Monroe Institute. This created some interesting results. After a good night's sleep (no longer pushing to gamble right from the start), the next day I found myself very intuitive. I would have hunches about where and when to go and what numbers would be coming up, etc. I think this was from all the meditating the week before. I won small amounts from the first and stayed ahead throughout the entire trip. This time I stayed at the more modest Sahara hotel. When I went to the Desert Inn free of "comp anxiety" I did very well there. I also began to shift the numbers that I would bet on, to those which are very hard to get statistically, such as a twelve which should only come up once in thirty-six rolls by chance. These numbers pay well, for example, $30 for every dollar bet on the twelve. And I was developing confidence that I could hit these unlikely numbers using PK with fairly good regularity. This trip I played more to enjoy the game rather than to be special. Concern about what other people thought and impatience were less of a problem.

One of the challenges for me in doing PK at the dice table is that the more successful you are, the louder and more crowded with other people the table becomes. It is hard to maintain a meditative state when this happens. This trip I experimented with a new image to address that problem. When things started to get raucous, I would image myself as a great eagle of light and soar high above the turmoil, still connected to the table, just as an eagle with sharp vision can clearly see dinner moving on the ground. I imagined the quiet of soaring high above and I was able to detach from the noise around me. This new image worked very well and I still use it successfully today.

I went to Vegas for trips in July, October, and November of 1995 and they went well with more consolidation of learning. I was able to tame my dragons more successfully! I was able to generate and manage the high energy needed for PK without losing my grounding. This also made the energy roller-coaster ride from home to Vegas and back again less steep. In earlier trips I would arrive back home very tired from running energy and experience that energy shooting out uncontrollably. For example, on the way home from the airport the big lights on the side of the interstate would blow out as I drove by and at home a half dozen light bulbs would blow the first day back. Then there would be a draining of all energy almost into depression. Everything seemed flat and slightly grey compared to the high energy shimmering and brilliance I would experience in Vegas. I think that I was running so much energy while in Vegas that on a neurophysiologicial basis my brain's dopamine receptors, which get activated during meditation, were being depleted, and had to have time to rebalance when home.

During these late 1995 trips there were some interesting PK phenomena that made me chuckle. I had patterned at home for hard six (3+3=6) to be my best number on a trip, and found upon arrival that I was checked into room #363. During this time the numbers that I was patterning for on the dice would show up often in room numbers, seat assignments, addresses, etc.

I went out with a psychiatrist friend one trip and after he watched me play we had lunch. In the restaurant, mimicking Freud by feigning a strong Austrian accent, he playfully asked me, "What was your relationship with your mother?" He was observing that I was not very trusting at the table and therefore more tense than I needed to be. He was correct. Difficulty trusting deeply was one of my dragons that was born early in my life. My mother was very diligent about mothering correctly. At that time the popular theory was to schedule-feed your baby. Even as an infant I had a high metabolism and would get very hungry between feedings. Despite intense crying that tore my mother's heart, she would not feed me until the next scheduled time. I think that this may have put in a deep program that it was not okay to trust the universe to give you what you need even on a basic level. Other experiences added to this feeling that you had to provide for yourself.

In Vegas these type feelings, which usually were buried, were coming to the surface and giving me the opportunity to heal them. It was obvious that with PK, lack of trust impaired the process, and deep trust facilitated a much stronger PK energy and also much greater abundance in terms of monetary return at the tables. After this lunch with my friend I took a nap and then meditated on what he had said. During the meditation I felt much angelic energy that seemed to be encouraging me to feel deserving of all good, and that the universe was indeed a loving and abundant place. I also patterned for hard ten (5+5=10) to be my target. I went down to the table with the image of myself as a child safe on my mother's chest. I immediately threw five hard tens in a row (which would happen only once in 60 million times by chance). I took this as confirmation that it was good to work on this issue of trust! And, of course, hard ten became my new favorite number and still one of my favorites today.

During my 1996 trips I was finally becoming more comfortable with $25 bets. One of the things that helped me get there was attending a craps tournament. In the tournament you were given $10,000 in fake chips to play with and whoever ended up with the most chips after three 30 minute sessions at the tables won the tournament. This opportunity to play with fake money was very enlightening. The only way to separate yourself out from the middle of the pack was to bet big and take wild chances. So I was making $500 bets with these fake chips and seeing the results. After the tournament was over it was much easier to risk a bit more real money and not feel so tense about it. On that trip I was reading the book *Pilgrimage: a Contemporary Quest for Ancient Wisdom* by Paulo Coelho and had a deep experience of God indwelling in my heart. Coelho inspired me with his statement that the true path has agape, practicality, and availability to all. And that God needs our help to manifest in us given we have free choice—the rest of nature just manifests God's presence automatically.

On another 1996 trip I started off with much irritation. I had a stressful mortgage signing the day before and then my car broke down on the way to the airport. I was crammed into a middle seat in coach on a long delayed flight. Irritation for me is a sign that my energy is rising so fast that my grounding is not keeping up with it and that I also have some fears floating around me. What this does is leave me very spacey (as if I had been drinking) and also oversensitive to stimulation. Noises become unpleasantly loud and lights harshly bright. It also seems like people are moving too slowly and are basically in my way. And often a series of negative glitches begin to appear in my life. This is not a good state in which to try PK. You get the PK but it is often the opposite of what you want, or "negative PK" if you will.

Highly charged states and negative emotion produce dramatically negative results. This is true in life as well. When I was going through my divorce everything in my house was breaking. The dishwasher, clothes washer, garage door openers, etc. What was happening was that in a highly emotional state I was thinking "broken home" and the universe cooperated by producing a broken home. The more the breakage happened, the more intense the feelings of stress became, and the more breakage happened. I was in a self-intensifying negative loop. These can almost be like the death spiral that airplanes sometimes experience. They can be very hard to pull out of. But I finally caught myself and changed my thought to "building a new life." When I did this, immediately many of the appliances fixed themselves and further breakage stopped. So if in your life you are having a series of negative events, it is good to check your emotions and thinking, and re-center yourself around calm emotions and positive thoughts.

That is what I did this trip. After two days of building irritation and consequently being punished at the dice table for it, I finally got the message and stopped and reset. I surrendered to the present moment, grieved a bit for the rough time I was having, and then re-centered around what I know about love. While eating Miso soup alone at a restaurant at the Desert Inn, just as I turned my emotional corner, the song *The Wind Beneath My Wings*, sung by Bette Midler came on over the speakers in the restaurant. I felt transported into God's love. It felt like God was saying to me how much he/she appreciated me being down in the darkness of this planet and how important it was to the plan that we manifest light in the darkness. After this experience I went to the tables and had a series of wins that brought me back close to even. The main lesson from the trip: Get your heart open first, and feel powerful, protected and loved, then attempt to manifest what you desire. I think this is a great lesson to apply throughout life!

Another thing that I was learning was that Las Vegas was a house of mirrors. By this I mean that the casinos were excellent at taking your thoughts, beliefs, and emotions, and immediately intensifying them, and then reflecting them back in terms of your experience. My experiences in the casino were a direct reflection of what I was thinking and feeling at the time. I think that this is true in all of life, but in the rest of life this feedback loop is slowed down and less clear. In real life this feedback can be so slow, in fact, that you miss the connection between what you are thinking and what you are experiencing. For example, one might be negative, angry, depressed, or fearful for days or weeks before the consequences of that type thinking manifests into reality by undesirable things happening. Also in real life if one tries to think positively it can be many weeks before a negative series of events begins to turn around. This can result is our feeling pretty careless about our negative thoughts and discouraged when attempting to change things for the better.

In the casino however, the consequences often occur in seconds or minutes. The quick casino feedback loop makes what is happening much clearer. So I would receive immediate evidence that our thoughts and feelings are highly important in forming our reality. Obviously it really helped to be positive. The kicker though is that such positivity has to be genuine. It was not sufficient to have "a stiff upper lip," or "smile and the world smiles with you" attitudes—you had to be fully present in genuine positive space. This of course is a challenge when things seem not to be going well. In order to thrive in the casino environment I had to develop a way to very quickly become aware of my thoughts and feelings, to express and release them very quickly if they were negative, and then to quickly build positive thought and energy. This practice in Vegas has helped me immeasurably in life to do the same process. While I surely am not perfect at it, the process is now often almost automatic. This in turn has made me much happier no matter what is going on. Now I release stressful things quickly that in the past I might have dwelt upon for a long time. This has dramatically reduced the number, duration, and intensity of negative events in my life and dramatically increased the times that are magically synchronistic and delightful.

I continued to consolidate my learning during my 1997 trips. By the end of 1997 my journal had become a personal manifestation manual that was a forty-page long record of my experience. It distilled my trial and error experiences into insights and recommendations that had been proven to work repeatedly for me. By this time, after more than three years of Vegas PK trips, I felt that I had learned quite a lot. And yet there was a feeling that there was even more to learn and that doing so would make the whole of my life experience much richer. I had a good sense of what was important to success in PK and what was not. I had shaved the time I needed to clear and raise my energy from four or five days in Vegas to about two days to be in peak energy, even with jet lag. I had smoothed the emotional roller coaster to the point where there was no let down when I returned home. Initially I needed to raise a very high energy to overcome many of the automatic attitudes and beliefs that stood in the way of strong PK. Now these attitudes, beliefs, and emotional patterns had been transformed enough that they were not such a hurdle. In fact they were much better in line with manifesting a positive reality.

I had learned the mechanics of the game of dice. I experimented with many systems of betting, discarded many that were commonly taught in the books on dice, and settled on an approach that was highly compatible with PK. Many systems that are taught, I could put under the rubric, "How to lose money less quickly." These systems are primarily defensive in strategy. One popular system (and its huge number of variations) teaches the player to place bets where the percentage of profit the casino takes is very low (in the 1.5 percent range). The problem with these systems is that those kinds of bet also paid very little to the player (for example $7 for a $6 bet). So with these type bets you usually had to either bet very large amounts of money or be there a very long time to get well ahead. It seemed to me that the casino was encouraging these type bets by taking a low percentage of the profits in order to keep the player at the table a long time—long enough for the probabilities of chance to kick into play. And those probabilities were always in favor of the casino. There is a saying in gaming that has much truth: "The player with the most money usually wins." It was obvious that the casino has the most money. Encouraging higher bets on these low pay out numbers puts most players in the position of betting too much on any one number and running out of money quickly. These players did not have the ammo to last through negative downturns, nor have the patience to wait for the right moment.

Other systems teach the player to bet for and against himself at the same time. These are called hedge strategies. They are much like the strategies that hedge fund managers use in the markets. These systems proclaimed that they will protect the player from large losses. Again, in observing hundreds of players over thousands of rolls, they just seemed to help the player lose money less quickly. There are other systems that have the player follow betting strategies designed to help him bet less when the table is "cold" and more when the table is "hot," then harvest profits in a disciplined manner. These strategies are a bit better but still as with all the systems listed, succumb to the laws of probability so that the casino eventually wins. All these systems, often with an amazing amount of time and mathematical analysis put into them, were based on the laws of probability which clearly indicate that the casino will win in the run long. In fact, it is the belief that the laws of probability can never be violated, that condemns these systems to failure.

In the game of craps, the player, playing in a chance fashion, and regardless of which system they use, will slowly lose their money the majority of time. But I discovered that there was something that was even more powerful than the laws of probability in separating the player from his money. It is the players' own beliefs and emotions! This is why on the plane to Vegas there are many excited people and on the way home the plane is usually very quiet. And if you asked how many won, only a few hands would go up. If the only thing in operation was the laws of probability, somewhere between a quarter and half of the people on the plane should have won. Usually my guess is that it is closer to five percent. What could be so powerful as to cause this?

The answer is that the player's beliefs and emotions strongly influence money management and how the average person plays games of chance. Perhaps the strongest influence for most people coming as tourists is that before leaving home, knowing that Vegas can be an expensive place, they carefully budget their money. They may say something to themselves such as, "I'm going to Vegas and I can afford to lose $20 a day, or $200 a day"— the number of zeros is not important. Having set out a clear pattern for manifesting "what they can afford to lose" in an excited but somewhat fearful state, that is exactly what they accomplish. They lose their stated budget.

Believe it or not very few players actually strongly and confidently expect to win and desire to win. Many are attracted more to the action than to winning. Winning takes more knowledge and more discipline than they care to develop. They are on vacation after all! And there is nothing wrong with that. They can see great shows, eat fabulous food, enjoy the action at the tables, and go home refreshed. Wanting to make money, fearing that you might lose it, and not having enough information to know what you are doing is usually a lethal combination for achieving abundance. This is true in the stock market, the real estate market, antique coin collecting, and business, as well as Vegas. Of course at any given time you can be very lucky and that is wonderful. But what looks like luck may often be preparation meeting opportunity, and then the guts to take a well understood risk.

I want to comment a bit further on luck. I do think that there is genuine luck, meaning that you did not do anything to prepare and perhaps don't even deserve it but the universe, angels, God, or another person basically reaches out and blesses you with good fortune. This good fortune may be as simple as a smile, an encouragement, or a direction. It can be as big as winning the lottery when you have huge medical bills, are out of work, and are sinking into despair. I think that the best way to invite this kind of luck or blessing is to feel deserving of it, to trust that it exists, to ask for it, and to allow it to come to you. My butt has been saved many times by this kind of blessing. And it is also true that wondrous things beyond my imagining have come via this kind of blessing. I love this saying which is purported to be an ancient Afghan proverb, "If luck is with thee, why hurry? If luck is against thee, why hurry?"

Another way beliefs and emotions effect outcome is that many players can only afford to risk a small amount without generating a lot of fear, and yet want to win big. Let's take a simple example. You find someone who will pay you $5 for every time you toss a coin and it comes up heads. They will fine you $5 for every time it comes up tails. Over many rolls, perhaps a hundred or more, assuming a balanced coin, you both should break even. This is because the odds are 50/50 for both heads and tails showing up. What happens in casino games is that on every hand (toss of the coin) the casino takes a percentage. This varies dramatically but let's use two percent as an average figure. This is like playing the coin toss game and every time you win you get $4.90 and every time you lose you pay $5.00. That is just ten cents per throw, correct? Yet if you toss those 100 throws and get paid the 50 times you hit heads, you will only be paid $245, and the other fellow will be paid $255 for his 50 tails. Even though you each won an equal amount of tosses, he wins $10 more. But you can see that at this rate, he doesn't win enough to build a grand casino and give you free drinks. Yet there are many grand casinos that are doing just fine.

What is happening here? No, the games are not rigged by the casino. They are very carefully monitored to be true to what chance would dictate. But the games are rigged against the player by the players themselves. The above stated, "I can afford to lose" thinking, plus not knowing what they are doing combines with a third factor—we could call it greed, but that is such an ugly word, and it does not quite fit.

What is happening is that the average player feels they can afford to gamble just a little but want to win big. If they changed this around to "I am willing to risk a lot and I just want to win a little," it would all work out much better most of the time. Let's go back to the example of the coin toss. The game is fifty/fifty but two percent taken for the house. The bet is still $5 each toss. But now the player wants to win at least $100, and does not want to risk more than $20. What happens? Assuming normal chance, the tosses will vary around the mean in probability language. Sometimes there may be three heads in a row, and sometimes three tails. But the person will most likely (in the sense of ninety-nine percent of the time) be $20 up or $20 down before they ever get $100 up. And remember when they are $20 down they are finished, as it was all they were willing to risk. This is what happens to most tourist players and quite a few of the regulars in Vegas. They lose their entire small stake before ever approaching their goal of the big win.

Now let's reverse this. The player is now willing to risk $100 to make $20. In this case they can patiently wait for themselves to get $20 ahead, even if at times they are $40 down. And the laws of probability now say that they would win most of the time. We can call this strategy proper money management, and even without PK this would allow many more players to come home winners. But the strategy is hard to implement due to human nature. For it to work you have to risk much more than you want to win and then be willing to be patient. And usually the more we have at risk the more impatient we tend to be! Yet this being willing to risk more than they expect to win is exactly what the casinos do. They are willing to risk a rare given player winning millions of dollars. They are very patient knowing that over the day and thousands of players, the laws of probability will even things out and they can take their percentage of each winning hand.

Much of what I learned in the casino applies directly to real life. This does too. This concept of being willing to risk a lot to gain a little applies to real life as well. I am willing to risk a lot to write a book and put in hundreds of hours in writing it. If the book entertains and helps a few people, I will be very happy with this result. Of course I will be even happier if the book is read by a huge number of people! How many people do you know in life who are searching for the big win yet only willing to risk just a little? This happens often in business, the stock market, and in relationships. In your experience, how does that tend to work out for them and perhaps for you? I am suggesting that a truly abundant and wonderful life can be created by taking risks for repeated small wins. And that some of those small wins will on their own turn into larger than anticipated wins. It may seem a big risk to ask someone out with the possibility of rejection, for the small win of a date with them. But in doing so you may meet your soul mate!

I would like to tell you a manifestation story. This happened when my energy was naturally high from going on many Vegas trips, doing the preparation work for these trips, and learning my lessons about how to create the reality you desire. I was sitting at home one day and thought to myself, "Gee, I would like to take my wife to Paris. She has never been and I know she would love the city with all its terrific museums and other sites to see. That would be a great romantic trip." The very next day the first email I read was from someone who I had trained at the Monroe Institute, asking if I would like to present a workshop in France. Up to that moment I had never been invited to present a workshop in Europe. I proposed my fee and they accepted it. In even higher energy at the prospect of the trip, I thought that it would be really cool to fly there and back first class. It would add to the romance and allow me to arrive refreshed enough to do a good job training. Next I remembered a business man who had recently told me that he had hundreds of thousands of miles on Delta, which was contemplating bankruptcy at the time. He was concerned that they may be going out of business and that he would lose his miles. I called him and offered to trade some miles from him for places in my workshops. He gifted me with enough miles (210,000) to get two free first class tickets. My wife and I excitedly planned a three-week vacation around the workshop.

This trip involved taking some risks: going to a foreign country, teaching in French through an interpreter, not being sure whether people would come and that the facilities would be adequate, asking this man that I did not know very well for the air miles, etc. But I was content to take these risks for the win of the trip. The anticipated win of the workshop turned into a much bigger win than expected. The workshop went very well, and during it we acclimated to the language and jet lag. Afterwards we deeply enjoyed our tour through southern France, then the beautiful Loire valley and finished by being in Paris for about a week. But the win became bigger still. From that workshop I received offers to do many others in Europe, including at the time of this book, several more trips to France, and several trips to Portugal and Germany. The last trip as of this writing was the opportunity to give a workshop at a five star resort right on the Mediterranean Sea in Cyprus. All the hosts of these events have been amazingly gracious, helping us see their countries from more of an insider view than a tourist. Many of the hosts and participants have become good friends. And lastly, the business man who gifted me the miles became a treasured business partner and friend.

Notice that I was willing to take risks to go for the small win. I was content that my fee for the original workshop covered some of the costs of my trip. If I had gone for the big win and asked for a large fee up front for the first workshop, probably none of this would have happened. I want to reinforce this insight because I feel it is so important. I feel strongly that the best approach is to go for the small wins and leave the big wins up to the universe or God. The universe wants to support us and give us abundance but it does require us to get out of our own way. Going for the big win is very difficult. Too much of our ego gets involved. There is too much temptation for fear and greed to sabotage our efforts. Repeatedly going for the big win, yet being scared to risk very much usually results in a pattern of discouraging losses. And at worst repeatedly going for the big win can literally be fatal. I think that this is one of the critical patterns that happened to my brother Peter leading to his suicide. Peter, in his struggle to get out of an ever-deepening financial hole, became more and more desperate for the big win. In Vegas you sadly see people who are behind and make crazier and crazier bets to try to get even with one big win. When you are feeling lack acutely it is almost impossible to attract that big win.

I want to note an important exception to the "go for small wins" theory. If the idea of a particular big win really excites your passion and it is in line with your heart and spirit's best desire for your greatest benefit and those around you, then go for it wholeheartedly. If it is right for you, and your passion is so great that it overwhelms any fears or limiting thoughts that you might have, then that big win has a great chance of manifesting. These large visions that are successful usually do not involve one just thinking of personal gain. They tend to be the visions driven by a passion to help others in a big way. Financial gain, fame, and power may come but they are not usually the goals that fire the spirit and cause the universe to help. The vision is often perceiving a need and feeling a passion to address that need. That is the way to become president, world peacemaker, founder of massive organizations to help humanity, etc.

It is disturbing to me that human beings engage in destructive and punishing behaviors. Why do we often work against our own best interest and the interests of the planet as a whole? This question led me to explore the nature of risk and how humans deal with it. There is a great book, *Against the Gods: the Remarkable Story of Risk* by Peter L. Bernstein, which explores this topic well. According to Bernstein, risk is a fairly new concept in human culture. For the Romans there was no risk, in that everything was ordained by the gods. Only very gradually has man begun to learn about risk, including the laws of probability. According to Wikipedia, Christiaan Huygens in 1567 provided the earliest known scientific treatment of the subject of probability. So we are not built to automatically assess risk accurately when it comes to the complexity of modern-day issues and systems. We are programmed to assess risk effectively in smaller, more nature-based environments, where decisions are usually made within seconds based upon the immediate circumstances. This risk assessment system is based more upon instinct and emotion than logic. We see a snake on the path and decide quickly not to step over it but to go a different way.

We continue to use this system now in our more complex society. This results in making decisions within seconds on very limited data and rationalizing that we have made a considered decision. Malcolm Gladwell's book, *Blink,* explains this well. We truly do go on first impressions and seldom change our minds from there. Fortunately, these quick impressions are often correct. Unfortunately, when there is a substantial risk, but that risk is rare or the consequence is not likely to occur for a long time, we assess risk less effectively. We usually will feel there is more risk from strangers and unknown places, yet most accidents occur at home and crimes against us are most frequently perpetrated by people we know. I know that flying is safer than driving, but it sure doesn't feel that way. We often underestimate long term risks and overestimate short term risk. This can lead us to engage in unhealthy habits than can take years to come back to haunt us. And we would rather avoid the short term risk of an unpleasant conversation, even through repeatedly doing so erodes the health of an important relationship. The Vegas gaming environment truly is a great place to practice confronting both short term and longer term risks, because you can keep the amount of money small and still learn the lessons. One can learn to meet risk with the correct tools: knowledge, energy, empowering beliefs, and the courage to act.

Casinos were not always a place to experiment with small risks. In the book, *Roll the Bones: the History of Gambling*, author David G. Schwartz relates that in the early casinos in Europe, members of the French court were expected to wager huge amounts, putting their estates at risk and then not crack a smile or frown when they won or lost. You can still see residuals of this attitude in European casinos. My wife and I took a tour through Germany, stopping at Baden Baden, known for its wonderful Roman baths and home to one of the oldest casinos in Europe. We walked in and it was quiet as a church. I was expected to wear a jacket and tie. All slot machines were missing from the main level. There were no dice games. We sat at a roulette wheel and on her first bet my wife placed ten Euros on number seventeen and immediately won, which paid 300 Euros (a one in 32 chance). We Americans both went "Yay!" and received looks of disapproval for our outburst. So we cashed in and left. The contrast with American casinos was dramatic. *Roll the Bones* is a fascinating tour of gaming through the ages and points out that as a society we have been gambling in various social games and organized houses on all populated continents since the beginning of recorded history.

CHAPTER 9

Honing the System

In these years of going to Vegas I had identified within a magical ever-changing milieu, what seemed to work, in terms of being able to use PK in the casino. I had learned through experience that money management was critical if you were throwing dice or playing slots according to the laws of chance. And one's beliefs and goals directly affected outcomes. A thought such as, "I can afford to lose X dollars a day," tended to produce that result. I also realized that management of assets was important even if you were using PK. I came to understand that the feeling of wanting to win big yet wanting to risk only a little was very deeply ingrained in our psyche and needs to be worked with. I had concluded that gaming that relied on the laws of chance was almost certain to be condemned to long term failure by this human tendency. But being able to do PK, even part of the time, created a way out of this quandary.

I gradually developed a method of betting and money management that was very different than the other systems that I had read about and tried—all those systems designed to help you lose money more slowly while fighting the casino's edge and the rules of chance. If indeed I could roll what I wanted through PK in defiance of the laws of chance, then the first thing was to select numbers which paid very well to be my targets, even if by chance they were unlikely to appear very often. For these type numbers the casino took a much larger percentage of the win. The rules were designed as if the casino knew that those were the numbers that could hurt them if a player had a "lucky" streak. In fact most of the incredible wins that I heard of, such as starting with $20 and ending up with $800,000 dollars, happened when the players were betting these unlikely numbers.

These next few pages are a bit complex and involve mathematics. For this I apologize. But it is the only way it can be clear about how and why I developed the system for PK targets and betting that I still use today. And comprehending this will help you understand some important principles for manifesting in general. I am not a math person, having always been better at words than numbers. Not to worry, there will be no test! If there were no tests in school, I might have even liked math a bit better myself.

As I mentioned earlier, the casino takes about 1.5 percent commission in dice when a player bets and then hits a number like six. This number is easier to roll than others statistically because out of 36 possibilities when the dice are thrown, there are five ways for two dice to come up as a total of six (3-3, 4-2, 2-4, 1-5, 5-1). Given this, the casino only pays you $7 for every $6 you have bet.

This contrasts for example with the number twelve. Statistically there is only one way out of 36 possibilities to get a twelve (6-6). Here if you hit a twelve the casino will pay you $180 for every $6 dollar bet. They are paying you at 30 to 1. Statistically they should pay you 36 to 1 because that is the actual odds of rolling the twelve. The difference between 30 to1 (what they pay you) and 36 to 1 (true odds) represents their seventeen percent commission on this bet. So you can see that if you bet six they will only take a 1.5 percent commission, but you will only get paid a small amount more than you bet ($7 for every $6). If instead you bet the twelve, they will take a huge seventeen percent commission, but will pay you a large amount if you win ($180 for very $6). These large commissions I believe are designed to discourage you from betting the numbers where they have to pay you a large amount if you win. Again, this is because you can really make some money in a short period of time on these unlikely numbers. And the casinos don't want that. They want you to stay and play a long time, because over a long time, the laws of probability and their commissions will work to separate you from your money.

But what if you are using PK? You really don't need to worry about the large commissions, but instead you can focus on the possibility of the large pay off. This is because with PK you can throw the dice to come up with the number you have selected as your target. And if you are strongly in the PK zone, you can have this target come up much more frequently than chance would dictate. This will allow you to bet small, thereby not triggering strong fear patterns, and yet win a larger amount. In the case of the number twelve, you would be paid 30 times your original bet. So as part of my method I settled on having some big pay-off targets. These bets are known as the "hardways" and "hop" bets.

A hop bet means that you call out exactly the number you are going to roll next and then immediately hit it on the next roll exactly as you have called it. For example, you call that the dice will land as 4-4. There is only one way in 36 that this can happen so they will pay you 30 to 1. So a $5 bet on 4-4 hop will yield you an immediate $150 if you are successful.

I also mentioned the hardway bets. These bets are for the dice to come up in pairs on any of the numbers 4, 6, 8, and 10. If the dice come up hardway on these numbers they will look like this: 2-2, 3-3, 4-4, or 5-5. You can bet these individually or as a group. If you want to bet eight the hardway, you would call out the bet "Hard Eight." This differs from the 4-4 hop bet in that you have more than one chance to hit your target. To be successful with a hardway bet you now have to hit the hard eight before a seven or a "soft" eight (3-5, 5-3, 6-2, 2-6) comes up. So with this bet you have many chances to hit the bet. You could next roll fifteen different numbers and as long as none were the seven or a soft eight, then on the sixteenth roll if you hit the hard eight you would be paid. This bet is more much likely to be successful statistically than the hop bet, so the casino would pay you about $10 for every $1 bet. This is in contrast to the $30 for $1 they will pay for the hop bet. But even after their high commission on this bet, it is still a very good payoff. A $5 bet on the hard eight would pay you $50 if you are successful. And you can have many chances to roll that hard eight, as that bet stays on the table until you either make it or not.

You can see then, why the hop bets and hardway bet became the skeleton around which to build my strategy. Both pay very well, allowing you to bet a small amount (reducing fear) yet win a large amount (increasing passion for success). But both of these bets, to be successful need to have very strong PK present. And PK sometimes takes a while to warm up. You need to settle down and get comfortable at the table, get used to throwing dice, acclimate to the other players and crew, etc.

Because of this need for warm up, I also added a bet called the "place" bet to my system. They don't pay as well but are statistically easier to make. I settled on place betting on the five and nine for complicated reasons that we don't need to get into. These place bets pay $7 on every $5 bet. And since statistically they come up 8 times in every 36 rolls they are more likely to come up than the hop or hardway bets that I selected as my framework. This gives time for small successes on the way to strong PK and larger success. This combination of challenging targets and easier targets serves PK very well. PK is results driven and likes the big score, but PK is also sensitive to tension or pushing, so it is good to have the small successes for encouragement too. If I picked only one challenging target, say twelve, I found over many trials that this would tend to freeze my energy too much. I notice this in other players too. PK flows best if it can follow the idea, "This or something better." This idea is also very useful in manifesting. It allows for many different outcomes to be positive, while clearly having a goal in mind. This approach is relaxed yet exciting.

The other thing that having multiple target does is relax the casino personnel. Casinos have to be on continuous alert for people trying to cheat. They are very vigilant with card games such as blackjack because there are so many ways to cheat. If you have ever seen close-hand magic you know that a skilled dealer of cards has the ability to deal off the bottom of the deck and many other tricks, faster than the naked eye can perceive. Blackjack dealers in Vegas have thousands of hours of dealing cards under their belt and could possibly be bribed into dealing to the player's advantage. Roulette wheels and slot machines can be tampered with. But in the game of craps the casino has lesser worries about cheating. There are multiple dealers all watching each other and cameras above to monitor for correct payouts and behavior of crew and players alike.

In dice there is one way to cheat that the casino has to control for vigilantly. It is called "loading the dice." If a person wanted to, they could take a die and drill a small hole and then put extra weight on that side. Such a die that is imbalanced in weight is said to be loaded. This would cause the die to fall more often than chance predicted to that side, thereby controlling the number that would end up on top of the die. The casino does many things to assure that this does not happen, including starting with fresh dice at the beginning of each shift, and destroying or clearly marking the dice used in the previous shift.

If you look closely at casino dice you will see that each die also has a distinct number embossed upon it, such as 5499. This number signifies the batch and is the same for all dice at that table. If a player or crew attempts to substitute a loaded die, the supervisor called the boxman can easily identify it as having the wrong identifying number. If the dice are accidently thrown off the table, for example, the boxman will pick it up, check the number and also spin it on its axis checking for balance. If you remember my story about my first big PK roll on my first trip, I had a target of six and hit it consistently and repeatedly for a few hours. This made the casino very nervous, because it is exactly how loaded dice would perform, favoring one number over and over. When the casino gets nervous there is unwanted attention directed toward the player who is making them suspicious. By selecting multiple targets for my system, I could dance from one number to another as feelings dictated, with the casino personnel relaxed because I was not hitting the same number too often.

Now that I had my targets and bets selected it was time to refine my money management strategy. We have already covered that I would be happy with small wins and delighted with bigger wins, but I was not out to make a killing. In fact my main interest in throwing dice at all was to experience and practice PK. I did not want to make a living at it and in fact there are much easier ways to make money, such as investing. Nor did I want to spend the majority of my time in casinos. A four-day trip every few months was enough to keep my skills up and provide an enjoyable break from daily routine, once my intense learning phase was complete. It is a question of balance, and I wanted my life to include teaching meditation, being in nature, family life, and time with friends, enjoying music, and many other things. Gaming was just a small part of the big picture.

So, in this context I developed a good money management system for my needs. First it was based on the $5 bet which is the lowest minimum for many bets on the dice table in Vegas. Next it would allow play for over an hour no matter what happened in terms of win or loss for the session. And for me that meant having about $200 available for each session. If I could not get PK going in a positive direction within that time-frame, it was clearly time to stop for that session. The $200 was what is called my loss limit. I would be happy with a gain of $20 to $50 dollars and would try, if ever ahead, to quit while I was ahead. Of course larger wins were possible and were welcomed. This may sound like a conservative and perhaps even boring strategy, but remember that I not as interested in the money as in experiencing PK.

Next, in honoring the human tendency to be more relaxed taking small risks, I wanted a betting system that allowed me to begin playing with the casino's money rather than my money as soon as possible. And that allowed any larger bets that occurred to be made with the casino's money not mine. So I developed a system in which once you have hit your target just one time, you would no longer have any of your money at risk on that target or number. Repeating this, once you hit the number the first time, you can no longer lose your money on that number. Sounds good, yes? How to accomplish this?

You can do this with a system called "take-press." Let's use the number nine as an example. You bet $5 on the nine, and you hit it the first time you roll. The casino pays you $7 for your $5 bet. You are now $2 ahead. This $2 profit represents the $7 you got paid, minus your original $5 investment. You take back your original $5 and keep it along with the $2 that you are ahead. Your original investment of $5 and your $2 profit are both now safe. You take the other $5 that the casino paid you and replace your original $5 with the casino's $5, betting on the nine once again. This whole process of taking all of the profits from the win is called the "take." You now, as promised, are playing with the casino's money instead of your own on the number 9. From here you have none of your own money at risk on the 9 yet can make large amount of money on the 9. How do you do this?

Well, you still have the bet on the nine (courtesy of the casino's $5). And your next roll is another nine. What happens? The same thing as before, the casino pays you $7. But this time you call "press." What that means is that you want to double your bet. Now you can do this with the casino's money (not your own) courtesy of the second $7 they just paid you. What happens is that they will give you $2 of this $7, and place the remaining $5 on top of your $5 bet, making it into a $10 bet. You keep the extra $2 as additional profit. This means that you are now $4 ahead plus have a bet, all with casino money of $10 on the 9.

You are in the PK zone and you hit another 9. This time you get paid $14 for your $10 bet and you again "take," meaning you keep all the profits. So you now have a profit of $18. The PK continues and you hit another

9. This time you "press," doubling your bet with casino money again and harvesting more profit. You now have a $20 bet on the 9 with casino money. You continue this rhythm of alternating take and press. I have done this and ended up with a $250 bet on the nine, never having risked more than my original $5.

No matter where in this series after the first win, that you finally lose, you cannot do worse than breaking even in terms of your own money. And all along the way you are playing with the casino's money and you are banking profits each time you say "take" and doubling your bet every time you say "press." If the series goes on a while, even though you might eventually lose when there is a large bet on the nine, that large bet is made up entirely of casino money and you have banked up many wins along the way. This is the take-press process of doubling to generate large wins. Doubling is a very powerful process. If fact if someone offers you a million dollars, or to pay you a penny on the first square of a standard 64 square checkerboard, and then double that penny on each square, you should take the penny doubled on each square—it will add up to much more than a million dollars by the time the doubling goes through 64 times. It would add up to 18 quadrillion dollars.

You can modify this idea of take-press and apply it to the hardway bets that are the other targets in my system, but here it is even sweeter because the casino is paying you roughly ten times your original bet instead of about twice the bet as they do on the placed 9. This allows you to press every time with the casino's money after the first roll. With the hardways let's say you bet $5 on hard eight (4-4). You throw a hard eight and the casino pays you $50. You can keep all the profits except enough to immediately press your bet, which will double your bet to $10, all with casino money. Where do you stand now? You are $40 ahead after the first throw. From there you can press your bet each time and you will be harvesting greater and greater profits: $100 on your bet of $10, then $200 on your bet of $20, all the time playing with casino money. When you get to a $100 bet on the hard eight you stand to win $1,000, yet again you have only put $5 of your own money at risk at the very beginning. This process is even more exponential on the hop bets that can pay up to $30 for every dollar bet.

If this sounds too good to be true and like a sure thing, well, it isn't. But there are some real advantages to this system. You know exactly what your risk will be (in our examples a $5 bet). This is very helpful in keeping control of your money and keeping your anxiety down. And you don't know how much your profit might be and this provides the excitement. You will not be successful every time and can, for example, try this ten times in a row and end up $50 down. But this also gives you ten chances at getting a really nice streak going.

So now I had at least a working understanding of the hurdles and helps that danced around PK. I had selected good PK dice target numbers. And I had a system for betting and money management. I practiced with these in Vegas on a few more trips in 1997 and was able to confirm that all of this together was a workable way to learn PK and to become more proficient at it. It was also very clear to me that such a practice was very beneficial in the rest of my life. My health, relationships, business, and abundance all were benefiting from the insights and the practice.

One part that still disturbed me was that all those issues that were so deeply ingrained in personality and previous experience kept popping up to be confronted repeatedly. Ego, personality, limiting beliefs, and negative emotions were my dragons, guarding the treasures of PK. And fighting several dragons at once was no fun. While facing one, another would circle around and sneak up from behind. To mix metaphors, fighting these dragons was like trying to put out a series of brush fires that just kept re-igniting. But through many cycles of confrontation and confirmation, I came to know that there was one thing that nearly always could transcend all the dragons. These dragons were quieted effectively by only one thing. They responded to this thing much like the way in mythology dragons respond to music. They respond by going to sleep. The PK dragons were no match for this magical and wondrous thing. These dragons were quieted by the miracle of an open heart.

Once I discovered this, things became much easier. Where I previously would face the dragon of fear with courage, I now melted the dragon of fear with love. And I learned many ways that triggered and cultivated an open heart. Beautiful music could do this. Focusing on all the people I love could do this. Remembering the love received from all of my pets could do this. The magnificence of nature, in the simplest flower or the grandest mountain could do this. Even just quieting down, breathing slowly and feeling my own heart space could open the gate to this miracle energy.

Finally all was in place, not for perfection, but for a positive and healthy path through the garden of PK and its wonders of abundance. It represented a positive and healthy life path as well. My good friend Richard Madaus who has written a wonderful book called, *Think Logically, Live Intuitively,* wrote an article on his dice playing experience. I am going to borrow the title of this article from him. You could call this path, The Yoga of Dice. The definition of yoga which literally means yoke, is the yoking or harnessing of the lower or more earth-bound qualities in the person with the higher, more spiritual aspects of the person. Here lower and higher are not meant to convey one is better than the other; they are just different.

As human beings we are designed to link heaven and earth and to be the sure bridge between heaven and earth. That is why it is said that the angels sometimes envy us, because being human is such a beautiful and privileged position. It requires an exquisite balance. If we spend too much time dwelling in earth, we become dull as dirt. If we spend too much time in the heavens we become detached and ineffective. John Welwood wrote an excellent book about this called *Journey of the Heart: Intimate Relationship and the Path of Love.* His point is that when we first fall in love, we are heaven and all is idealized. Then in the daily life of paying bills, snoring in our partner's ear, and arguments we are integrating this experience into real earth life. The key is to balance these poles and not lose either heaven or earth, and then the relationship will grow, thrive, and endure.

This practice of and experience in blending heaven and earth is why the Yoga of Dice could also be called a Yoga of Love, for it is loving to yourself and to others to express the whole of our nature, both enlightened beast and enlightened spirit. Discovering this in the casinos of Vegas was very inspiring to me. If you can discover this in casinos you can find it anywhere. With my system of betting and money management, with knowing that PK exists and is the same energy used in creating our dreams and healing, and with knowing love can transform our dragons of ego and belief, I felt called to teach this yoga to others. And that is the story presented in the next section of this book. The yoga of dice has much in common with other yogas or paths. It invites us to be fully in each present moment, it requires discipline, it yields tremendous benefit, and it can be very helpful to have a teacher.

I looked forward to teaching this for many reasons including the strong desire to share the magic of PK and how Vegas could be a classroom for advancement into human potential. Another simple reason was that these three years of learning by myself were very lonely. In fact I am a bit concerned that this first part of the book may come across as self-absorbed. Yes, I made friends with many along the path, and the crews and other personnel knew me by name, but essentially at the tables and in my meditations I was alone in my process. What fun it would be to play with others with similar goals and awareness! And what power might be generated by encouraging and supporting each other? As I contemplated teaching this, I was filled with excitement.

PART 3

CHAPTER 10

Ready to Teach

Don Juan is quoted by Carlos Castaneda, in *The Teachings of Don Juan*: "…ask yourself, and yourself alone, one question. Does this path have a heart? If it does, the path is good; if it doesn't, it is of no use."

I was convinced that at least for me this path of PK dice had much heart and would be an interesting one to follow for the foreseeable future. I felt it would be very beneficial to me. I felt that, if it could be taught it would be helpful to others, in terms of their manifesting and healing skills as well as learning about how consciousness affects reality. I was ready to teach but was anyone ready to learn? Many had expressed interest in what I had been doing but there is a big difference in being interested versus being committed. For my teaching to have the best chance of success, I felt that I would need to find students who were very committed to learning this subject because it was so challenging to our usual belief systems and behaviors. It has been said jokingly but with great wisdom that, "In a bacon and eggs breakfast, the chicken was interested, the pig was committed."

I felt that the best way to teach PK was experientially. An academic lecture would not really convey how it felt to be in this process and would not teach the person that they indeed could do psychokinesis themselves and how it felt to do so. I knew that the deep levels of healing and transformation that potentially were the fruits of this work would not be tasted unless the person walked this path fully, and personally engaged in the journey and the outcome. So it was clear to me that the way to teach this was to develop a workshop that was held in the hotel and casino and from the start had people hold the dice in their own hands and attempt PK.

I had questions about whether I would be able to find a receptive casino, that people would be willing to come and risk their own money, and that the process would be a healthy and positive one for them. I was fairly confident that in a few days workshop, I could teach the rules, betting, and money management needed to play rudimentary craps.

One of my biggest concerns was whether I could give people enough guidance in a short workshop on how to handle their own dragons. I was sure that these dragons would surface quickly in the context of gaming in a casino. One way to look at the dragons was that, though they took many forms, they were all actually manifestations of fear. There might be issues of performance anxiety, fear of risk and loss, being accepted by the group, being responsible for rolling with other people's money at stake, doubts about their deservingness to experience abundance, fear of being powerful, and many other issues. Even if the people that attended such a workshop were very nice and naturally open-hearted people, all the fear that would be triggered might make it very difficult to be in an open-hearted space. It is not the space that we automatically go to when feeling threatened. And from my experience I knew that approaching this with a wide open heart was critical to success. The dilemma is voiced well in the song, *Devils and Dust* by Bruce Springsteen:

> *"Fear's a powerful thing*
> *It'll turn your heart black you can trust*
> *It'll take your God-filled soul*
> *Fill it with devils and dust."*

I wanted to do everything possible to bring a group of people together that might meet this challenge with as much grace as possible. Given that I could teach the game of craps and my strategies of betting, I did not feel that it was at all important for the participants to already be craps players. If fact, I felt it probably would be a disadvantage for them to be highly experienced with the game because what I was going to teach was so different from the way most people play craps. If they were already experienced, I would probably have to spend a lot of time and energy helping them unlearn what they already had learned about the game. And they might strongly resist my "deprogramming" if success at the table was not immediate with this new approach to the game. After all they would have their own money at risk.

My workshop would rely on meditation to clear and raise energy and would also demand much self-awareness. So it seemed that inviting people to attend who already had some experience with meditation would be a good idea. In the workshop there would likely be long hours of group interaction over a period of days. This was because we would be relying on group support and energy to accomplish our goals. People who enjoyed and were good at being an active participant in an intense group situation would also be a good choice. In my experience such people usually were good at establishing personal boundaries, yet easily able to empathize with another person, and happy to extend themselves to be helpful to others. Given the challenge to belief systems and emotional patterns that such a workshop might cause, I also wanted them to be psychologically strong yet flexible. I would be talking about and encouraging people to connect with the spiritual side of themselves, in order to pull in the highest of energy. People willing to do this would be welcome. It would help if they were not rigid, judgmental, nor proselytizing in their beliefs.

Obviously I did not want anyone in the workshop who had a compulsive gambling problem! Nor did I want someone who had a higher chance of developing such a problem, such as anyone with an addictive personality, major depression, or a desperate need for money. It would be good to have people attend who were comfortable taking risks, both interpersonal and financial. It might be difficult to handle folks whose main purpose was to gamble and make lots of money in such a group, because the emphasis was not gong to be on making money quickly. Rather the goal would be to support one another in learning about PK and its potential for use in healing and manifesting abundance of all kinds, not just financial.

The challenge then was to find psychologically healthy people who were experienced in meditation and did well with intense group interaction. They should be self-aware and spiritually open, yet interested in something that involved gambling and be willing to take interpersonal and financial risks.

As I have mentioned I started training consciousness exploration programs at the Monroe Institute (TMI) in 1991. And that Robert Monroe was very interested in psychokinesis and manifestation himself. He had asked me to keep him informed on how my Vegas trips went, which I did from when I started them in 1994. He was always eager to hear how my last trip to Vegas went. When I would go up to the Institute to train a program, we would always find time to sit together and talk about my discoveries. We shared other things as well, including our progress through the grieving process, his missing his wife and my missing my brother Peter. I remember a conversation in the fall of 1994, where we were sitting on a hill overlooking the beautiful land with its pastures in the foreground and the mountains distant. We were watching turkey vultures soaring on the thermals. Bob always like to fly and in fact was a glider pilot and for a while ran his own small cargo airline. This afternoon we sat in admiration of the freedom of these birds above, warming ourselves in the late autumn sunshine. Bob had established his Institute based on the principle that we were more than our physical bodies, after he had experienced for himself what he called out of body travel or OBE. And he often compared his OBE experience to the joy of flight.

The conversation turned more intimate than usual for us. He said that he was still filled with great ideas and passion for his work but that he was lonely and nearing 80 years old and did not like the increasing physical dependence he could see coming, as he was having trouble with the heavy physical work on his place, such as bringing in the wood for the winter fires. This was my last strong memory of him. On Saint Patrick's Day, March 17 of 1995, Bob released his physical body and winged his way home. After Bob died, his daughter Laurie Monroe was recruited to take charge of the Institute as president, as I continued training there and began to consider teaching others about PK in Vegas.

Laurie did a great job of pulling everyone together at TMI after the shock of Bob's death. With the help of an experienced crew of staff and trainers, she first worked to assure that the Institute would continue to thrive. The senior staff led by Franceen King developed a wonderful program called Exploration 27 which investigated, through meditation, the states of consciousness involved in the non-physical or spiritual areas that one might encounter after physical death. The program launched the summer after Bob's passing. I was a trainer with Franceen King and Karen Malik for the first Exploration 27. It was an immediate success.

I can remember Laurie talking to us at our first trainer retreat the winter after Bob's death. She brought up the model of the Disney Corporation. After Walt Disney died, the company continued and also began to try new things, some of which bombed and some of which were home runs. Laurie said she would not be afraid of trying new things at the Institute and did not expect everything to always work out well. She encouraged our creativity and many new programs were born that continue successfully to this day.

In 1997 when I began to ponder where I might find participants for my teaching in Vegas, I thought of inviting Monroe Institute graduates. In my experience as trainer at the Institute I found almost everyone attending there to be self-aware and spiritually open. As a group they fit the bill perfectly in terms of psychologically healthy people who were experienced in meditation that did well with intense group interaction.

Given the context of Laurie Monroe's encouragement of creativity, I thought that it would be appropriate to discuss this idea with her. Her response was positive and enthusiastic. This would not be an official Monroe Institute program but I was authorized to invite Monroe participants that I had personally trained over the years, to attend such an event. Her words were, "This idea is in line with my father's interests in manifestation. I know you to be an excellent trainer and I trust your judgment and ethics in putting together a quality program. As long as you remain in integrity I will support you." To her credit Laurie continued to support me even when she received feedback from some associated with Monroe equivalent to, "How could you use the sacred energies we access in Monroe programs to do something as crass as gambling?" Even though I knew my Vegas journeys had been highly positive for me, I had pondered this question myself long and hard before deciding to teach. I took the question into deep meditation and while doing so felt a very warm and loving presence say to me with a sense of light humor, "Son, haven't you learned yet how much fun it is to light a candle in the darkness?" For me, all is sacred from the highest heavens to the lowest forms on earth. There is no differentiation at the deepest level between the sacred and the profane. It is all part of the amazing construction of consciousness that Bob Monroe called the "Earth Life Experience."

With Laurie Monroe's blessing I moved forward with plans and approached the Sahara Hotel and Casino. By then I had been going to the Sahara for nearly 25 years and had many connections there. Still it was a bit challenging to explain what I wanted to do to the casino staff. I settled on a story that was true as far as it went. I told them that I trained people from around the world in meditation and that I wanted to give these people a real world experience in which to practice their meditation skills outside of a retreat center and in a stressful environment. I thought that the game of craps would be an ideal setting for this. I would bring them to Vegas, spend a day teaching about the game and preparing by meditation, and then we would try our luck at the dice tables.

Brenda who was my host at the property became my liaison for this project. I asked the Sahara hotel for a large two-bedroom suite in which to meet. I preferred this to a regular meeting room. In my experience as a workshop facilitator no matter how thoroughly I explained that for the meditation exercises I required a very quiet space, I could not achieve the silence I needed in a regular conference room. And noise is very distracting when trying to meditate. When I tried hotel conference rooms, invariably some other group would be meeting next door for a sales meeting with loud cheering and music, or the kitchen would be located nearby, or there would be a lot of traffic noise transferred from the hall into the room. My worst experience was in Toronto where I was assured a quiet room and arrived to find that we were meeting right above a subway station with trains rumbling by loudly every few minutes, shaking the whole building. So as I planned my Vegas workshop, I wanted to be on a floor of the hotel that had bedrooms. I had found that during the day Las Vegas hotel guest rooms are uniquely quiet. People were usually gone from their rooms sightseeing or in the casino. And if they were in their rooms they tended to be sleeping off the previous night's festivities.

Next I asked the Sahara for specific times when we could have a dice table all to ourselves. They arranged this by having the crews arrive early or stay over and then reserved a table for us using these crews. I wanted a table to ourselves so that we could be sure that everyone at the table was properly prepared and on board with a program that would be conducive to PK. Finally I asked for a discounted rate on guest rooms for all my participants, called a casino rate. On most Vegas properties the hotel and casino, while related to each other closely, are run as two separate entities. Both the casino and the hotel have to be efficient and show a profit on their own.

The hotel obtains revenue from room rentals, with conventions being a significant part of that revenue, and restaurants, show rooms, and other services helping to generate additional income. The casino derives most of their profits from the gambling that occurs on the casino floor. But there is a special relationship between the two divisions in that each requires the other to thrive. Few would come to the hotel if there were no casino, and few would come to the casino without a place to stay close by. Given this relationship, the hotel allows the casino a certain number of rooms that can be given out at steep discounts or complimentary. These rooms are given to players who bring enough action into the casino that the casino expects over the long run that their play will be highly positive to the casino's bottom line.

Some of the rooms set aside for special players are indeed lavish. They are the high roller suites and can have every amenity conceivable, starting with private jets picking the player up, limos from the airport, and a private lounge to check in. This can then extend to private elevators, top floor views, and over 3,000 square feet of space in the suite. The first level of these discounts is called the casino rate. Casino rates apply from the cheapest rooms to most luxurious. Regular rates are called rack rates. One of the things that is unusual in Vegas compared to most hotels is that the rates vary wildly depending on time of year, day of the week, holidays, and the number of conventions in town, etc. A room that may go for $29 some nights of the year may be as high a $300 on another night. Millions are at stake every day in this dance to set competitive rates and provide attractive amenities for the player. The rates now change by the minute, much like airfares! That is why I wanted to negotiate a casino rate for my players even though the casino had never seen these players before. I needed a stable and fair rate, so that I could tell people what the cost of the seminar would be and not have a convention book at the last minute causing the rates to jump dramatically.

To get a casino rate, usually a fairly modest level of play over a few days is required. To get a full room and meal comp for a basic room, meaning the room and all meals are free, one is required to gamble a minimum of 4 hours a day with an average bet that might be $50 for one property and $150 for a luxury property. As one's gaming goes up from there, then the luxury suites become available.

There is very sophisticated computerized tracking of these systems now through what is called a player card. The player card gives the player many things depending on level of play including access to VIP lines at restaurants and shows, restaurant discounts, select parking, etc. The card accumulates points much like an airline frequent flyer program does. These points can be converted back into cash, casino play, or to pay for rooms and meals. The player card is able to track the player electronically at all table games and slot machines and at the end of the year can even give you a exact print out of the casino's estimate of your gaming performance, including average bet, how much money you came into each session with, win/loss, duration of time at the games, etc. This monitoring occurs across all the properties that the parent company owns, anywhere in the world that they own them.

This monitoring contrasts in sophistication with the old days when I started in Vegas before computers were prominent. In the seventies when I started, record keeping was by hand and the hosts were trusted to cultivate and manage their player/customers with much more freedom of discretion. Casinos were more loyal to their players and consequently players were more loyal to them. By 1997 when I started to teach in Vegas, computer systems and player cards were already quite a presence, but the casino host still retained more power and autonomy than they do today. At that time most properties were individually owned. Now most are owned by large multi-national corporations. For example to the best of my knowledge at the time of this writing, MGM corporation owns twenty-nine major properties in Las Vegas as well as others around the world, and gaming is just one division of their company that includes many other activities such as movie studios. On the Las Vegas strip, it is as if a giant game of monopoly has occurred over the last ten years and MGM has Boardwalk, Park Place, and much of the other property as well.

My understanding is that the takeover by corporations extinguished any last vestiges of mob ownership of casinos on the Vegas strip. It allowed the huge multi-billion dollar properties to emerge as the dominant force on the Strip, and removed any last chance of being physically hassled by the casino. Imagine if, in the current environment, a casino employee took you out into the alley and twisted your arm about payment of a debt, etc. The lawsuits and bad press the MGM Corporation would be exposed to would be horrendous. That coupled with highly developed security forces in casinos is why I feel physically very safe in Vegas. I felt comfortable bringing in people from all over the world for my workshop and knew that they also would be safe. And yet I miss the folksy human touch that existed in the old style Vegas.

In doing this PK workshop, I also felt that the casino would be quite relaxed about our play. Given that we were planning to start with mostly $5 bets, we would be fairly low on their radar. The scale of money flow in Vegas is hard to grasp. It is rumored that MGM will often have over two billion dollars in their vault on a given weekend. The casino cashiers office, where you covert your chips back into cash is called the cage. It is usually located at the far back of the casino, away from any doors. This is done so that someone cannot enter a door, take a few steps and quickly rob the cage at gunpoint. I remember going to the cage once and chatting with one of the ten tellers lined up there. I asked her, "How much money do you carry in your drawer?" She smiled and countered, "Guess." I guessed, "$5000?" She laughed and said, "What do you think this is, a small town bank? We each have $100,000 in our drawers." She may have been kidding me but I will never know. They certainly were not going to let me come around back and count it!

I successfully arranged an agreement with the Sahara that included good room rates, meeting rooms, reserved tables, and dates for a three-day weekend in October 1998. From my own experience and my journal notes I began working on a framework for the workshop. I felt strongly that the first day should just be getting to know each other and building group energy. On this day I would present the rules of the game, discuss our strategies, talk about PK and lead meditations to raise energy. We would not even go into the casino as a group that first day. I planned the second day around two sessions at our reserved tables, plus more meditating, debriefing our experiences, and fine-tuning the process. The third day would be much like the second with two more sessions at the tables, and then we would finish with a closing circle where we could recap and hopefully celebrate the experience. I also developed a preparation manual that people could study before they attended so that they would have some knowledge about what we were going to do.

The workshop would be limited to eighteen persons including myself, as that was the maximum number of people that could fit around the dice table at one time. Also this seemed a good size for generating powerful group energy and yet being able to keep a handle on things. Keeping a handle on things was a concern. When I would go out with my family, it was hard to keep track of them and have them show up when we agreed to meet for a meal. Someone was always going off and getting into something exciting and losing track of time. This was fairly easy to do—there are no clocks on the casino walls and plenty of distractions.

Next, it was time to announce the group. I came up with a title for the workshop, the Inner Vegas Adventure™ workshop. At the time I was thinking of doing the first one and seeing how it went. Little did I know then that I would be doing about sixty Inner Vegas Adventures over the next fourteen years, and as of this writing that the workshop would still be so popular. We have had people attend from all over the world including Australia, Japan, Iran, Israel, Cyprus, Spain, Portugal, France, Germany, Austria, Russia, Latvia, England, Brazil, Canada, and of course the USA.

At that time many people did not use email, so I developed a one-page flyer and sent it out to the people that I had trained at Monroe Institute. I invited Laurie Monroe to come. She accepted and wrote a cover letter for the flyer letting people know that, while this would not be an official Monroe program, she warmly invited people to attend. Within days the group was full. Some of the most seasoned, intrepid, and curious explorers of consciousness that I knew signed up. As the time for the workshop approached, I was very excited and more than a bit nervous. There were some thoughts such as: "What am I doing, bringing these nice folks out to Vegas and having them risk their own money at the tables?" And, "What am I going to do if there is no PK?"

CHAPTER 11

The First Inner Vegas Adventure Workshop

October came. It was finally show time for the first Inner Vegas Adventure. I am relying on my journal of the first workshop to help me tell its story. From here on, names will be changed to protect privacy. I want to go into detail to give you a feeling of the structure and what was experienced in this first workshop.

I arrived Thursday. The room was not ready so I went to the pool and reset my mood after the hassles of travel by meditating on all the blessings in my life. This left me feeling grateful, calm, and confident. I then checked in and discovered that Brenda, my host, had gotten me a really nice suite with a balcony on the 21st floor which was the top floor of the hotel. I unpacked, took a nap, and met with Brenda to go over the plans. Everything was in order. Surrendering to jet lag, I went to bed at ten and awoke Friday at 4:30 a.m. As I tried to open my heart I was aware that I was feeling tension about the workshop. So I meditated while listening to a Hemi-Sync exercise called *Sleeping through the Rain* and cleared my feeling of nervousness. I had a nice breakfast with some of the participants.

The workshop started Friday morning at nine, with everyone arriving on time. They liked the roomy suite with its views of the desert and its large outdoor balcony. People seemed in a great mood and very excited. Six people had some experience with casinos and eleven had none. There were eleven men and six women in the group. Two people came directly to the workshop after meditating in the desert for a week. Folks ranged from their early twenties to late sixties, with the majority being middle-aged. Their homes were in Nevada, New York, Virginia, Indiana, Texas, California, Illinois, Wisconsin, Minnesota, and British Columbia. We had one father and son team.

The first day of the seminar flowed well. It had been a good idea to have no pressure to gamble that day, as people were getting settled in from their travels and time zone changes. Most of the participants were able to follow my description of the complexities of the rules of craps. A few seemed a bit lost after this. The group liked my presentation on how to do PK with dice, as I was able to throw the dice so that they came up on our targets right in front of them (Whew!). We meditated using Hemi-Sync as a group. To do this I had arranged to have pillows and blankets delivered to the room so that they could lay down on the floor comfortably on a mat made from a blanket, put their headphones on, and use their Walkmans to play the meditation cassette tapes.

In the afternoon I live-voiced a guided meditation for the group on how to manifest the reality they desired, and particularly at the dice tables. I was tired by late afternoon with jet lag. We took a break at five for dinner which was good timing. There is a slot machine in Vegas that is linked throughout most of the casinos, called Megabucks. Its jackpot was at 24 million dollars. We gathered after dinner and went down for a tour of all the facilities of the casino, as part of their orientation, and then went to Megabucks to play together. Each person tried $21 in the machine, which at three dollars a pull gave them each seven tries. This went okay as a way to get the groups' feet wet and to point out how scattered everybody's energy was compared to what we were aiming for in terms of coherent group energy. To be fair, most of the participants were very tired by then. It had been a full day. After the day's program Laurie, Sam, and I went to Desert Inn and then Sahara to play some craps. I did well on my initial roll and it felt good to get back in the game.

Saturday morning it was time to give my pep talk to the group, as we would soon be going down to the dice tables for the first time. My talk covered what I had personally found useful in doing PK at the tables. I reminded them to approach this with a light-hearted attitude—to feel that it was child's play. They were free to follow their intuition and participate only to the extent that they were comfortable doing so. I encouraged them to trust themselves and the universe to create something magical. I suggested they think of their gaming stake for the session as a gift from their greater self or spirit, to themselves, in order to play and learn. I advised that they bet low enough so that they could focus on their own energy and learn, without the money being a distraction or creating fear. I asked them to love themselves and one another.

I reminded them that in our group each person can bet as little or as much as they want without worry or comparing themselves to the person beside them. I mentioned that at the dice table, we would be like a chain of energy. And in this chain, the weakest link would not determine the strength of the chain; rather we would only need one strong link (good roller) but the more strong links, the merrier. I credited them with what I genuinely felt for them. "Out of 100 points possible here, you receive 95 for just showing up and having the courage to try something so different."

I used the image of the dice table being like a big sand box. The money, converted to chips, was just the sand we would play with. And I reminded them to be grateful for having enough "sand" to come and play. We would not just be throwing sand around but would be focused on building something magical. Just as with kids in a sand box it was best not to worry too much about what you were building, rather just let it flow naturally. Lastly I said, "As much as possible, just get out of your own way. Your ego does not know how to do this. You can't consciously force the dice to roll in the desired pattern. Some part of you does know how to do PK, so let this higher part of yourself do it through you."

The first dice session for the group was at noon on Saturday. This time was chosen to coincide with peak sidereal time. One study had suggested that at 13:30 sidereal time, PK was at its strongest and at 18:00 hours at its weakest. This was thought to be true because at 13:30 sidereal there was less electromagnetic interference that might interfere with PK. I wanted to have every advantage going into this first session that I could. According to Wikipedia: "A sidereal day is a time scale that is based on the Earth's rate of rotation measured relative to the fixed stars . . . Both solar time and sidereal time make use of the regularity of the Earth's rotation about its polar axis, solar time following the Sun while sidereal time roughly follows the stars . . . sidereal time at any one place at midnight will be about four minutes later each night, until, after a year has passed, one additional sidereal day has transpired compared to the number of solar days that have gone by." So, sidereal time progresses roughly four minutes per day compared to solar clock time. On this particular day, Saturday 13:30 sidereal time occurred at 12:26 p.m. Vegas time, creating a two-hour window from 11:26 a.m. to 1:26 p.m. where PK should be particularly good. And there would be a poor PK or declining window at about 4 p.m. to 6 p.m. that day.

The group went down by the pool to get some fresh air after meditating and to ground their energy. There was quite a bit of excitement and a good bit of nervousness about what we were about to attempt. We assembled at the dice table. There was great group energy for about a half hour at the table and then the energy dropped and scattered. Each person became preoccupied with the mechanics of trying to play this new game that they were learning. When this happened there was greater interest and attention being paid to self-interest than to the group, or who was rolling at the moment. All participants had a chance to roll in the ninety minutes that we stayed at the table. The first half of the table had good small wins, and then we began to have small losses.

We went back to the suite to debrief the experience. It was apparent at the table and in the debrief session that I was asking a lot of them in their attempt to play the game for the first time. They were trying to keep track of all the rules, betting, and money management, and at the same time trying to keep individual and group energy high and coherent. I actually was very pleased with how much progress was made in learning the game. People looked frazzled after this first attempt, so we delayed the next planned craps session in favor of a good long rest. I knew from personal experience that playing craps and attempting PK when tired was a recipe for disaster.

We reconvened at 7 p.m.. I warned the group about getting fuzzy and unfocused, and forgetting our tools for grounding. I urged them to stay strongly in the present moment. I had realized during break that we actually may have gotten exactly what we wanted in the first session. It would be natural for each person to want to try to actually hold the dice and to roll themselves. And we accomplished this in our 90-minute session. The trouble with this manifestation is that, in the game of craps, the longer one person holds the dice the more money is made by everybody at the table.

What happens in the game of dice is that after a point number is rolled, which are the numbers 4,5,6,8,9, and 10, then the object of the game is to roll that point number again before a seven is rolled. Sevens are expected to be rolled statistically once in every six rolls. This is more frequently than any other number. It is challenging to keep rolling without hitting a seven at the wrong time. This is why most of the time when you see someone roll they hit the seven at the wrong time (called sevening out) very quickly. Often this sevening out occurs within three to six rolls and in about five minutes of play. When that happens, the casino wins almost all bets on the table and the player who had been rolling loses the dice and everyone has to start over. The shooter who had been rolling passes them clockwise to the next player and another attempt is made to win bets before the seven comes out at the wrong time.

With PK we are attempting to keep the energy high, grounded, positive, and relaxed, because that is when PK is strongest. And in this energy we focus our intent to keep hitting our target numbers for a long time before the sevening out. When we do this, each time we hit a target number that we have bet, we get paid by the casino. As you remember from those pages loaded with mathematics, we are using a take-press strategy which means that we are taking a profit each time we hit our number, and every other time we hit the target, we double our bet. In this way, in a long roll we can start with a small bet of $5 and as the roll progresses, we may end up with several hundred dollars profit each time the number is hit, because we have had the opportunity afforded by the long roll to hit our target many times and double our bet many times.

When PK is strong, you tend to roll exactly what you are thinking. One of the challenges, as the money begins to pile up on the table, is to not think of the seven because in doing so you may well roll it. Since everyone knows that the seven will end the streak of profit taking, it can be tough not to have the thought of seven cross someone's mind in the group. Especially bad, yet natural to do, is to couple strong emotion to the thought. Often that emotion is fear as in, "Oh, I hope I don't roll a seven, look at all the money out there that everyone will lose." That is an almost sure way to roll the unwanted seven.

There is another factor here though that must be mentioned. Within the high energy needed for PK something interesting happens with intuition. For most people, as they develop the energy needed for PK, they find that their intuitional sense becomes much stronger at the same time. People who claim to have never had a hunch begin to get them. Other people who are aware that they have intuition find that their hunches come more often, and that the intuitions become clearer and stronger. Indeed the hunches often approach an absolute knowing of what is going to happen next.

So in PK, if you have your energy high and your heart open, and no fear is present, and all of a sudden while minding your own business the thought of seven pops into consciousness, then often this will be an accurate intuition about what is about to happen next. This gives the person two powerful options. The first option is that they can attempt to reset the energy and choose another reality. We have learned that there are many ways to do this. It can include something as simple as getting a hug from the person next to you. This tends to both ground you and open your heart further. Then you can take your time to select another reality or number to roll. Having that new number strongly in consciousness, about half the time causes it to be what comes up next.

The second option is that when you receive a strong intuition that seven will be coming next, you have the option to say, "Down on my bets" and protect your profits that are on the table by de-activating all your bets. When the seven rolls you do not lose the money that you have on the table, rather it is returned to you. In a group setting such as Inner Vegas Adventure, people can share their intuitions and help each other to either reset the energy toward another number, or take all their bets down as a group. So in Vegas as in life, it is a very useful skill to be able to differentiate intuition from fear, and then have the courage to act upon intuition.

As we prepared for our second dice session I encouraged the participants to release the thought, "I want to roll" and to support the person who is ready to have a great roll. I asked them to see each roller doing great for at least fifteen minutes or longer. In a normal non-PK game you see someone able to hold the dice for fifteen minutes about once in every twenty rollers or so. With every passing minute it becomes more difficult to avoid that seven that should come up once in every six rolls. So when someone manages to hold the dice for twenty-five minutes, it is quite exceptional.

We went to the tables for our second session at eight that evening. Lessons had been learned and the group strived to create a very high and coherent energy. They were more familiar with the rules of the game and how to handle their money, so it was easier for them to focus on the energy. I had told them that while the rules take some time to learn, that learning is only about twenty percent important in PK dice. Being able to generate and hold the coherent energy is the other eighty percent. A person can know the rules down pat and have fancy and complex bets to make, and if the energy is not there they will lose. Conversely, if a person doesn't know the rules and strategies very well but has the energy they will win. And the person who both applies the correct strategies and has the energy will win much more. The group absorbed this idea well and achieved a much sweeter energy than on our first attempt. We stayed at the table for seventy-five minutes and were much less frazzled at the end.

There are many possible ways to generate high energy for PK. I presented the group with options. The important thing was to be genuine with how you were feeling. Some examples would be: If you are feeling very light and playful, then roll from the energy of your inner child. If you are feeling strong perhaps roll from a feeling of warrior. If you are feeling magical, imagine yourself as the powerful good witch or wizard. What these have in common is that they are in line with how you are genuinely feeling. Besides this, you are in the present moment, you feel entitled to be there, and to be supported by the universe as you play out whatever flavor of good energy you have chosen.

I noticed even in this first group that in general men and women each tended to favor a different energy and produce a different result. They could each shift to the other energy but one just seemed to come more naturally. Women in general had an easier time with letting go and surrendering. They could more easily enter a sweet loving space, feeling support from everyone, not only their friends at the table but also angels and guides. Women tended to like to roll any happy number and not think too much about what would be next. When in line with this type of feminine energy, they would look very relaxed and throw a lot of different numbers (except the seven) over a long time, hitting our targets along the way, interspersed with other numbers.

In contrast men in general tended to adopt a more active and focused position with clearer intent on a particular target. They seemed to connect with support more from dominion and brotherhood. They tended to produce a much more focused result, but perhaps not roll as long. Men at their strongest may do something such as roll nine 9's in a row, if that is their target number. And right after achieving this goal they might seven out. Both energies worked and both could be used by either gender. So, for example, when I was feeling kind of quiet and tired of using my own energy, I could surrender into feeling a supportive flow, and join with this flow to produce good results. If I was feeling very strong and powerful, I could move into the dominion type roll.

From my notes from this second session, Ann rolled beautifully from an inner child space. I noticed that all the women did well from feminine energy. Roger had dreamt of hard 4 the night before, and then made four hard 4's. Most of us made money this time. Hardway targets (2-2=4, 3-3=6, 4-4=8, and 5-5=10) began paying, particularly when our energy was aligned. There were lots of nines, which was Laurie Monroe's favorite number.

In our debrief of the session, I congratulated the group on their progress from first session to the second. I encouraged them to add an "all is one" feeling for next session, and to align with their own God-nature and go from there. If more than one number has money on it, one way to include all targets at the same time in your intent was to think "happy numbers." I mentioned that the dice like to dance—let them dance and create their own ballet. When PK is strongly present, the dice actually move gracefully through the air. I reminded them that each was capable of a great roll. While one person was rolling, all the rest of the table had to do was to send energy to the roller, which might feel like sending someone a healing and encouraging energy.

Sunday was the third day of the workshop. We began with reports of the previous evening's excitement after we had disbanded as a group. Several people had fun on the slot machines, others saw a show. We discussed perceptions and questions. People were reporting that they were having a great time. We meditated together again using Hemi-Sync to reset energy.

Our third session together started again about noon. We went ninety minutes in this session with two long rollers after picking position by lot and patterning for long rolls. Women had both of the long rolls. One woman had a twenty-five-minute roll and the other a thirty-minute roll. A roll of this length usually only happens once in about fifty attempts at a table where people are playing dice normally.

In debrief I shared my joy. It seemed to me that the participants' PK abilities were like beautiful flowers opening more fully. I was very proud that the session was completely free of pouting, whining, and victim energy when there were glitches. And this is not easy when there is money involved. Instead people were consistently caring for one another, open, and courageous. I congratulated them for "walking the talk" with a sense of fun and delight. I let them know that some may feel finished and to respect this. We had our closing circle. Much love, happiness and excitement about what had been learned was expressed. People were very grateful for the chance to get to know each other, and felt that new deep friendships were formed. Some folks had flights to catch and some felt very complete and a bit tired. Others still wanted to play again. So those who still wanted to play agreed to meet after dinner.

We went to the dice table at eight in the evening Sunday for our fourth and final session as a group. Our second roller rolled thirty minutes hitting the hardways, and the next roller fourteen minutes. Then two rollers later Rick, looking like he was practicing all that was preached and glowing from within, started a fabulous forty-five-minute roll, consistently rolling the hardways. It was great—we would call out a number and he would roll it like a divine short-order cook. Four rollers after this, Rick's father Roger rolled for thirty-five minutes. I made about ten times profit for the session on my seed money. All of us won handsomely. The mood, energy, and caring at the table was perfect. We tipped the dealers well. I think they made $2,500 in tips. How this happened was that once we were in the zone and hitting the hardways regularly, we would place a $25 chip as a tip for the dealers on the hard ten. This way they would be playing with us and win when we won. When we hit it, it paid ten times the bet, so the crew would receive $250 as a tip. And we were successful at doing this repeatedly for them. Needless to say they were very happy with us and were enjoying the game as much as we were enjoying ourselves!

I was still awake at 2:30 a.m. filled with energy while writing in my journal about the day's events. All four long rollers in the fourth session were men and they were very precise in hitting our targeted hardways. The group PK in this first workshop seemed to follow the same process as when I would do PK individually. I personally did not have any great rolls during the workshop. I think that my sense of responsibility and pre-occupation with teaching and coaching everyone kept my own PK zone from developing. I was quite self-conscious when I rolled. While I knew that everyone was cheering for me, I felt some obligation to perform for the group. As the workshop ended I decided that my lack of rolls was just perfect in that I clearly destroyed any guru mythology and empowered the group members to step up and create through their own power and not just ride on my coat tails. The workshop experience, even with all the responsibility on my shoulders was much less lonely than playing by myself. I felt deeply blessed by all the wonderful heart energy that was shared within the group.

Another special thing about this first workshop is that I don't think that I had had as much fun and laughed as much in a long time. In the backwash of my brother's suicide, life had become very somber and serious. This laughter was a true blessing from heaven for me. Early in the workshop I told the story of meeting a participant at Monroe. This man had been gaming successfully for a long time. He reported having won a major jackpot in slots on every birthday for the past six years and two on his latest birthday. He sent me a copy of a check from one the jackpots that was over $155,000. He accomplished this feat in a special way. Before gaming, he first would use dowsing rods and a five-foot strip of adding machine tape paper. He would write percentages on the paper, and ask the question, "Today, how strong will my peak PK be?" Then he would walk along the strip until the dowsing rods crossed, and look down to see the result. If the rods indicated eighty percent or better, then he would go to his next question. On a second five-foot long strip of paper he would write down the hours of the day. Walking along the strip he asked the question, "What time will PK be the strongest for me today?" He would note the time indicated and play then. He reported that four out of the last five big jackpots occurred at the time he predicted. Needless to say the odds against this occurring by chance are astronomical, way over a billion to one.

We had several exciting conversations during breaks while he was at Monroe. As we shared strategies I let slip that one of the things that I did was to wear silk underwear while gaming. In my explorations of PK I had found that certain energies were important to the process. In fact it was ideal for all the energy centers of the body to be open and filled with good energy for PK to work well. The first energy was to be grounded or connected with the earth. This allowed one to more easily affect the physical because you were strongly connected to the physical in the present moment. In the energy language of the Indian system of the chakras, this would be a vibrant first chakra or energy center connection, located on the body in the perineum area. Caroline Myss, a medical intuitive and world renowned lecturer has translated this chakra concept into western terms, looking at each chakra as a kind of bio-computer. Her book and CD's called *Energy Anatomy* describe this in detail and I think are excellent reading for those interested in energy work.

The next energy that I found to be very helpful in PK was the energy of the second chakra, located in the genital area and associated with sexual and creative energies. This energy helps because it is also the strong life energy, and PK and manifestation use a lot of energy. Silk underwear felt good to this energy center. My jackpot winning friend looked surprised and then delighted when I told him this—he had discovered this same thing and wore silk underwear while gaming too! We had a good laugh over our "secret weapon."

The third chakra is associated with power and is located about two inches below the belly button. The fourth chakra is the heart center and located near the heart. I found that along with the first and second, that the heart chakra was particularly important in PK and manifesting. It is associated with love of self and others. It contains the energy needed for positive manifestation and is the intersection point between earth and spirit energy. The fifth chakra is near the throat and is associated with self-expression and speaking truth. When this center is open it allows the person to access greater intuition. Since PK and manifestation are forms of expression, this chakra is important too. The sixth chakra is located between the eyes and up a bit, where most people would locate the third eye. It is an area of receiving intuition and also projecting energy for PK. And finally the seventh chakra at the top of the head is associated with connection with spirit and feeling oneness with all life which also was helpful for positive PK. So, earthly and sexual energies are conducive to PK when held in the context of an open heart and a feeling of oneness with all.

Now back to my story. I was telling this first Vegas group about these energy centers and wearing my silk. They seemed very interested in anything that might help them be successful at their first PK experiences. Then during break on the second day of the workshop, Laurie Monroe and I were taking a walk along the Vegas Strip, taking in the sunshine and talking about how the workshop was going. Most people have heard that you can get just about anything you want in Vegas. On our walk we stumbled upon an intriguing looking shop and went inside. We came out with a small package and continued on.

When we arrived back at the hotel for the afternoon meeting I announced to the group that I had good news, we had found some silk underwear and were going to give it to the first man that volunteered to model them in front of the group. There was some nervous laughter and one brave middle-aged man named Neil thrust up his hand. I gave him the package and he disappeared into the bathroom. While he was in the bath I told the group what we had found. Laurie and I had selected a pair of men's underwear that was made of red silk with a G-string back. The front was shaped like an elephant with white furry eyebrows and a substantial trunk. Neil was gone a very long time! The group waited with baited breath. When Neil came out he was wearing his jeans. Redder than the purchase, he said, "I'm wearing'em, but I am not showing'em." The group exploded in laughter.

Later in our fourth dice session when Rick had his forty-four-minute roll and his father Roger began his long roll I was standing next to Roger. He told me that he was going to roll from inner child energy. Roger was in his sixties, but as he rolled he looked just like an innocent ten-year-old boy having lots of fun. About halfway through his roll he suddenly became anxious, turned to me and said, "I have just thought of seven, what do I do?" The group quieted to hear my advice. I looked Roger right in the eye, raised my right arm and waved it, mimicking an elephant's trunk, and let out a trumpeting roar. The group exploded in laughter. The crew looked really surprised and puzzled. Their reaction just made us laugh even harder. And Roger kept rolling well for another 15 minutes, having shifted the energy of seven through a good laugh. Our energy during the workshop was light-hearted, happy, and at times even a bit bawdy, but all in good fun.

I felt strongly before starting these seminars that I wanted to have the workshop tangibly benefit people who were less fortunate. I envisioned that just by our meeting to learn about PK and abundance, other people would be comforted and their lives made a bit easier. Encouraging generosity is very much in line with the energy needed for PK and positive manifestation of abundance. In fact, it is a good idea to be generous with anything you would like to see increase and perhaps that you feel you currently don't have enough of. So if you want to have more time for yourself to do the things that you enjoy, paradoxically it is good to donate your time to helping others. This also goes for donating attention, energy, and good cheer, etc. What you are generous with tends to then show up in your life more abundantly.

Holding money too tightly implies that there is a lack of it to go around. And feelings of lack (which contain a fear of loss and deprivation) tend to produce more lack. Generosity also is a natural response to the feelings of deep gratitude for all the blessings that we do have. And such gratitude is a very powerful energy for PK and abundance creation.

In this first workshop I started what we called our "blessing bucket" to hold donations for charity. People were invited, with no pressure and completely anonymously, to contribute anytime during the workshop to the charitable cause that we selected as a group. This concept was very well received by this first group and enthusiastically supported by each Vegas group since then. At this writing we have contributed nearly $100,000 to charities through our blessing buckets that were set out in the Inner Vegas Adventures and other manifestation workshops that I have led. Our charities have included individuals in need, as well as funds supporting organizations such as a start up of a local animal shelter in Nelson County, where The Monroe Institute resides. Other charities we have donated to include:

Doctors without Borders which delivers medical care in some of the worst war zone areas in the world.

Smile Train which surgically repairs cleft pallets for children in underdeveloped countries, helping them to avoid becoming outcasts in their society.

Central Asia Institute which establishes schools for boys, girls, and women in areas controlled by fundamentalist Muslim governments where women were prohibited from schooling and government schools often foster terrorism.

Amnesty International which seeks to prevent torture and intervene where torture is occurring.

Right before the start of this first workshop a dearly-loved man who worked at the Monroe Institute had experienced a seizure and had driven off the road and down a steep ravine. He was diagnosed with inoperable brain cancer. We decided that Dave would be our first beneficiary of the blessing bucket. We collected $650 for Dave during this first inner Vegas Adventure even though most of the participants had never even met him.

I want to share a letter that I wrote to my original participants the week after returning home.

"Dear Inner Vegas Adventure One Group:

Thank you for a wondrous weekend. I surely had beliefs turned into knowns and was so happy to see such heart-space develop in the midst of a casino. For me group PK is now a directly experienced fact, and that inspires a wealth of group healing and manifestation possibilities.

The craps crews and bosses came up to me and said how much they enjoyed our group. They commented that they had never seen such positive and loving energy at a craps table, and that they wanted the number for the Monroe Institute, etc. So we made a difference, walking the talk, and inspiring others. Dealing with "real life" since back has been a little left-brained for my taste but still there is a satisfied heart-open glow. The beauty here of the mountain forests changing for fall is excellent for the soul.

I thank you in a big way for having the courage and

curiosity to go, for hearing what was said, and for sharing your truth and caring for each other. You maintained priorities, had faith in yourself and the group, and allowed your belief systems to stretch. Thank you for supporting me, for donating $650.00 for Dave's wellness, and for my new Star Trek Hat!

When I was at the table for that last session and proof of man's ability to change physical reality through energy and intent was being manifested, I experienced a profound moment—the satisfaction in seeing this dream fulfilled was total. I really can't find the words to express my elation and thanksgiving at that moment. Afterward some asked whether I would do another group. I probably will. But that night, it felt too sacred to even contemplate a repetition. I hope each of you feel as blessed by the experience as I do. Love, Joe."

I received much positive feedback about the group, which was very satisfying. A participant, Gary, wrote about his experience and graciously gave me permission to share his thoughts publicly. Gary's letter and sentiments like it, assured me that this experience could be very positive for others, and that the gaming was just an excuse to pay careful attention to what was needed for PK and to practice opening our hearts.

"Joe Gallenberger was my trainer at The Monroe Institute. I learned that he was offering a workshop on psychokinesis and healing in Las Vegas. He stated that the energy in both areas was the same, and Vegas provided an environment that could challenge and confirm these manifestation skills. Our classroom would be the casino and the craps table.

"I didn't know what to expect and naturally went in hopes of winning lots of money. I had no idea that the course would exceed my expectations by the magnitude it did. We spent three days meditating with Hemi-Sync® tapes, and learning about PK, healing, manifestation, and the game of craps. We worked vigorously with affirmations, visualizations, and empowering beliefs. We moved into a steadily higher energy state of joy, unconditional love of self and all others, dropping ego, balancing male and female energy, centering, and then into deep gratitude and trust. By the third day, I was in a greater/finer energy state than I had ever experienced before. This seemed true for the rest of the group as well. Several of us kept the dice for almost an hour without throwing a losing number. The group had opened the psychokinesis window—we could roll exactly what we wanted, when we wanted it. What heart-open fun we had!

"Several days after returning home, I was still in that exquisite energy. I moved into an awakening of my Kundalini energy, particularly in the lower chakras. As this settled down two weeks later, I received the gift of being able to instantly take away physical pain in people by simply touching them, serving as the conduit for healing. I learned that PK energy and healing energy are the same. It is an energy that flows best when you open the heart, have love and joy, and are playful, grateful and trusting . . .

"Then, I went to Joe's second Vegas workshop. There, my heart chakra opened wide and remained that way. Just a few weeks ago, I went to a third workshop where I experienced an even greater opening of my higher chakras, and a deepening of my healing, manifestation, and intuition skills. In these last two groups, I also saw others moving into their healing power. After the second group, one woman, upon arriving home, bent her silverware as easily as if it were a cooked noodle. I have heard other participant stories of terrific heart, intuition, and healing experiences. I'd encourage anyone to experience an Inner Vegas Adventure for themselves — it is amazing, life changing, and totally fun.

"For me, I feel that I am at the beginning of a magic journey into deeper surrender and gentle healing power. So thanks, Joe, for sharing your love and knowledge. You are truly making the world a better place.

"Love and joy to all,

"Gary"

CHAPTER 12

Working on the Tapestry

I am faced here with the challenge of how to present the essence of the next sixty Inner Vegas Adventure workshops. I am looking forward to presenting this because in doing these workshops, it is as if I have been working on a tapestry where you work from underneath. And writing about them, gives me the opportunity to turn the tapestry over and see the overall picture. And you get to see what the design looks like with me. I hope it will be a beautiful picture!

I kept a record of each group by making notes during the workshop, and by doing a journal at the end for the participants. I sent it to them when they returned home as a memento of our experiences together in Vegas. I will share some of the individual group highlights that illustrate points that I want to make about the process. Out of respect for brevity I will leave out many things that happened during all these interesting times. But I will cover pivotal changes, insights, and events that occurred and also how these experiences were affecting my life at home.

As the seminars proceeded we found ourselves at different casinos. Many of the people came back for multiple workshops, often a dozen times or more. They found the repeated experience valuable as a learning tool about their own consciousness and how they could use thought and energy to create reality. They reported that these adventures were wonderful fun, and they especially enjoyed having the opportunity to meet like-minded people from all over the world, and have a unique experience.

As we progressed, the format changed a bit but always remained a three-day seminar. We began to discuss more how to use these energies for emotional and physical healing after finding, like Gary did, that dramatic spontaneous healings were occurring, as well as the ability to heal others. Gradually we evolved more sophisticated behaviors at the tables. For example, early on we would all make a group Om sound at the table to combine and raise our energy. We found that making that unusual sound freaked out some of the crew and other customers. Still, sound is powerful thing, so we changed to more Americanized sounds such as the cheering you might hear at a sports event. This worked just as well without upsetting anybody.

I am very happy to report that from my point of view, every single group was able to witness PK at the dice table and often on slot machines. Since this PK effect was at times fairly subtle, I would not be surprised if some participants would not agree with me on this. But in the large majority of groups the PK effect was clear for everyone to see. As the groups continued, there did seem to be the same general rhythm that we saw in the first group. Most of the time the group's first session is a little rough with small losses, and a feeling of being frazzled at the end of the session from attempting to focus on so many things at once—the rules, money management, and PK energy. The second session typically would be better, and the third better still. Sometimes the fourth session, if there was one, was great if the energy was still high, and sometimes it was pretty flat if people were tired and felt completed. But this pattern had many exceptions, such as the first session having someone who exploded immediately into strong PK and rolled for an hour right from the start.

Over the course of all these workshops, while PK was always present and there was much learning about healing and manifestation, winning money was less predicable. This was because each person was in full charge of what they bet and when. And sometimes losing early on, for example, might put them into fear a bit. They would pull back on their betting and when things finally got going positively, they would be reluctant to bet when they could have made good money. The beginner's groups in general usually have a few people for whom the take-press idea of betting is just too complex. I would tell them to relax about it because tension and self-consciousness was such a killer of PK energy. I would advise them to just go, and bet the same amount each time. This did help them relax and do better but this level-betting did cut into their possible profits. The net result is that at times by the end of a typical workshop some people had made money and some didn't.

All together over the course of these sixty workshops we have had perhaps four times that most everybody lost at each session of the workshop. Even then, people's financial losses tended to be small. And they still expressed much satisfaction with what they had learned. What seemed to be happening in these groups was two-fold. First, at the table people tried just a little too hard, which is tempting to do if there have been some losses. Second, in these few groups there were great challenges to beliefs and emotions going on for the majority of the participants in that group. All groups face issues such as their feelings about money, and feelings about taking a risk. Added to this is often a fear of power, anxiety about performance, issues of not feeling worthy to receive abundance, and many other limiting beliefs and emotions to work on. This focus on fighting their dragons often results in great healing by the end of the workshop but tends to pull energy from being available at the tables. In the four workshops mentioned these issues surfaced more intensely and in more people, than in an average group.

I would like to give you two examples of the inner work that participants sometimes face. In one workshop a woman began feeling very ill the first day and spent the second day resting on a bed in the suite where we were meeting. What surfaced finally to her awareness was that as child she had been able to do PK, and then someone in her family died and she thought that she might have killed them. This childhood perception made her shut down all her power in life very strongly. Once she shared this perception with the group, we sent her healing energy to transform this limiting belief. During her Inner Vegas Adventure she was not able to roll well, sevening out immediately while she was processing this issue about power being unsafe. After the healing she was then able to roll well by herself but not in front of the group. Later she attended another workshop and by then was able to roll very well in the group and had experienced a surge in power and her effectiveness in relationships and career.

In my second example a woman came to the workshop about a year after the death of her daughter. She arrived depressed, having trouble sleeping, etc. By the end of the workshop she was feeling much better, and was smiling and open to life again. She was very appreciative of this. But she had not rolled nor bet well during the workshop. When she returned home, within the next few weeks she found herself winning repeatedly on penny slots. She hit jackpots of a few hundred dollars to a few thousand. In just a few weeks after her Inner Vegas Adventure she managed to accumulate

$38,000 in winning jackpots. She returned to other Adventures to continue her learning.

Another factor that was present in two of the groups that lost every session was that I discovered later that we had people secretly drinking alcohol. We have a strict no drinking rule in Vegas, not because I am against it in general, but I had found that alcohol was antithetical to the energies needed for PK. Alcohol tends to ruin grounding, that strong connection to the present moment and to the earth. And although it can be relaxing, it impairs the concentration needed to track the game well. Further, alcohol is dehydrating and in the desert environment it adds to the tendency to dehydrate. Lack of hydration can produce headache, spaciness, tiredness, and irritability. Again these are all PK killers. When registering, participants are informed of this no drinking policy in writing. In addition to the individual effect on the drinker, keeping such a secret from the group has bad effects. When a group is so strongly bonded with each other, secrets work against the energies of honesty and integrity that help positive energy flow.

In more than a handful of the groups, everybody has won every session they played during the workshop and therefore all won strongly for the whole workshop. But typically as mentioned before, we might start with a small loss in the first session, then break even the second, and then make money the third and fourth sessions. So at the end of the most typical workshop most people tended to be ahead a little bit, and a few down just a little or about even. I have always made it clear that winning money during an Inner Vegas Adventure is not the main reason to attend, nor the main focus of the workshop. In any event a definite financial win cannot be guaranteed because I have no control over peoples' individual betting decisions, or how strongly we will experience PK. This general result of modest wins for people attending Inner Vegas Adventure is fine with me. I do not want to tempt people to drop their life's work and try to make money in casinos, nor trigger an underlying compulsive gambling addiction!

Another thing that became apparent quickly and continues today is that when people return home from the workshop they report many miracles of healing, manifesting, and abundance in their life. One woman returned home to find that she had been commissioned to do several large statues in bronze for a university, where before she had no luck getting her work accepted. People sold houses quickly that had been languishing and for great prices. Others were promoted or found exciting new jobs. Some reported finding their soul mates. These type results are very gratifying to know. Even the small victories such as being upgraded unexpectedly to first class on the flight home are fun to hear.

As 1999 approached there was much healing between my ex-wife and me. This was very important to me in that we had been great friends and business partners together. I dearly hoped that we would both be happier apart but could remain friends. As of February 12th I wrote in my journal, "I have enjoyed every day so far in 1999. There has been a shift in me towards inner peace."

Two weeks before my next Vegas workshop I was driving home from work at dusk on a country road. About a mile from my office I noticed an owl sitting by the side of the road and as I approached, it took flight right across my path. A few miles further down the road the same thing happened again. I entered my driveway thinking, "Boy, I must be getting doubly wise!" I forgot about the other thing owls tend to be omens of. Two nights later I had a very clear dream. In it I had entered what looked like a very clean and luxurious mental hospital. As I went through the dining room, I noticed that all the crystal was shining on the starched white table cloths. There was a great sense of peace within the place. I proceeded up a grand stairway to a landing and looked out the back window. I could see beautiful gardens, then fields, woods in the distance, and finally way far off I could see the whole earth as a beautiful globe. I thought, "This must be what heaven is like." And just then my dream was broken by the phone ringing.

It was my dad telling me that my mom had just died. Mom had been in a rest home for the previous two years with dementia, so it was not a total shock. I got up, lit some candles in the darkness, put on meditation music and connected heart to heart with her. I felt that she was being loved and cared for, and felt her strong love for me. I sent her my blessing for peace and clarity in her transition. Compared to my brother's death by suicide, my mom's death was much gentler. She and I had been very close. The main thing I missed was our late-night talks in the kitchen, being the night owls in the family. After her death I learned that I could sit down with pen and paper and just begin writing, making up a dialogue between her and me. I started as simply as, "How was your day, Mom?" I would make up an answer and pretend that she asked me back the same question, and I would tell her about my day. Often in these sessions, after a few made up sentences, it would seem that she really was answering me in my mind, as I wrote her part. It was not as satisfying as having her here to hug and to see her smile, but it was a consolation nonetheless.

I did my second Inner Vegas Adventure in February of 1999. The group had filled quickly with a waiting list, after word-of-mouth spread about my first workshop. Here are some highlights: The first craps session had erratic energy, and people were very tired afterwards. This was very much like first group's experience. No great rolls but all stayed within budget. For the second session we drew lots for table position and gave our first roller energy before we left the meeting room. He went to the table in high energy and had a thirty-minute roll. The second shooter did fifteen minutes, the third ten minutes, and the fourth fifteen minutes. Energy held better this second session (which was similar to the first group's experience).

Right before the third session we put each person, one at a time, in the center of a circle and sent them energy through an Om chant. The first three rollers at the table rolled for an hour combined. Everyone made a profit this session. We noticed that the elevator kept getting stuck on the ninth floor and lots of nines were thrown. These odd synchronicities between what would happen away from the table, and what would then happen at the table continued through most of the groups that I have taught. We learned that such synchronicities were a sign that our energy was high, and an excellent guide about what to do. I have found this true as well in life—that intuition and synchronicities happening with greater frequency is a sign that you are living in your intuitive heart, and are excellent guides about what to do next.

This is one of the delights of the energy path that I have been on for these years. About a year after our beloved dog Brownie died, I felt we were ready for a new pet. As I researched breeds I was very drawn to Labradoodles which are a cross between a poodle and a Labrador retriever. I loved the poodle breed's intelligence and playfulness, and the retrievers' easy disposition and loyalty. Labradoodles also were supposed to be hypoallergenic and shed-free. Brownie had been a major shedder, so this was a definite plus. At the time I first researched Labradoodles they were a fairly new breed and cost about $2,000 for a puppy. This was out of my league for a dog that would live in the country and be exposed to the risks of that life-style. Besides I did not like puppy mills and would only consider an animal that was home-raised, and I knew of no one in our local rural area doing this. After doing the research my intuition was to wait.

Several months passed and I basically forgot all about the dog idea. I then found myself in a store and drawn to a local magazine that I had not read in years, called the *I Wanna*, in which people can advertise items they want to sell. So I bought the magazine not knowing why, except intuition, and went home to scan it. I quickly came upon an advertisement offering to sell two labradoodle puppies for $250 each.

I said to my wife and kids, "You want to go look at a puppy?" The kids jumped at the idea, my wife was wondering what had gotten into me. We went to see them. We pulled up to their street which was named Kendra Drive, and Kendra is my daughter's name. There were two ten-week old puppies left. The owner was getting married the next day and these two females were left from an eight-puppy litter, the mom's first. The puppies were raised inside her home since birth with lots of affection.

The puppies' mom was a beautiful yellow lab and the father a grand champion white poodle. The puppies were the cutest bundles of wagging fur one could ever imagine. We got down on the floor with them and were mauled with kisses. My wife immediately scooped both of them into her arms and said, "We have to keep them both." Now I was the one surprised. I thought of my brother and his wife, Dianne, who lived next door to us on their own nine-acre place. I said, "Let me call John and see if they might want one of these cute little critters." He and Dianne agreed to meet the pups, if we brought them home.

We quickly settled on $400 for the both of them. Asking their date of birth we found out that the puppies had the same birthday as Dianne. On the way home we had a short discussion about names, while each of my kids held a puppy. We ended up keeping the names the owner had given them, Luna and Kodi (short for Kodiak). It was a very happy day.

Kodi seemed the gentler of the two and also was a bit cuter by being the even fluffier ball of energy. I offered her to my brother and his wife, and they said yes immediately. As the kids played upstairs with Luna that night, I checked my email. The first email I opened was from someone in England with pictures of dogs in Halloween costumes. After checking my email, I went to play my favorite computer game called Bookworm Deluxe which is basically like Scrabble. The bonus word as I opened the game was "doggy."

Luna and Kodi have been amazing pets (except that they do shed). The "girls" get to play together most days, running like the wind through the woods surrounding us. In fact, as I write this I have just come in from playing with them. At seven years old they still have a lot of zest. They have added immeasurable pleasure to our lives. And look at all the signs that they were meant for us! I find now, that if I keep my energy high and my heart open, when important decisions come along that have the potential to greatly enhance my life, multiple signs and synchronicities guide me well. I just have to have the courage to follow my intuition, and great blessings usually follow. This is indeed a magical way to live and reassures you that the universe is there to support you.

This topic of signs is an interesting one. You really can ask the universe for signs to confirm which direction you should take. At one time my wife and I were thinking of moving to Oregon. We were pretty conflicted about whether to do this because we really liked our home in North Carolina, yet most of our best friends were on the West Coast. We put our house on the market but had gotten little response. Approaching Christmas time I asked for a sign whether we should leave the house on the market. Shortly thereafter I was sleeping soundly when suddenly I heard a tremendous bang and the whole house shook. My daughter's brakes had failed when she went to leave for work and she had hit the side of the house with our truck. The wall was pushed in and all the brick had cracked and fell onto the hood. We had to take the house off the market for repairs. In retrospect the fact that the house not attracting buyers given that it is a very nice property, was probably the sign I should have respected.

Given what I was learning in Vegas, I would often tell groups that, "Fear is expensive, love is priceless, choose wisely." Years later in meditation I asked for a sign about some important decision. My exact words were: "Universe, please give me a completely clear and concrete sign." The universe obviously has a sense of humor. Two days later the postman delivered a package to me. When I opened it I found out that it was a gift from a participant. They had printed my saying, "Fear is expensive, love is priceless, choose wisely" on a wooden sign and sent it to me. I got my concrete sign and it was indeed a good answer to my question.

There is a psychic that I know who works on very important government and private questions. I was present when he told a group in a lecture one evening that he uses finding a feather as a sign that whatever he is thinking at that moment is the correct answer. I left the meeting and went outside into the dark, wondering if that could work for me, and a feather fell directly out of the night sky into my hand. So I use seeing a feather as a good sign for me as well. Within the past year I developed a yen for a new piece of stereo equipment. It was a beautiful black deluxe CD player and quite expensive. I went down the driveway to get the mail thinking about whether I should purchase this luxury. On my way down to the mail box and back I found twenty-six black feathers of all sizes. Usually on this walk I see none. Later that night I made my case to my wife that I would like to buy this CD player. At the end of my presentation of all the good reasons, I pulled out all the feathers with a flourish and said that they were a clear sign that I should buy it. She responded, "What did you do, shoot the bird?" We both laughed. The player has been a great source of enjoyment ever since!

In the second Inner Vegas Adventure before dinner on the last night, I asked the group to create a monetary gift for themselves much like a present to take to a wedding or party, and then let go of pushing for any particular outcome and just enjoy the party. We went down for our celebration session and held the table for over three hours and stopped before everyone even had a chance to roll once. Fabulous energy flowed consistently throughout the session.

We tried a new strategy that session that became an integral part of every Inner Vegas Adventure since. We decided to have a designated "energy person" stand next to the roller and hold energetic space for the roller. We also had a "shielder" person stand behind the roller to block any on-looker's energy that was not in light-hearted joy. This process came to be known as our energy arch. Since that group we practice this in the room before going to the tables. The idea expanded into two people standing on either side of the roller. They face each other for a moment, gaze into each other's eyes and connect soul to soul. Then they ground this high soul connection with earth energy and bathe the roller in energy within that space. The roller just needs to step into this invisible arch, relax into the wonderful energy that is flowing between these two people, and throw the dice. If the roller doesn't want to keep track of money while rolling because it might be a distraction to their meditative state, the people within their arch can do their betting for them. The roller can turn to their arch for help with grounding or ridding themselves of the seven-energy. The arch also can take care of the shooters' more mundane needs, getting them a drink, and tipping the dealers for them, etc.

In a gothic cathedral whenever there is a high arch there also is a support for the arch called a flying buttress on each side of the arch that helps strengthen that arch. In a similar fashion with our energy arches in Vegas, we have two more people, one on each side of the arch, that support the arch's intent. These support people can also help with practicalities and shield the shooter from any negative energy coming from onlookers or crew. Adding the relatively simple device of our energy arch greatly improved our PK power at the tables. It helps the roller settle down more quickly and not be so distracted by the turmoil at the table. And most importantly it helps the roller be able to sustain the high energy state needed for PK much longer because they are being supported energetically within the arch.

So in this celebration session using the energy arch, many people rolled twenty minutes to a half hour. And we developed very powerfully aligned heart-energy. During this workshop many folks worked on healing others in the group of minor physical complaints with great success. I was again thrilled with the seminar outcome and noted in my journal that I thought it is phenomenal that we are able to get so far in just three days while also dealing with jet lag, and learning about casino games.

During this second workshop there were several energy challenges to me personally and some for the group. For me I was still coming off the sadness of my mother's funeral and the drain of a bad cold. Also when we were in Vegas I got a call the second night there that my teenage daughter was caught having an unauthorized party at my house in my absence. I wished on hearing the news that I knew how to fly, because I wanted to fly home and throttle her. It is a good thing that I do not know how to fly, because by the time I did get home I settled for a lecture and a long grounding. Given these challenges I was happy to see that the techniques that we were practicing in Vegas even worked when there were significant blocks to good energy.

In this workshop each time we went to a table to play there were hassles with dealers, yet we overcame this with much good-natured kidding and tipping until the crews became friendly. In our group we had a person who was highly irritating to many of the group members including me. This was causing us to not do as well at the tables as we perhaps would have. I reflected that, given we were trying to be loving, that our irritation and judgment would hurt us all. And in Vegas that was bound to be expensive. The group then as whole moved into an unconditionally loving acceptance of this person, and that person became our best roller for the whole workshop—making us lots of money. This illustrated to all of us that we always have a choice in how we react to challenges. It demonstrated the power of love to transform interactions with others instantly. I love how Vegas offers such clear and immediate feedback on whether or not we are taking the higher path.

After attending both of the first workshops, Laurie Monroe was confident that the Inner Vegas Adventure was a powerful, constructive, heart-open way to experience a new level of group consciousness. She broadened the invitation to participate in future Vegas workshops to the general Monroe Institute graduate population (versus only people that I had directly trained). I also decided to send people a questionnaire before they attended an Inner Vegas Adventure, so that I could more finely tune each group experience to the participants' individual needs, interests, and experience.

CHAPTER 13

So Long, Sahara

There was much interest expressed during the first and the second Adventure groups for a graduate program. So I began working on putting one together. I decided that attending such a graduate group would be by invitation only. I wanted to personally select those individuals who had learned the game of dice and money management fairly well, so that there would be less distraction from building good energy. Those invited would also be selected on the basis of their ability to give and receive love easily and to play well with others in the intensity of the group experience.

In a graduate group, all attending would have already witnessed PK in action. I thought that this might be very helpful because of the dramatic difference in power between a belief that something is possible and knowing that it is real. I felt that in such a group of experienced people, we would be released from having to spend so much time learning the game. We could use this time to build and align our energy faster. This freedom from learning so much detailed content might aid in the formation of even higher heart-energy. In physiological terms, there could be less left brain activity and more right brain or integrated functioning. That would allow us to get to the tables faster and be more powerful there, with the aim of making better profits.

Profits in the graduate group could also be increased by introducing several new money-management and betting strategies, including when to take profits out of the game. In the introduction seminars we just left money out on the table until the run ended, and by doing so there were many times when we had significant winnings swept away. In the introduction seminars, the emphasis was on strategies to conserve money so that everyone could play a long time.

There was a limit to how much information I could give people in the introduction workshop before they were overwhelmed. In a graduate group we could also try new strategies such as not having everyone rolling in order each session. Rather we could amp up a few rollers who knew they were ready to roll, by sending energy to them in the privacy of the suite before heading to the table. Other participants that session might be prepared ahead of time to send energy to the whole table, or be less active and more in touch with their intuition, so that they could guide our bets at the table. A concept came to me in a meditation after the second workshop. I felt that if we each focused on "all is one," perfect balance, etc., and then targeted the hardways, this might work well. We would in effect be targeting unity, harmony, and balance as expressed in doubles. This was a way to blend several targets into one intention. Such a unity concept might be an easier focus to maintain versus selecting individual numbers and constantly shifting which number we were sending energy to for any particular roll.

We had our first graduate Inner Vegas Adventure in May of 1999. It was a smaller group of eleven people. We emphasized group alignment and consciousness more, both during and between meditations. The first dice session Friday night at the Sahara went well with much calmer and smoother energy than in the introductory groups. It made a big difference that people already knew how to play the game and had seen PK.

Felix started Saturday morning by telling us the story of what happened after his first Inner Vegas Adventure. Felix is a very generous man, often putting substantial money in the blessing bucket before the group even went to the tables. When Felix was very young he knew that he was supposed to remain unmarried and accumulate enough money to live on by the time he was thirty. This was so that he could devote the rest of his life to more important things than earning money. He succeeded in his plan. When he was thirty years old he bought a small office building and began living in a basement apartment in that building.

In the last workshop most everybody won except Felix. He stayed a day after most people left. He went for a walk along the Strip and ended up at a casino where there were gardens in the back. His energy was so high that the birds flew to him, fish swam up to his end of the pond, and turtles crawled out of the water towards him. It was like he was a modern-day Saint Francis. With all the love he was feeling, he asked the question why did he not have a better result at the dice tables?

Then Felix headed back to the Sahara on the trolley that travels down the Strip. He sat in the back on one of the wheel-well seats, facing inwards. At the next stop a homeless man got on the bus and sat on the well opposite Felix. This man began to sing and carry on, and soon all the people on the bus were singing along with him and having a great time. Then this man locked eyes directly with Felix and said to him, "You've got to love life, you've got to love life!" Felix felt a chill of recognition—that was the answer to his question about what he needed to do to receive more abundance. The man got off at the next stop and Felix got off at the stop after him at the Sahara. The group loved this story and we discussed how easy it was to get bogged down in the trials and duties of life and forget to celebrate its amazing gift. Felix's story pointed to the wisdom of opening the heart and loving life while playing craps. In fact it was great advice for living all of life.

We played our second graduate session on a field trip to Desert Inn. We played for two hours and most made money. Saturday night we played again at the Sahara and focused more on sending energy to the shooters rather than focusing on numbers and this worked better. Because we were again more relaxed, there was more accurate intuition about what would occur next. Sara had a great thirty-five-minute roll, hitting several hardways in a row. In the middle of her roll she realized that she had not been betting the hardways herself. On hearing this we each tipped her $50 because of all the money she had made us. She made an instant $500 and she learned about giving and receiving in a new way. Filled with gratitude for our gift she continued rolling well. Then the pit boss came up, pointed his finger at Sara and said, "Still rolling?" She immediately seven-ed out. This pointed to the need for the group to help the shooter re-set if there was any thought of seven. That session Felix rolled forty minutes with many hardways. Everyone won 400 percent to 1,200 percent of their budget for the session.

Sunday morning the group experienced a meditation during which most members felt a deep connection with each other and a feeling of angelic presence. There were many tears of gratitude after this meditation. Then things shifted. The casino supervisor called my room just after everybody had dispersed for lunch and said that our table was going to be ready at noon, one hour sooner than planned. We rushed to re-gather and were fragmented, in low energy, and in some irritation. We started to play with me rolling. I rolled exactly what I was thinking, made two hard fours quickly, but could not get seven out of my head, and had a hard time selecting among multiple targets before each roll and finally seven-ed out. Then with another shooter the boxman was disruptive, asking the shooter as she was rolling, that if hardways were harmony, what was seven? We were able to reset energy a few times and then succumbed to his energy. We played for about an hour and stopped with most players down a little bit.

Sunday afternoon as we meditated, in my mind I claimed dominion over the group and put a big energy shield around the group—"This is my group and I reject any interfering forces." That night the Sahara didn't open a table for us as promised, so we went to the Desert Inn. The energy was calm, happy, and trusting, and we rolled well. We rolled two and a half hours with about every other roller hitting numbers. All made money on that session. People's intuitions were correct about ninety percent of the time. It definitely worked best for the shooter to manage their PK and the rest of us to send energy. We effectively used the image of our higher selves hanging out in the beautiful chandelier above the table playing with us and sending support. I woke up for the flight home singing, "You've got that magic touch, the touch that heals so much".

Interwoven through the weekend was the beauty and heart of many members graciously giving healing to other members in many ways, including taking the time to give each other energy treatments and massages. I felt that we had learned much about PK and healing in this first graduate group and had a lot of fun doing it. We have done a graduate group, which we now call Inner Vegas Reunion, once a year for the last twelve years.

My next Inner Vegas Adventure group was in September of 1999. I want to talk about it a bit because it showed me what would happen if I did not practice what I preached. What happened was not pretty, although there was much learning and the final outcome was quite wonderful. An abundance exercise designed to remove any feelings of lack or guilt was added to the home preparation materials. The exercise came to me in a dream, when I asked before bed to have a deep healing of anything that might be in my way in creating abundance. Most people found this exercise very useful.

Friday went well with great energy quickly developing in meditations and good group alignment. Folks caught on well to the craps practice in the room. On Saturday the group energy was more aligned and cleaner than earlier groups. In our first craps session we rolled two hours and ten minutes and got around the table once with two people not shooting. People were not quite as frazzled and tired as in earlier groups, even though this first session went longer than in the other groups. With trust and heart energy forming earlier in the weekend, many folks began to find significant personal issues surfacing quickly. People supported each other to clear these issues. The people having these challenges each did a magnificent job embracing their responsibility for their own moods and perceptions, and getting the help they needed. The courage and heart people were showing was tremendous to see. Within this high energy others began to have "first-time-ever-for-them" experiences, such as new abilities to perceive information and energy, and to project energy for healing others.

Prior to our second craps session Saturday we sent energy to the two group members who had not rolled in the first session, and who were going to roll first. Again there was good energy alignment, despite negativity in the Sahara crew members. The first roller rolled for thirty minutes with clear PK, plus there were several more extended rolls by others. The session lasted two hours and twenty minutes with not everyone rolling once.

By Sunday the small and larger hassles with the Sahara were mounting. Some of the rooms were rundown, showers were going from freezing to scalding, elevators were slow and stopping at incorrect floors, food service was slow. When the group went down to our third session, the main casino boss came over and took me aside and said that they would no longer rate our play for comps because, "we were not betting enough and we were driving the crews nuts." This sounded like bull and I responded to him that we had been promised that we could earn comps, so that people would have a chance of at least some reduction in their hotel bills. I asked that we be treated fairly by previous agreement, but they were not budging on it, so I let it go and reset my energy.

The session started with beautiful group energy. We were aligned, peaceful, lovely, and sweet, and many participants saw a cone of white light form above the table. The crews were initially quite negative but we kept beaming them, including them in our circle of light, and they all turned around to be positive. Several group members had great runs, being very much in the zone and glowing. The person that did the best had one person sending him energy, someone else betting for him, and another telling him when the dice were ready, so that he could keep his eyes closed and build energy. Everyone was happy with the third session. Personal issues such as worthiness, having to do everything right the first time, and fears about full self-expression, kept surfacing and being processed lovingly throughout the day.

I take what happened next directly from my journal of the workshop:

In retrospect, our rushed preparations for the last session were a "perfect imperfection." It set in motion a tumbling of incidents that energetically we (and your fearless leader, specifically) were unprepared to deal with. I am going to go into detail here because it turned into such a valuable lesson in negative PK or manifestation. I think this lesson is relevant not only for Vegas but in our lives in general, particularly when our energy gets whacked by stress. In this story it may seem that I am beating myself up—I am not. I fully realize that I am human, that we have all been there, that there is nothing to feel guilty about. I also feel that it is likely that we can learn a lot from this fourth session that will serve our futures well if we pay attention.

We went down for the fourth session and the table was not available. The shift boss (whom I had known for years) took me aside and said there would be no table. I told him we were promised one. He said that nobody had promised one. He did this in a cold manner with no attempt to be helpful, and immediately walked away. I felt like he had called me a liar. Being in a highly sensitive state, and not well grounded, I reacted with anger and grief. It seemed to me the last straw. I would not be coming back to this casino.

This was a big deal for me. I had made many friends among the

Sahara staff in the twenty years I had been going there. The Sahara was also the first place I had experienced PK while gaming and had become like a second home to me. With my emotions boiling I went upstairs to find another casino with an open table. I had difficulty getting one (another missed sign to stop and regroup) but finally did find a table at the Stardust. The hitch was that we had to be there in twenty minutes. I returned even more stressed to the group waiting down at the tables. I presented our options of staying at the Sahara and waiting for a table to possibly open up, or going to the Stardust. I asked for feedback but did not listen to the one person who had the courage to say they were not comfortable moving. I didn't consider the disruption that it would cause new players to move to a different location with different chips, table size, and betting odds. The group, though uncomfortable with the plan change, followed my lead, assuming that I knew what I was doing.

By the time we got to the Stardust I had broken several important rules that I know by heart—to be prepared, be in high energy and grounded, and look for signs that you are proceeding correctly, such as everything flowing well. Also, I blew through the rule to express emotion and not suppress it. I was still having deep feelings of betrayal and sadness in relation to the Sahara and anger at being shamed in front of the group by the staff. So my ego was in a full-swing pity party. Next I broke the rule to always listen to others and care for each person's view as if it was my own. But my heart couldn't be heard over the roar of ego, now in full command of what seemed to it to be an emergency situation. My ego was shouting that my group's chance at having their final glorious session was threatened.

I believe things still could have righted themselves except that I went on to break other cardinal rules. As I suppressed my emotions they turned to a mounting irritation with everything. In my personal Vegas journal in the boldest, highest letters I had written, "WHEN IRRITATED, STOP IMMEDIATELY, UNDERSTAND WHAT IS GOING ON AND RE-GROUP." This was written in bold because that particular dragon had vanquished me so often. When things get rough I tend to get impatient rather than to relax and reassess. This impatience implies a lack of trust that the universe is unfolding as it should in response to my thinking and feeling. I eventually developed a mantra that has helped me immensely.

I now say, "Patience Sweetens Passion" to myself quite often when I am getting thrown off-balance by irritation.

But that night at the Stardust I didn't stop the cascade of negative emotion and thinking. Soon I was becoming irritated at a dear friend of mine at the table, basically for being happy and expressing it by being boisterous. Breaking the next rule, I didn't express this for the usual fear of hurting someone's feelings and knowing that it was really me, not her that had the issue. Yet, it felt like her problem and therefore the problem was now outside myself. So I moved further away from taking care of myself and instead put energy into changing her. If I had spoken, saying, "I know this is my stuff but you are bothering me," I know she would have got me back on track as we processed the issue. Sharing with anyone what is going on, and really listening to their response transforms things—that is one of the great gifts we can give each other at any time. As a therapist I have known this and lived this for twenty years, yet when stressed it is amazing what we can forget!

Of course the fourth session opened with several people rolling lousy. I had tripped and fallen and the group tried valiantly to harmonize and reset its energy but stumbled as well. No one strongly said "there is an elephant in the room," and we all plodded along, making the best individual and small group efforts that we could, but not clearly calling for the large group to address what was going on. The group energy fractured. The session went on for two hours as we pushed ahead. But weak positive PK turned to negative PK so that by the time we left the Stardust we walked out the wrong door and got lost and scattered on the way back to our hotel, tired, confused, and worn out. This was a perfect reflection of our status as a group at that moment. We did finally manage to all get back to our meeting room. Still much love and support was expressed, individual to individual through all this stress.

The next morning on Monday, even though the group was officially over, I called the remaining eleven group members together to process what had happened. Feeling quite sheepish about my behavior and saddened that this group had not had a joyous last session, I was received in this meeting with an unconditional, powerful, and peaceful loving by everyone there. Even though I felt that I had let everybody down, there was no blaming and shaming. All heard me fully as I talked a long time without interruption. When I was done each person also had a chance to frankly express themselves.

We shared many great understandings and healing of personal issues. We came to several insights. Most of these were really things to remember, that are easy to forget when stressed. We reaffirmed that you can't ignore the basics such as being ready and aligned. That it is always worth it to take the time to shift any irritation through speaking your truth. Trying to be nice when feeling otherwise just does not work. There was a strong feeling in the group that this was a very useful lesson delivered with love that would benefit many participants personally and the future evolution of the Inner Vegas Adventures. We decided that several modifications will be implemented in future programs such as: 1. We would establish a buddy system to encourage self-expression, self-care, and right energy, while swimming in these intense energetic waters. Before the workshop I would assign everyone an energy buddy. This would be another person in the group with whom they could share goals and talk to about concerns, if they were having trouble bringing up issues to the whole group or to me. 2. We would pay even greater attention to preparation before gaming throughout the workshop and add a debrief session after the last gaming, even if that session occurred after the formal closing of the group.

We also discovered some new things that might be tried in future groups. We had one person, Mary, who tended to freeze when it was her turn to roll. But if Mary stood with her eyes closed, she would see geometric symbols that were highly accurate, for example when she saw a cross, fours would be rolled. So in the next graduate program, if it feels right, we might divide tasks, so some people would be betting, some rolling, some giving energy, and some connecting with guidance, and then split the profits. This may take group love and interaction to a new level. So far everyone had always controlled their own money. Betting and rolling for others might produce a better effect. Also in future Inner Vegas Adventures we might encourage people to go to a table alone and roll several starts to get more familiar with the feel of the dice before we went to the tables as a group. I always warmed up like this when I was learning the game. It is very challenging to start off well immediately. Often I'd roll several short series until I settled down, and then have a great roll.

We finished this meeting with good feeling, great respect and affection for each other, and hugs all around.

I spent the rest of Monday cleaning up the meeting suite and then rested up. After not gambling all day, after dinner that evening George, his wife Mary and I went to the Desert Inn, sat by the pool and entered a very soft, peaceful, almost sleepy state. I did a little energy work on George. We decided to try to gamble from this state of deep peace and also to apply all that we learned from the night before, particularly speaking our truth at every moment and being open to any guidance. We might just roll a few times each and would stop anytime we felt agitated in the least. We went to the Desert Inn tables and there was one empty. After a quick trip to the restroom we got back to find the table closed. Rather than going to an open table with others playing, we simply walked away and checked guidance. I felt pulled to go back to the Stardust to set a better energy pattern there than we had left with after the fourth group session. George asked for a sign and immediately got a pulsing in the head. We joked: "Was it two pulses for yes and one for no?" Mary got her symbol for fours. We took these as sign to go back to the Stardust.

As George picked up the dice, we were still in this gentle open mood, unattached to outcome. From the first roll he got a great series of hardways, sixes, and eights. As best as I could count, he rolled at least 7 hardways, 6 eights, and 6 sixes. During his roll occasionally Mary or I would speak our truth, unafraid of distracting him, and redirect his energy. I continued to sense his energy easily and redirected it anytime that I felt it was wavering the slightest bit. For example, one time when I felt he was about to roll a seven, I pointed out the song that was playing softly in the background: "You can't hurry love, you just have to wait, it will come easy, just a game of give and take." He slowed down, smiled, and threw a hard ten. Four came up often and with Mary's intuition, we were on it. George was getting a clear physical pulse in the head before each hardway he rolled. We slowly increased our bets, always maintaining the sweet energy and staying totally in non-efforting. The chips ceased to equal money. The casino had become very quiet, or else we tuned it out completely and it just seemed that way to us.

When George finished rolling, I picked up the dice and did the same. I enjoyed a perfect roll from the start, everything graceful, plenty of hardways, finally moving to the place when I knew exactly what I was going to roll as the dice left my hand. Others had joined the table so we stopped and walked away, the two of us having held the dice only once each. I had risked about a hundred and walked away with $1,300. George and Mary also made great profits, none of it made on one big bet, just slow and steady. The crew was quiet, positive, and helpful throughout. They smiled and said "great job" as we left. They looked like they were in reverence of us. Not too many players walk away while they are winning!

As we cashed out our winnings we looked over and saw a bank of three Megabucks machines. These are known for never paying out much or often until it pays the big multi-million dollar prize. One could put $100 into this machine and never get one decent pay. But as we saw these machines this evening we were filled with excitement and delight. We took this as intuition to play. We decided to put in $21 dollars each, which at $3 a pull would give us each seven chances. As one of us played, the other two would send that person energy.

George's money went without a jackpot. Then my money went until I jokingly made a pelvic thrust at the machine—it immediately paid a small jackpot. We were laughing by the time Mary put in her money. Nothing happened until George said to her, "Make love to the machine." She blushed and immediately got a small jackpot. We all laughed and were in a very open-hearted mood, bonding as friends. On her next pull George put his head on her shoulder and softly said, "Now you have a guy giving you head." She pulled and immediately got another small jackpot. I then put my head on her other shoulder and whispered to her playfully, "Now you have two handsome guys giving you head." She immediately hit another small jackpot. By this time several people had come over to see what all the laughter was about and noticed that Megabucks was actually paying coins to the player. George next whispered to her, "Now you have a crowd watching," and she immediately got another small jackpot. All Mary's jackpots had been in a row without any intervening non-pay hands. We left the machine with a profit. We took this as a sign that the Stardust would be a great place for our next workshop and an affirmation that what we were learning really works well when our energy was right. And the Megabucks experience was a great reminder that second chakra energy in the context of an open heart is a powerful energy indeed!

We went back to the Sahara and processed what happened. It felt like a great healing had taken place. We stayed in trust and didn't struggle or push in any way, and the energy opened. Afterwards, I remembered that I only once before had experienced this soft, still, surrendered playing, also with great results years before—guess what, that session also occurred at the Stardust! The experience was like standing in a gentle snowfall at sunrise. As I wrote this down in my journal, Sandy from the second Inner Vegas Adventure called. She reported going down to buy a lotto ticket and picking her six numbers, then asking for one random ticket, and the computer kicking out a random ticket with five of six numbers matching her chosen ticket. Whether this was PK or intuition, it was a millions-to-one shot. Isn't it a great universe?"

CHAPTER 14

The Platinum Arm Club

It was clear to me after our last experience at the Sahara that we were no longer welcome there. I am not sure whether it was the consistent level of our winnings, or our usual behavior at the tables including chanting an Om and cheering even when we were losing. This could have generated complaints from other players. But whatever the reason, the signs were dramatic that we should move on. I met with several people at the Stardust and settled on George as our host. He was quite a character and operated more from the old-time Vegas model. His family had been in the casino business for a long time. I explained to him what I needed in a meeting suite. He showed me a suite that would work perfectly. I asked for tables reserved just for our group. He agreed to give us a try. I felt very odd to be leaving the Sahara after two decades of playing there. I was very attached, and wondered if we could do as well in another place.

Our next graduate Inner Vegas Adventure was in October 1999. It was my fifth trip within the year and my one-year anniversary of starting the workshops. Many of the people attending had been to several of the workshops, so we were building a nice reservoir of experience. My wonderful girl friend and soul mate, Elena, was coming out for her second trip to the workshops. Elena would eventually become my wife. In this group there were more women than men for the first time. On the morning of my flight to Vegas I woke up from a dream where I was singing the tune from the Wizard of Oz but with one important word changed. "We are off to *be* the wizards, the wonderful wizards of Oz." I took this as a good omen!

We decided to be more discrete at the Stardust table with energy sending (less loud Oms) than we had been at the Sahara. We were using the "energy buddy" system for the first time to help keep communication open and support high. We emphasized that this time each person could speak their truth at any time—no being nice just to go along—in hopes of developing more group wisdom.

We started our first formal healing circles in this workshop. Throughout the workshop, once the PK energy was raised to a high level, we invited anyone in the group to request healing. If they made a request we put them in the middle of a circle while we sent healing to them. They had the option of sharing where they would like us to focus our energy. Often this would be to part of the body that needed healing. But occasionally we would be asked to focus on relationships, emotional issues, to help shift limiting beliefs, and to enhance qualities of character such as increased capacity for forgiveness. Any request was honored.

For many people it was a big deal just to ask for help, and to be the center of attention and good intention. These circles became an integral part of the Inner Vegas Adventures and have resulted in many miracles of healing for body, mind, and spirit.

Once the person had shared their request, I would start the meditation by calling on the group to remember that they were free of all limits, and of great light and love. Each time my exact words would be spontaneous but often included components such as: "Okay, now please connect with the beautiful energies of mother earth and bring these energies into your heart. Now connect with the energies of highest spirit and bring these energies into your heart. Now connect your heart with the hearts of everyone in this group, where as one, we begin sending our highest and finest energy to this person who has requested our assistance. Affirm that you are open to the highest of healing energies to come through you for this person. Seeing this person in their finest health, and sending energy for all they have requested and for their highest good, we begin with an Om."

We found that this structure worked well. We leave the person in the middle for about six minutes with me letting them know when time is up by saying gently, "Let us know when you feel complete." This takes the pressure off of them in terms of feeling that they might be taking too much of the groups' time. When they feel complete they get up from the middle and re-join the outside circle. We ask them to stay in silence, knowing that their time in the circle is a catalyst and that the healing will continue. We usually do three people in sequence. Then we go back to the first person and ask if there is anything that they would like to share about their experience of being in the middle. Often people indicate that the energy was very tangible to them, such as that they felt very hot, they felt tingly all over, they felt like they were floating, or that their hearts were filled with gratitude. We ask the full group to wait and share any feedback for the person in the middle until at least a day had passed. This is to give the person in the circle further time to integrate the experience.

Working this way with three people takes about a half hour. It builds a wonderful energy within the group, characterized by peacefulness, harmony, and an open heart. It is a deeply respectful, even prayerful space. Our feeling is that while participating in sending focused healing energy this way, you also are receiving healing, so that even if you are never in the middle you receive great benefit. Immediately after being the focus of healing, people who have been in the middle often report dramatic healing. Reports of further healing continue over the next hours and days. We have had people with polio, fibromyalgia, and other chronic pain conditions burst into tears, as they tell the group that they are now pain-free for the first time in decades. Many people have had their tinnitus clear, or report being able to hear better. Sore shoulders, knees, feet, and backs have improved often to be completely pain free. Emotions such as anxiety, depression, shame, bitterness have shifted. Limiting beliefs have been transcended.

Occasionally people have requested that we send this energy remotely to a loved-one in another location. We often receive reports back that this remotely located person felt strong energy and experienced excellent results. Often people on the rim of the circle report that they feel the presence of the person's loved ones, or angels and guides. Occasionally the people on the rim of the circle receive messages that are helpful to the person requesting healing. These healing circles have been one of the most satisfying parts of doing Inner Vegas Adventures to me, and one of the things most treasured by the participants. The healing circles provide a great balance to the energy of the casino and allow participants to see this energy in action in another very practical and beautiful way.

In my experience these healing circles are effective about sixty percent of the time. This is higher than expected by just placebo effect. The placebo effect (where the person's own beliefs create healing instead of any external drug or surgery causing the effect) may indeed be another form of energy healing. Placebo effect usually causes about thirty percent positive response in controlled healing trials when evaluating drugs or surgery. Energy healing may be one way out of the expensive and often toxic treatments that are currently offered in western medicine.

Don't get me wrong. When I broke my leg falling on the ice, I deeply appreciated having an ambulance pick me up and a surgeon skillfully thread a titanium rod though the bone under anesthesia so that I could walk again in a few months. In terms of acute care and prevention of contagion, modern medicine has done wonders. It is generally less effective with some chronic conditions. And many conventional approaches, particularly for conditions such as cancer, are highly toxic with little supporting evidence that they significantly improve or prolong life. Hundreds of thousands of people die each year in the United States from conventional medical intervention. This is more than from wars, car accidents, terrorist acts, and murders combined. The best approach may be to clean up traditional medicine's act in terms of cost, medical errors, over-use of drugs, etc., and then combine it with energy healing. I know emergency room doctors, for example, who have been to the Monroe Institute and now quietly practice energy medicine at the same time they are treating trauma in the E.R. by conventional means. They report excellent results.

We sent healing energy to two people in our first formal circle during this workshop. Then we went to play our first session at the Stardust. In it, the first person we sent healing to rolled twenty minutes, then the other person sent healing had a thirty-five-minute roll, hitting mostly hardways. It soon became clear that being in a healing circle was often a great way to prepare for rolling dice. This was true when the person experiencing healing took the time to ground their energy before rolling. If they neglected this they often were "flying too high" from the energy of the healing circle to roll well.

On Saturday morning we did another healing circle for three members. All felt powerful energy being sent and like they were floating. In our craps session after the healing, one of people sent healing had the best roll within a very good session. It looked like we had made the transition from Sahara to the Stardust in a fine fashion! The rest of the workshop went well with one highlight being a group member's making a weird bet called the "hopping buffalo" which has odds of 6 to 1 against making it. Over the trip she placed only six hopping buffalo bets and made them each time they were placed—this overcame odds of 46,656 to 1 that such a thing happened by chance—so intuition and PK were definitely flourishing.

On the day after the workshop the remaining folks gathered in the evening and reported some great things. One couple had gone to the baccarat tables and made a few thousand using intuition. That evening five of us did our preparation work by the pool at the Stardust, sending energy to each other. We looked for signs about where to go, as we tried to decide between the Stardust and the Desert Inn. The first thing that I saw was a latex glove on the ground, with its middle finger pointing to the Desert Inn across the street. Well, that sign could be taken either way, so I threw my Stardust room key up high up in the air with us deciding to go the Desert Inn if it landed face up (heads) and the Stardust if it fell face down. It came down and hit George squarely on the top of his head and fell face up.

Felix (of "You've got to love life!") had a vision on his long drive to Vegas that sometime during this workshop he would experience a series of three hardway tens, and that he should bet them big. Monday afternoon while taking a light nap, I asked what had happened to Felix's vision of tens, since he had not rolled them during the workshop. I received the impression that Felix still had his hardways coming even though the workshop was officially over.

As we started our fairly long walk to the Desert Inn, I had the intuition that Felix might not have enough money to play in a relaxed fashion there—it was a more expensive casino. I mentioned this discretely to George and the man who had won thousands at the baccarat table, and they both handed me a hundred. I turned to Felix and extended my hand to give him $300. He kept his hands at his sides stiffly and said, "I've never taken anything in my life." We kept walking and I whispered to the other two guys, "Pin him!" They let Felix get ahead of them and then came up behind him. I turned, looked Felix directly in the eyes and said, "Felix, there is a big difference between taking and receiving." He melted and received the money gratefully.

As we walked a bit further the guys pinned me and said, "Joe, you have been coming out to Vegas for years alone and now you have to set yourself apart from the group in the trainer role. We want to give you the gift of coming out to Vegas. We will take care of everything for you and all you need to do is just relax and enjoy yourself in our good company." Now I was tearful with gratitude at their wonderful offer and the love that was being extended.

We arrived at the Desert Inn glowing and a table opened instantly as we walked up. Several of us had great narrow PK rolls. These rolls including folks rolling our target number, which was nine, many times in this session. Our first player rolled six nines in a row, then the next person rolled nine seven times in a row, and finally Cindy rolled our target eight times in a row. This was particularly special because Cindy felt that she had not done well in either the introduction or graduate programs so far because she was dealing with heavy fear issues surfacing from deep in the past. These issues made it very difficult for her to express herself. This night became a great victory over a thirty-year inhibition against expressing her power.

That night, during the Desert Inn session, Felix was the last roller. He rolled hard ten, then soft ten, then hard ten, then soft ten, then hard ten and immediately sevened out, just like his guidance had said that he would. These were just some of the magical happenings in this second graduate workshop. Going over the group, my impression is that at least eight out of fourteen people made major shifts during the workshop in areas of their lives that had been stuck sometimes for decades, and nearly all shared experiences during the workshop that had deep impact for them.

My wife Elena's story merits special mention. Elena was raised by Russian Orthodox parents. She still speaks Russian to her mother today. Her parents survived the trauma of World War II. Having experienced deprivation, they taught her not to be frivolous with money. Elena did not care for competitive games. As a parent she was uncomfortable playing Chutes and Ladders with her kids. Perhaps this is a bad example because every parent knows that that particular game becomes spectacularly boring after the hundredth time—yet young kids love it. Elena had been to Vegas once before she met me and did not like it much. But she accompanied me on an Inner Vegas Adventure to be with me and see what I was doing out there.

When I met her, Elena's energy was clouded by grief. She has lost a child to brain cancer when her beautiful girl was six years old. She then had the challenge of breast cancer herself and was recovering from surgery. She and I initially spent much time just resurfacing from grief, me for my brother Peter, and she for her child, Erica. It felt to me as if we saved each other from drowning in sorrow. We both functioned for our children's sake but had lost much of our joy in life. Awakening to joy and beauty together formed a deep bond between us.

On her first Inner Vegas Adventure, Elena found herself very uncomfortable with the whole idea of gambling. She lost about eight dollars her first session and was distressed, the second session she lost about fifteen dollars and became more distressed. Next she won twenty-five dollars and did not seem very happy with that. I pointed that out to her that her negative reaction to loss was much stronger than her positive reaction to gain. By the third day there, she took me aside privately and said that she wanted to go home. With my encouragement she stayed. Nearly every time she would hold the dice as the shooter, she would roll a point, then seven out immediately on the next roll. Her rolling pattern was a pure example of negative PK. Her antenna were up so strongly about loss, that she knew most every time someone else was about to roll a seven. The group began teasing her, bestowing on her the honorary title, "Queen of Sevens."

This pattern continued over several workshops and she did not like it. She had found that she loved meeting the people, the healing circles, and going to shows. And she particularly loved being by my side when I had a wonderful roll. She said that she could look into my eyes and see a change of color there which indicated that I was about to explode into a monster PK roll. I loved having her by my side to share the experience and she was excellent at grounding me, just by putting her hand on the small of my back. And she guided me well about when to slow down and reset my energy because she felt a seven. I didn't always listen but she was right about ninety-five percent of the time. But she hated it when it was her turn to roll and kept repeating the seven-out pattern within group sessions. We tried what seemed like everything to break her negative PK pattern. At least she was learning that losing money at the table or slots, while unpleasant, was not the end of the world and that the money usually came back in some other way.

Finally she moved from feeling like a victim and resisting what was happening to a place of anger, and then to a stance of power. She took the bull by the horns and went off by herself to roll in downtown Vegas where the tables were cheaper and no one knew her. She began by betting the seven and purposely trying to roll it. Once feeling dominion of the seven in this way, she moved into a new relationship with the dice. She returned to the group and in the dozens of workshops that she has attended, became one of our strongest rollers. She really began to enjoy the dance of the dice, and eventually even the slot machines.

One turning point for Elena was in a group where she, George, and Mary (of the Megabucks story) and I were the only experienced rollers. The first session had not gone particularly well. We decided that we four experienced people would start the next session. George started and sevened out immediately, Mary passed unexpectedly and I, surprised at the pass which was not part of our plan, sevened out quickly. So, the dice came to Elena within minutes of us starting, taking her also by surprise. We settled down before her roll with me on her left side and George on her right as her energy arch, and Mary behind her to form a wonderful cocoon of energy for her. I took charge of her betting so she did not have to worry about that.

After shaking off her nervousness, Elena began to roll and went into the zone, feeling very sheltered and comfortable in the energy cocoon we had built. She began to feel waves of bliss and felt so close to us that she felt she merged on a soul to soul basis with us. She also reported afterward that she felt completely connected with God-Source. I shielded her from what I was betting for her because as time went on I had some big bets out there. Everything just felt right. Elena rolled a spectacular ninety minutes without hitting a seven at the wrong time!

After this experience of deep sacred time at the table, Elena began to really enjoy playing the game. She has had many rolls from sixty to ninety minutes since, in the thirty or so workshops she has attended with me. I love going out to a casino, just her and I, where we are not known. I usually start and often do well. Then the dice pass to her. Most crews expect that she was just there for my support. Then she picks up the dice and has a monster roll, amply demonstrating that she understands the game perfectly and will not be rattled by distractions. We sure have fun in those moments! At the Stardust, Elena became the big crew-favorite with her classy good looks, her generous and fun demeanor and her dynamite rolling. Whenever I took a trip to the Stardust alone, everyone—the limo driver, the bellmen, house-keeping, the crews, and the supervisors, all would look around expectantly and say to me, "Where's Elena?" When I explained that she was not on this trip, their faces would fall like I was chopped liver. I am so proud of her in the casino (and elsewhere) knowing the grief and reservations about gaming that she has overcome to be where she is now.

There are two more stories that I would like to tell about Elena at the Stardust that show why she was loved there. In the first story, we walked in on the housekeeper cleaning our room as we arrived back from lunch. Elena started a conversation and noted that the woman seemed tired and depressed. The woman was from the Caribbean and said that she had been cursed and had been depressed and sleepless for many months. Elena imme-diately pulled off her treasured amethyst earrings and gave them to the lady, along with one of our cassette recorders and some of our Hemi-Sync tapes designed for relaxation. Elena said to her, "Please take these earrings, they will protect you. And please listen to these tapes. We will send energy for your healing." The next day when the housekeeper found us, she was beam-ing. She reported that her depression had lifted and that she had her first good night's sleep in a long while.

One of our favorite dealers at the Stardust was a gentleman from Vietnam. He would always grace us with a wonderful smile and bow deeply to Elena. One time he stopped us as we were going to the tables and pre-sented Elena with an orchid from his garden. She thanked him profusely. He then told us a story of how when he had moved in, his neighbor, a Vietnam vet was highly hostile to him. Our dealer friend responded by bringing him food and flowers repeatedly while ignoring every insult and threat. The man finally came around. Our dealer finished with the wise words, "No greater victory than making enemy, friend."

In the fifteen years we have been together Elena has become my best friend and business partner. When she is in Vegas with me she supports me in countless ways: going shopping to bring in food for the group, helping me set up the meeting room, keeping it clean and handling hassles. She is my sounding board when I am in frustration, doubt, or impatience if things are stressful within the group. She is highly available to individual group members to go to lunch, to go out shopping, and to process their issues, giving wise and respectful counsel. Then at the tables in the introductory groups first sessions, she takes the end of the table opposite me, holds great energy and coaches people along. We have seen many of the good Vegas shows together. We usually spent another day in Vegas after the group has gone home to just relax and enjoy the city and ourselves. Through the years of child rearing these trips were wonderful respites and a great break from the quiet rural life that we lead. When I travel internationally, I take Elena along the first time that I go to any new country, so that she can help me with the group and we can have a nice vacation after the workshop.

I want to end this chapter by illustrating what an accomplishment having a ninety-minute roll is, such as Elena had. As you read the article note that up to the time I am writing this book, we have had more than a half dozen rolls of ninety minutes or better, and more one hour plus rolls than I can remember.

"Welcome to the Golden Arm Club, where membership is earned by hour-plus dice-throwing."
By Kirk Baird, *Las Vegas Sun*, May, 2003

"Henry Lee doesn't cast an imposing figure. In fact, perhaps the most striking feature of the 72-year-old is his smile. A tall, thin man with a roof of white-gray hair, he's cordial, a bit shy, and full of quick, easy guffaws. The Terminator he's not. Unless you're a casino operator. Then you look past Lee's grandfatherly demeanor, as he stands by a craps table casually attired in a Hawaiian shirt and blue slacks, and to his right arm. Longish, moderately sinewy and tan—the result of his living in Honolulu—Lee's arm has done something only slightly more than 100 people have accomplished since 1989 at the California hotel-casino: thrown dice for more than an hour straight during a craps game.

"If it doesn't sound like much, John Repetti, executive vice president and general manager of the California, begs to differ. Most people hold onto the dice between five and 10 minutes, he said. And out of the tens of thousands of craps players who come through the casino each year about 18 people manage to make the 60-minutes plus. That averages to about 1 1/2 per month. "I betcha there are more holes-in-one on a golf course," Repetti said.

"Because of the enormity of the feat, a club has been created to recognize these people with the special touch: the Golden Arm Club. Created in 1992 the club was born after one casino patron, the late Stanley Fujitake, held the dice for a staggering three hours and six minutes. The Golden Arm Club has 116 members, including one who just joined last Thursday after holding the dice for one hour, six minutes. There's also the more select Platinum Arm Club, started in '99, which is reserved for those who've held the dice for more than 90 minutes, or for more than an hour on two separate occasions. The membership for this club stands at four.

"And since 1996 many of the members of both clubs return to the California for an annual reunion. The idea is to get those players with the golden touch, along with those patrons who are more apt to spend money on the tables, Repetti said. The match has been marital bliss for the casino so far, pushing the business in the "pit"—the nickname for the area with the craps tables—to its busiest period, other than Super Bowl weekend. David Lebby, vice president and assistant manager of the hotel-casino, said: "We made a holiday out of a non-holiday.

"Which is why Lee and fellow club members, such as Margie Masuda, are here. Masuda, 63, from Pearl City, Hawaii, has the distinction of being the only woman in the Platinum Club by virtue of a one-hour, forty-three-minute roll during the Super Bowl this year. And Dottie Fujimoto, 71, from Ewa Beach, Hawaii, held the dice for more than an hour twice: once in '97, again a year later. (Fujimoto is not eligible for the Platinum Club because her first one-hour-plus roll was before the club was created.) And Kenneth Sano, 73, and Dennis Peterson, 59, both of Honolulu, held the dice for one hour and 12 minutes, and one hour seven minutes, respectively.

"The members gather at the California, which caters to Hawaiian tourists and local residents from the 50th state, to socialize, play the game, and see if they can match or even better their feat. No one came close this weekend. And certainly no one came close to matching Fujitake's feat—and probably never will, Repetti said. A former pit boss for the casino in the '70s, he came up through the ranks and has seen many "hot hands." "But I've never heard of anyone shooting for three hours," he said. "If there was a Guinness Record (for craps), Fujitake's roll would have to be a record."

"Roll of the dice. Fujitake was a slender man of 65 when he had his moment in the spotlight. It began about 1 a.m. on May 28, 1989, and ended at 4:06 that morning. In between he held a pair of dice for a stint that lasted longer than some sporting events, NBC's Thursday prime-time lineup, most any movie without Kevin Costner in the credits and the flight time for a jaunt from Las Vegas to Dallas. It was long enough to attract the attention of a throng of admirers who surrounded the table four-deep and, after several phone calls, caused Repetti to leave his home and come up to the casino to begin signing checks. In all, the casino was out more than $1 million, with the biggest winner receiving a little more than $100,000, Repetti said, "That night was the biggest single loss for the California, period" from a table games perspective, he said. And the man responsible, Fujitake, found himself in the "middle of the pack" in terms of winnings. But perhaps as importantly, he had a newfound status as a celebrity. The quiet man from Hawaii who simply "blended in" with his surroundings soon could not escape the attention. Fujitake was all the talk around the casino, and word got back to his home state before the sun had begun its ascent. Everyone was abuzz with news of the man with the golden arm.

"In the morning, when Repetti presented him with a check for his winnings, he said he asked Fujitake about his accomplishment. "He said he dreamed that he won lots of money," Repetti said. "He rubbed his arm and said, 'This arm is golden.'

"Fujitake was right. He held dice for more than an hour three more times, although never coming close to his record-setting roll: his best was one hour, 36 minutes in 1997. But he tried, until passing away Thursday—ironically the day before the reunion—at the age of 77 after a long illness. "At least Stanley knows he went out a champ," Repetti said. "He was the king of the dice tables of the California hotel. Knowing Stanley, that was important to him. No one ever beat his record." But that doesn't mean they don't try.

"One last hand. By his own admission, Lee had not been doing well this weekend. Ten, fifteen minutes tops, and then he was out. Nonetheless, he persevered. Then, early evening on Sunday, he found himself in a bit of a groove. Standing at the far end of a craps table, the table full with players—many of whom knew him—Lee was throwing well. There was a certain energy in every throw—a long pause as he stooped over the table, and then let loose with the dice that almost always struck the far end of the table and rolled to a verdict: live to throw again or crap out. The money he bet on each roll was his own. For at least 15 minutes the gambling gods were smiling on Lee, his "golden arm" making himself and everyone at the table very happy. "That-a-way Henry," one friend routinely called out when each roll came up good. Others were eager to chime in with shouts of encouragement as well. Lee was happily in his element. And it was easy to see why. "I like to make money," he said. "(But I) enjoy the game." And now he was doing both. With each turn taking longer because of the amount of chips being exchanged on the table, Lee seemed to focus more and more. If there is such a thing as a "zone," Lee was nestled comfortably in its bosom. The funny thing about that zone is that at some point it ends. And for Lee it stopped around 20 minutes, or roughly 57 minutes short of his best. The Terminator was through. Still, it beats the time he rolled for 59 minutes before crapping out, missing out on becoming a Platinum Club member by 60 seconds. It's something he good-naturedly acknowledges irritated him. "There's nothing I can do," he said. Except keep playing and hoping for the best."

CHAPTER 15

The Stardust Years

I would like to continue my story with some highlights of what I think of as the "Stardust Years." Our next group was in January of 2000, a brand new century. We had survived Y2K. We had a full group of eighteen with twelve men and six women. Many of the men had an engineering background, while many other participants were in the financial and investment fields. This group had the strongest left-brain representation of any group so far! By the end of the group I felt that this program was held in part as a gift to the engineers from the Grand Engineer, because so many of our engineers experienced a strong expansion of their belief systems concerning risk and the bending of statistics used to predict the "random events," such as metal fatigue, that they used in their profession.

The new methods we introduced to Inner Vegas Adventure such as the energy buddies and energy arch contributed to us having our first ever winning first and second table sessions in an introductory program. All through the weekend, the Stardust's location, VIP check-in, ambiance, friendliness, and efficiency served us better than our old casino, the Sahara. Afterwards, my host at the Stardust, George, remarked on how many of the casino staff and crew had come to him telling him how sweet a group we were—with a wonderful positive energy. We were more than welcome back.

Our first dice session was an apt lesson in holding energy. We had developed a tradition in these groups that I start off as the first roller of the workshop. If I did well we were off on good footing. If I sevened out quickly, then I was able to devote all my attention to supporting the group without having to worry about my upcoming roll. When we got to the table there was a crew that we had not played with before. Since the play goes clockwise I stood at the very corner of the table next to the baseman. I said hello to him. He was obviously in a lousy mood. When he asked where we were going to start I pointed to myself. He announced loudly to the group, "Well folks, here's a fellow with a big ego—we usually allow a woman to go first." His name was Dick and I began to think that he was very appropriately named!

Dick next started hassling me that there were too many people at the table and that we could not all play at the same time. I explained to him that we had permission to play all eighteen of us at the same time. He accepted this and handed me the dice but kept grumbling about it. I was standing within inches of Dick. I put a big shield of energy between him and I. Elena was at my other side and I had an arch standing behind me.

I began my roll a bit shaky from Dick's harassment, but Elena put her hand on the small of my back to ground me and center my thoughts. I could feel my arch sending energy. The group also formed a very sweet and supportive energy, filling the table with light. I rolled for a while, struggling but holding my own, with my thoughts going back to Dick every time he grumbled about something. Then I realized, I do have a big ego. All I had to do is admit it and relax. I immediately felt more comfortable and began engaging Dick in conversation between rolls. I ended up rolling for over an hour, hitting target after target. When I finished, Dick said loudly, "Now I know why you had him start—what a great roll!" Then he bowed to me and smiled. I returned his smile and bow and said, "Thanks for the help," meaning it.

This session was a personal victory for me. With a lot of help from the group, I was able to keep my energy right despite ongoing adversity. It was also the first time that I can remember rolling a monster hand in front of a Vegas group. Since starting Inner Vegas Adventures I had found myself feeling responsible and self-conscious in the groups compared to when I took trips alone. It seemed that everyone was watching me with extra attention to see how I would do, and also often upping their bets just because I had the dice in my hand. And my reaction to this was involuntarily muting my personal PK. The crew cheered us as we left and Dick became one of our favorite crew persons, from then on always being gracious to us. He even became quite a luck omen for us. Whenever he was the stickman on a crew, it seemed that we won. When he grabbed the stick to start his time at that position, we all thought, "Dick on the stick," smiled, and raised our bets to take advantage of the good luck that he brought us. I recently found out that Dick has passed away. We will miss you Richard, rest in peace.

Although it was approaching midnight and I had a 4 a.m. wake-up for my flight home, I felt like playing one more time and patterned for a quick but precision roll. I went to the table with my four friends still well-wishing me. I immediately started rolling a great series of points and hardways, risking $150 and coming up twenty minutes later with about $1,700. It was a great way to end to a trip filled with communion with friends.

In the fifth Inner Vegas Adventure we experimented with remote sending of a target number to the group. The following story reveals the power of remote energy sending for PK or for healing. Laurie Monroe sent energy from Virginia for Phyllis to roll three nines in a row on the last session Sunday night. As it turned out, Phyllis decided not to roll that night. I remarked to George, "Well I'll just transfer those nines to me." The next morning, Elena and I went to the tables right after breakfast, still a little sleepy, and immediately each had a hot roll, with very narrow focus and high PK—hitting several hardways each, and each rolling a long series of nines, without even making nine the target. Every time we put a tip for the dealers on a hardway, we immediately rolled it. We both won about 400 percent of what we risked.

Later, Elena and I had an incredible dinner at the Desert Inn's best restaurant (free and courtesy of the Desert Inn, because of previous play). What a great way to feel abundant—"money for nothing and the food for free"—to paraphrase the song! We then met George and Mary at the Desert Inn dice tables where Elena, Mary, and I each had nice PK rolls, back-to-back. Within them I rolled five nines almost in a row, then Elena rolled five nines in a row, and another two nines, then Mary rolled four nines. This was in spite of fairly abrasive, invasive energy by a man standing next to us at the table. We extended our thanks to Laurie!

This remote sending of energy for healing or PK is a fascinating area that we have continued to explore. The most dramatic example was when a friend of mine who had been to previous Inner Vegas Adventures was taking off for Antarctica. I asked him for a favor. Would he please, once he was there send us energy to roll any number that he selected? I asked him not to tell anyone what the number was. He agreed to send his intention at the time when we were having our next workshop.

During the workshop I forgot about my request to him, but I carefully recorded what numbers the group threw. In that workshop we made an amazing amount of nines (about forty percent of all numbers thrown). By chance nine should come up as eleven percent of the numbers thrown. There are two ways to make a nine on dice, as a 4-5 or a 6-3. Both are equal in difficulty so you should have a fifty/fifty split between these two types of nines. In this workshop, eight-five percent of the nines we threw were 4-5. When I got home I checked my email and opened one from my friend in Antarctica. He had selected 4-5 = 9 as the target to send to us. So it looks like the energy involved in PK is independent of distance, if one's belief system allows this to be so. Modern physics supports this idea through the concept of non-locality. It says that everything is connected to everything else regardless of distance.

In the May 2000 Inner Vegas Adventure we incorporated this idea of remote energy sending. We asked the folks back home who had been to previous workshops to send us energy for a great workshop and lots of eights, nines, and tens expressed as 4-4, 4-5, and 5-5 on the dice. This worked really well. These numbers were thrown at well above chance. We also began experimenting with taking down our bets when the group felt a seven was coming. This had been hard to do in the past. People would have the intuition that the good run was about to end with a seven. Yet no one wanted to say anything because they did not want to be the party pooper and jinx the table by putting out a negative thought.

Because no one was saying anything about their intuition, when the seven came, even though we had made money on a good roll, we would all have a lot of money on the table to lose. Having all that money out there first creates excitement, but then an ever increasing tension builds, as there is both more to gain and more to lose—even though it was the casino's money. We had taken out our initial investment off the table long ago.

We decided that a good model to bypass this reservation was to speak our truth about sensing the seven. When a farmer plants a field with corn, on a certain day the crop is perfect for harvesting. If it is left there it loses peak freshness and then rots. In dice, when we initially bet it is like planting seeds that we hope will return a bountiful crop. At some point in a long run there is a shift in energy and you can feel that it is about to end with the seven coming at the wrong time. We decided when people picked up that feeling they would announce to the group, "The corn is ready!" We could then harvest our bets before the seven came and feel great gratitude for all the abundance created. We tried this in the workshop and were successful. This is a victory of wisdom, intuition, and action over the ego-tendency, fueled by greed and fear, to just keep pressing on and hoping for the best.

In the August 2000 group we had two new features. It was the first group where not everyone had been to the Monroe Institute before attending this Inner Vegas Adventure. We also had one fellow, Tim, who had attended before bring out six members of his family to try the experience with him. During our meeting Saturday morning Angie commented that "Craps" spelled backwards was "Sparc." We laughed and decided that "sparking" versus "crapping out" was a great way to express our feelings after rolling a 2, 3 or 12 on a come-out roll, which is a losing roll. We also had many indications that when PK energy is high, signs and synchronicities abound. Helga reported a late night phone call at exactly 3:03 a.m.—no one was there. Ben then reported a dream about a 3 x 3 pipe angle. We wondered if these were hardway six messages and decided to stay alert. The group went down to the tables for a 10:00 a.m. session. Helga had a beautiful manifestation of her phone call from the night before when she called a hardway 6 out loud and immediately rolled it!

We continued our healing circles with Robert feeling a dramatic turnaround in his energy, from tired and depressed since his surgery, to positive and "being his old self again." We gathered for our healing circle with Tim being the recipient. Tim had been suffering for years from a severe chronic illness. This may have been the highlight of the weekend for many of us, as we experienced a very beautiful and profound timelessness during his healing. Many were moved to tears, as visions of angels, golden light, and Christ energy surrounded Tim and radiated back to us. We were doing the healing in silence with eyes closed. To me it felt like an amazing light, with a Christ-like feeling of compassion, entered the room over Tim's head, went into Tim and then shot outward into everyone's heart. I burst into tears with the power of the experience and when I opened my eyes I saw that most of the group was crying as well. The power of this circle was probably enhanced by having six of Tim's family there with him who loved him deeply. It was a very sacred moment.

After closing circle, by popular demand, I attempted to light a fluorescent bulb through PK with the group watching. I was not successful until I said, "I quit" then the bulb immediately lit—showing the importance of forming intent, then letting go. The Stardust staff again was extremely impressed with our Adventurers' positive energy, generosity, and good humor. Several asked us about how to meditate. We again lit a candle in the darkness!

We had another guidance message manifest into reality before we left Vegas. Elena had a meditation vision of me standing to her left, with me rolling, both of us on all the hardways. In the vision I rolled a five then immediately a hard ten. Elena's message was to bet the hard ten as a "hop" bet. Later that evening we were at the Aladdin and it happened exactly that way! Then Elena and I both had great rolls at Caesar's. All these rolls on Monday were extremely focused with an amazing number of (4-5) nines being rolled.

All weekend long I was attracted to the signs for the twenty-first floor where we were staying. I felt that the 21 signs were a strong message. But I concluded that the sign meant that I was supposed to play Black Jack, also called "21." I didn't want to play Blackjack, so I dismissed the invitation and failed to look for other meanings. On our last night I had a run at Caesar's where (2-1) three and (4-5) nine alternated six times in a row! Turns out our room number was 2109 and reflected this three-nine series perfectly. Elena followed my roll at Caesar's with her own long roll of mostly nines. A player on the opposite end of the table walked away with about $15,000 profit on Elena's roll.

During this trip I experimented with trying to access guides, spirit, or Higher Self by sitting down, being quiet and just starting to write in a stream-of-consciousness. This is what I wrote while in the light meditative state: "Dear child, take time this time for self, to collect self and be guided. Let it be new. It can be created in splendor. Again trust it to come to you. Hardway tens, yes. Have more fun. The auto-writing is a good way to connect. There are new friends here for you. This is fun and a play time. Your mate loves you—trust this as well, and be yourself."

I then asked what was most important.

> "Knowledge and connection. Let the group help. At home you can coast some in reality, in Vegas it is created in each moment. Do this for self; we will help Hardway ten if you see it as a star system. The seven is just fear like Casper the Friendly Ghost. Yes, roll from your strong heart joy—travelling light today in the eye of the storm. Say to yourself, 'I am an abundant man who prepared and took a chance.' Stand with your council in brotherhood at the feast table."

I asked what has been in the way.

> "Tension, tight holding. What is needed is fearlessness. You are loved, you are abundant, remember this and relax, allow, allow. Just do it—it is the next step. Play to win. Fear of loss has to be lower than desire to win."

In our October 2000 Inner Vegas Adventure we had our oldest participant so far. Alvin, at ninety-seven years old inspired us all with his energy, wisdom and love of learning. We had several dramatic healings including a healing of Diane's shoulder with immediate alleviation of pain, Don reported that he could hear better out of an ear that had been nerve damaged for twenty-five years, and Lyle reporting a spontaneous healing of pain he had been experiencing in his back and shoulders.

I found that a very common fear in new players was that the casino will dislike us if we win. This belief works against winning. Therefore, I discussed how the casino is glad to have us there—we have positive energy, we are nice people, we fill rooms, we gamble, we bring in other players to the tables (a table often fills immediately after we leave, and when a couple of us start at an empty table, it often fills up quickly). When we are playing, the casino has films of the rest of the casino near us filling up with players that are attracted by our positive energy. The Stardust casino actually changed all their craps table felts to make the hardways boxes larger to accommodate our bets and winnings! The Stardust personnel, from cleaning persons through waiters, dice crews, VIP, all looked forward to our visits because of the positive energy. The dice supervisors have seen the quality of our play and say they know that we will win $40,000 + from them in the some future session, but they still welcome us.

In February, 2001 we began using a newly expanded, home preparation manual that included dice and many energy preparation exercises. This helped get folks up to speed more smoothly and rapidly. A strong theme of physical healing emerged during the workshop, as one third of the participants were facing significant health challenges. Wonderful shifts occurred, with these participants being able to feel significant energy being sent to them during directed healing sessions. I received a report that one participant who had been having much trouble with numbness and weakness in her legs, was able to take a long walk and feel greatly improved strength for the first time in many years.

After cleaning up and resting from the workshop, I went to the tables at the Stardust by myself and had two great sessions. In the first, as soon as I got the dice, I started with a series of six winning 11's and 7's on the come out, and then made 11 points in a row, in rapid succession. After resting a bit I went back, bet the 6, 8 & 5, and immediately rolled a series of 11 sixes, 11 eights, and 5 fives, with very few other numbers between. The coolest part of all of this was that during this roll, I felt for the first time exactly what the essence, nature, or feeling of eight and six were. When that perception was in my consciousness, no other number could possibly roll. I was one with the number. I discovered that each number has a distinct feeling or nature. This is hard to put into words but I will try.

While I was standing there, all of a sudden I just knew what the essential nature of the number eight was. Eight seemed to have a consciousness and an important place in the universe in terms of helping to hold all of physical time-space together. Eight seemed to be a living being or consciousness, almost like an angel or deva. I thought of Plato's world of ideas, where there is a perfect form of everything that exists. I was very fascinated by these perceptions. As I have mentioned before, I do not even like mathematics. Yet here I was feeling awe at the beauty of eight and its place in the universe. While I was in this contemplative state, another part of my consciousness began to notice that all I was throwing was eights— in fact I threw eight 8's in a row. Despite feeling perfectly content to just enjoy this new relationship with eight, my curiosity got the best of me and I wondered if I could feel this same level of depth with another number. I shifted my attention to six and felt the same beautiful thing, six as an angel or deva and its place in holding the fabric of time-space together. While perceiving this I threw six 6's in a row. This feeling of union of consciousness with a number has never repeated as strongly and clearly for me, but I often can feel a glimmer of it. And when I do I almost always throw that number on the dice.

In March 2001 we had our smallest group yet. Despite the group's size, great energy was generated for the healing circles and the gaming. Every person in the group was ahead financially at the end of the workshop and wins continued afterwards as well. I had a one-hour roll followed the next session by a forty-five-minute roll. Tim had two forty-minute rolls at the Stardust. Many folks also experienced clear intuitions about what number would roll next. We used a new intuition exercise where we rolled dice in the room, asking for series that we could see manifest at the tables, such as 12, 3, 2, 2.

As we rejoined Sunday morning, Paul related a dream he had last night where a white-haired dealer gave him the sequence of number's (5-7-5-6-4-5). We went out for our fourth dice session about 10 a.m. I had a twenty-minute roll, followed by Mary rolling about thirty-five minutes. During these rolls, Sam realized that the sequence of numbers in Paul's dream was being rolled. We bet the sequence and saw it come in for great profit. The dealer at the end of our table during the sequence was the same man that appeared in Paul's dream! Several other sequences that were intuited came in during the workshop. It's awesome when miracles can be repeated!

After cleaning up and resting from the workshop, I went to the tables by myself and had several winning sessions, rolling tons of 8's and 5's which were my targets. The best part of all of this was that during this roll, I experienced, as I did last trip, the essence, nature, or feeling of 8 and 5.

When that perception was in my consciousness, no other number could possibly roll. I was one with the number. In my last session of the trip, I picked up the dice, bet and quickly threw seven hardways.

Our twelfth workshop was unusual in that Elena and I arrived just seven days after my father's funeral, and our energy was tired, distracted, and sad. We had gone to Dad's ninetieth birthday party, a few months earlier, just a few days after people were permitted to fly again after the 9/11 terrorist attacks. I was leery about flying then but felt strongly that we should go. The party was a wonderful event. Dad was in great health and actively socialized with family and friends from all over the country. It was the last time I saw him alive and it was a wonderful last memory. The week of his death, in keeping with the theme of this chapter, he had won at poker with his friends, won at slots at his local casino, had lunch with my brother Mike, and put out the fixings for dinner, and then died quickly of a heart attack. When I touched base with him on the other side, his message was, "Dying was easy, like stepping from one room to another. Then he joked, "Death agrees with me, I should have done it a long time ago!"

I still sometimes call on him when I am at the slot machines which he loved. One time I was walking by the slot machine called "Wheel of Fortune", based on the popular TV show. While I was thinking of the times that I arrived home for a visit and found my folks watching this show, the machine shouted its signature call, "WHEEL-OF-FORTUNE"! Feeling my dad's presence I sat down and immediately hit a $1,000 jackpot—thanks Dad!

In the Saturday afternoon meditation Elena had the same vision of the hardway 8 she'd had the day before, with heart racing and sweaty palms (pay attention signs!). This time several people had some very nice PK rolls, including mine for twenty-five minutes. All rolls were precise with points being made almost immediately, which is very indicative of PK. Elena's vision happened exactly as she had seen it.

In all but a couple of workshops so far we had a winning Monday for the folks who stayed the extra day. These Mondays are more relaxed with the workshop being over. This shows that letting go of intent is an important piece of manifestation. We focus on learning during the workshop, then let go, relax, and play. We have discovered that play is one of the best ways to learn. In this workshop, for the first time, I asked that the participants to email me with any after workshop reports when they returned home so that I could include them in their journal. We received these wonderful reports.

On Monday Elena and I had a strong intuition to connect with Stan. We saw him having his breakfast and sat down to chat. We agreed to meet in an hour by the tables. There, Bill and Don joined and we went to play, feeling good. Stan got the dice. He rolled for forty-five minutes hitting lots of points as well as 6, 8, and 9 repeatedly. Ann had an earlier vision that Stan would roll three 12's. When Stan rolled a 12, he, Joe, and Dan remembered and hopped the next two 12's, which came in a row. We were thrilled with Stan's incredible roll and each came out $600-$1000 ahead.

Brenda and Simon went out as a team, played just the pass line and whatever hardway number came in. Between rolls they chanted quietly and focused on how much the dice loved them, letting go of winning money (and therefore hopefully the fear of losing). Simon rolled for a half-hour, and then Brenda held the dice for ninety minutes (adding another member to the Inner Vegas Adventure's personal "Platinum Arm Club"). She did so in beautiful energy with precise hitting of targets, and no sevens out of sequence. A direct quote from her: "Another interesting twist to this story is that a funny little man came up and was watching the dice go around. When they came to us he started to bet. He told us that he never played craps before, but was led to the table. He only had twenty dollars and left with over $500. When we finished, I looked at him and handed him ten dollars in chips and blessed them (not quite sure why I did that). He put five dollars on this wheel and won the jackpot. Simon and I were walking away and he called us back to see it. We ended up having a snack with him. He told us that he had had a near-death experience and after that he gets guidance on what he should do and that was why he was led to our table. He said that he never accepts money like I gave him but he felt that it was blessed and that he also should play it on the wheel of numbers. It was a great experience."

Don stated, "Intellectually I've felt for a long time that anything is possible. Our being together in Las Vegas helped me to bring together the ideas I've had about God, love, magic, and the possibilities for this world, and make those ideas more emotionally real—more experientially real."

In May 2002 we had our fourth graduate trip, which had been renamed, Inner Vegas Reunion. Everyone at this workshop had attended at least one previous Inner Vegas Adventure. As things evolved and shifted we began to employ new energy exercises and ways of focusing.

On Sunday Erin brought up the issue of losing energy when we are not behaving or feeling as our egos think we should. This resulted in a heart-opening discussion. We prepared in the morning for our casino session by doing healings and sending Om's to our rollers. Our goal this session was to devote twenty percent of our energy to the game's logistics and eighty percent to holding group intent. Group energy was much more coherent, grounded, and expanded during this session. As a result everyone ended up ahead financially for the session. Clear intuitions were flowing for many of us. Arnold held the dice for at least a half-hour in a very focused way, where each time he rolled the dice, he waited until we all were aligned with him, brought earth energy into his heart, waited until the energy came from spirit into his heart, then released the dice. Melisa followed with a beautiful fifty-minute roll, also in the zone. Coincidentally both Arnold and Melisa were receivers in our healing circle, immediately before going to this session.

On the last day we gathered for intense healing work with several remote healing requests, including a person with a brain tumor, a teenager facing neck surgery and biopsy, and my brother, John, who had been diagnosed with Inclusion-Body Myositis. All three healings were accompanied by tears at the love and energy present in the room. Several people received insights into what would be helpful for these people. Other group members also received healings. We then had our closing circle with many celebrating the caring, harmony, and beauty of our group experiences, and expressing great gratitude for the healings and insights experienced and shared. From my point of view we had risen well to the invitation to be impeccable and create from a grounded/expanded heart space in each moment. We saw how the real-world chaotic dice table provides clear immediate feedback on this process.

After our October 2002 workshop I ran into Cindy, who works as a dealer at the Stardust. She had received $3,600 from our blessing bucket in a previous Adventure group to help her with expenses when her daughter was seriously injured in a car crash. We had also sent healing energy to her and her daughter at that time. Some of her friends died in the wreck, and she had one leg crushed and the other amputated. The money we collected helped Cindy to take off work and stay home during her daughter's rehabilitation. Cindy and I hugged, and she burst into tears as she expressed her gratitude. Her daughter is doing much better and in fact had gone on Oprah recently to talk about teenage driving. Right after hearing this great news and very open-hearted I went to the tables and had a beautifully precise roll on our targets.

Our February Inner Vegas Adventure was a wonderfully winning weekend. February 9, 2003 was the designated day for a worldwide group meditation for peace led by 100,000 people who had learned to bend spoons as a sign of our power to affect the world. Our group joined in this world prayer. We created a beautiful ritual space to symbolize the earth. The group experienced a very powerful meditation that ended with us holding hands in deep sacred space. Many felt a shift during this meditation with perceptions of connecting with all who embraced peace in the Middle East, and with the power of love to transform the Earth. Note: the next morning I heard on the news that the UN was now more hopeful that Iraq would cooperate with inspections. We raised over $500 for the organization sponsoring this world prayer, to go towards a retreat center for psychic children to receive psychological support, and to be encouraged to use their gifts for peace.

Calvin had a fifty-minute roll in the morning and in the evening we had another wonderful session with Georgia rolling a beautifully grounded thirty-five minute roll with point after point of 5 and 8. I then had a twenty-minute roll with several hardways, followed by a twenty-minute roll by Mary, who also rolled several hardways. During this session, as well as the last one, the crews were very slow because we were getting paid on almost every number thrown, so the rollers had to hold energy for a long time between rolls. Everyone did a great job with this. The group cashed their winning chips in once again, with more goodbye hugs exchanged before parting as a group.

This group bonded wonderfully, stayed on task, and was extremely supportive of one another. Irritations were gentled by non-judgment and acceptance. We all held the goal of individually expressing the peace we wished for the world. It was highly unusual for so many people to have good rolls in one session, but this group consistently had twenty-plus-minute rolls in all but the first session, as well as on their own in smaller groups. Within this loving space, many people worked with their issues of receiving, deservingness, and openness, and had many new break-throughs, and healings

After workshop experiences: While Elena went for lunch and retail therapy, George and Joe more than made up for it with a royal flush win ($1000) at their friendly poker machine! At the Hilton, Elena had a roll with four hardway 8's, two of them in a row and eight 8's in twelve rolls. Then, Joe hopped a hard 8 on his first roll and it hit! He followed this with the same roll as Elena—eight eights (four of them hardways) in twelve rolls. More blessed synchronicity and PK.

> *John:* "Thanks again for an amazing weekend. It was the best weekend spent in many years. Spending time in heart-space and reconnecting with my center was both refreshing and enlightening. Not to mention some very special times in what I would describe as being in the company of heavenly hosts and universal energies. As for my ego, it had a message for me, and I am processing that message this week. I realized I need to accept, and know that I DESERVE love. I believe I do, but I have never accepted at face value deserving-ness of love, sup-port, and adoration. Till now I thought I had to earn, trade, or borrow it. Thank you."
>
> *Robert:* "SUPER session—thank you again. I'm looking for-ward to May. Little by little I am finding the energy. On the return home we had a big open house at work. It looks like it will result in a budget increase and maybe a raise, even in these tough budget times. Also, two days after I got back we had an "instant" resolution of my aunt's estate that has been dragging on without movement for nearly three months. The energy is GOOD!"
>
> *Mary:* "I came home to my lover, who was very happy to see me, with tons of red and white roses everywhere, and he said I

looked very pretty, alive, and YOUNGER! What I experienced during my first time doing a twenty-minute roll at the craps tables, in the midst of lights, bells, hollers, and whacky casino vibes was my first genuine contact with an energy of the universe that was timeless, noiseless, vibrant, centered, empowering, and fully expanded. It is what they call the FLOW. You can talk about it all day long, but until it is a real live twenty-minute experience, it's hard to comprehend. I GOT IT! And now, I'll be able to be there, in that fully centered and empowered state whenever I so choose. And from a long time meditator and healer, I tell you this state was DIFFERENT. In all truthfulness, those twenty minutes were, so far, the most important experiential moments of higher consciousness that I have experienced in a long, long time."

CHAPTER 16

The Yoga of Dice

Our May 2003 Inner Vegas Adventure was a terrific experience in coherent and powerful heart energy. I want to go into a bit more detail about this experience because of how magical it was, and how it shows the evolution of Inner Vegas Adventure as the process was fine-tuned over the previous two years. After describing this group, even though there have been dozens more Inner Vegas Adventures, I think I will have given you a sufficient taste of what the Adventures are like.

All three official group sessions in this workshop had major PK rolls of extended length. Everyone won each of these sessions and was ahead financially for the trip. We were immersed in the energies of healing beliefs, emotions, and the physical body. Our "blessing bucket" raised $1,515 for the Central Asia Institute.

On Friday, previous workshop attendees George and Robert assisted me in preparing the suite for the workshop. After setup, the three of us "Musketeers" went downtown, had dinner, and rolled dice. Robert moved into a zone of impeccability, throwing thirty consecutive rolls. George followed that with a good roll of fifteen. The energy of long rolls and abundance for workshop was in place!

On Saturday the full group appeared eager to begin. For many, the workshop began well before arrival with energy rising and issues surfacing. People reported a strong feeling of protection and light as soon as they arrived in Vegas. The workshop targets of 5, 9 and hardways were established. Many had great practice rolls. I showed how we would hold energy as group and had a roll where ten of twelve numbers were winners and four hardways were thrown. Robert and George sent healing energy to my knee which was hurting badly after kneeling during this long demonstration. Total pain relief was achieved in fifteen minutes and lasted through the next day. As we ended for the evening some group members went to observe actual table play in the casino and to roll at least once. The Three Musketeers came upon Marty and Alice and tested their intuitive skills. I successfully "hopped" (one roll bet) three successive rolls by Alice. I hit her hard ten, moved my bet to a hard four, hit that and then doubled my bet on a hard six—hitting that as well. George and I followed this with a 700-quarter win on a poker machine. Several others played at the Riviera with good success. They reported a dour table upon their arrival that was moved into a smiling and pleasant space as they played. Alice reported doubling her original buy in at the table before retiring for the evening.

On Sunday morning, Gene, a casino supervisor at the Stardust and my friend from the Sahara, met with the group. He encouraged everyone to have fun, and thanked the group for choosing the Stardust. Following a Hemi-Sync tape everyone felt smooth and in harmonious energy, and ready for our first session. I rolled first and immediately moved into openheart energy and PK with a thirty-minute roll. The group was excellent at avoiding distracting behavior and holding a coherent energy. One hundred percent of participants won this first session, many at four times their investment. Marty had a dream of two 12's in a row (900 to 1) he bet it and they came in. Many ventured into the world of "hop" or oneroll wagers that were high risk and high return. Success during the first workshop session was an excellent omen. All agreed that they had seen PK and intuition in action!

After break I talked about the power of healing energy and its relationship to the "zone" from which PK, intuition, and long dice rolls appear. In all these cases, it seems to me that one moves to a place of peaceful timelessness, which in sports is called the zone, by dropping from the mind into the heart, from a left-brain linear time focus to a right brain eternal-now focus.

The group agreed to continue the same order at the table during our second session. Several rolled out quickly. Derek was next. He felt very good from a healing circle and wanted to roll. The group affirmed his desire. He rolled beautifully. After thirty minutes he reported to me as part of his energy arch that he had a deep and growing need to go to the restroom. I told him, "No, you don't'!" Derek transcended his "out of bladder" experience. He rolled an incredible one and a half-hours! Derek joined our growing Platinum Arm Club. The game supervisor commented that he had never witnessed such a roll in his five years of Casino work. The Stardust joined our party by treating the entire group to a nice dinner.

Back in the suite quick tallies were made of our success. Many made fifty times their investment on Derek. I had rolled first in this workshop as usual. Because we were giving everyone their first turn at the dice, I had not yet rolled again because everyone so far had been so good that the dice had never come back around to me. Some decided to see if the group could prevent me from rolling again during the workshop. If this happened, it would be because those who had not yet thrown would also roll the dice a long time. This intent was shared the next morning amid heart-open laughter and teasing.

Monday the group assembled in the suite still holding the energy of play and abundance. We placed the remaining rollers in a healing circle before heading down to the tables. Marcia kicked off the session with a very respectable fifteen-minute roll and passed the dice to John. He rolled 5's and 9's and hardways with great regularity. John moved into a zone of impeccable joy and rolled for fifty minutes. Carla finished our session with a beaming smile, and moved into complete deva and fairy magic energy. During the de-brief John noted that during the roll he had been higher than he had ever been in his life and that included several "runner's highs" from ultra marathons. He felt grounded but couldn't seem to feel the ground itself. Again all won for the session and many made fifty times their investment on John.

In closing circle, powerful energy and gratitude feelings were present. Many reported strong healings around life patterns and wanted to return for another workshop experience. Folks were confident that their new energy and experience would manifest in life situations. Many in this group arrived tired, fearful, or scattered and yet we were able to quickly form a coherent, gentle, positive, powerful, and compassionate energy. It was also noted that since this circle officially ended the workshop, we were victorious in me not throwing again! After dinner our platinum-armed

Derek said he was feeling good. The decision was instantaneous to support him fully. He had a precise PK roll of thirty minutes.

On Tuesday those who had stayed an extra day decided to play a bit. I threw a hardway dominated twenty-minute roll. The dice then passed to Robert who found himself a gentle flowing energy. He threw for forty-five minutes. Wonderfully supported by the energy of the small group, PK space opened like a flower. Several folks reported seeing the numbers before they appeared.

The three musketeers had a quiet room service dinner, expressed much love and appreciation of each other, went out and had several more great rolls. After Robert left, George and I continued with good precise rolls. We finally got so naturally high, we lost grounding and couldn't even handle our chips without dropping them, so we moved to the slots laughing so hard and being so silly that when John found us all he could do was politely smile and shake his head.

My family joined me for vacation on Wednesday and we had a wonderful time. Between sightseeing and shows, I continued to roll very precise profitable rolls with great consistency. I want to comment on how healing it was for me to have George come into my life. He quickly became a best friend and nurtured me in ways that I had not felt since my brother Peter died. This was so healing for me, in that exceptional male friendships are a rare treasure. I have never laughed so much with anyone and felt so free to let myself be outrageous. We even had a great time shopping for clothes together (which I usually hate). We were dangerous in the store, picking out tons of stuff as our wives shook their heads. It was a good thing that we were hitting the dice and slots well to defray our spending spree. George raised wolves and even named one of his wolves after me. George is an excellent example of the amazing blessings of friendship that have been part of doing these workshops for me.

At home reports:

Sara: "In extreme gratitude to you and in honor of the beautiful Native Arizona land upon which I live, I intone that the Inner Vegas Adventure was a wonderful ceremonial blessing with craps being the celebration dance of joy after the sweat lodge cleanings of class exercises and the tribal prayers led by tapes, all of which gifted each individual with infinite enlightenment . . . The spiritual and emotional value is priceless. Joe's expertise in psychology provided a much needed therapeutic experience as well as beautiful growth of personal enlightenment. What a cleansing, learning, joyous, uplifting experience!! Thank you fellow co-creators. Peace and joy."

Shirley: "Thank you. My experiences of Vegas with the group will remain dear to my heart. My intention is to hold this magic/love as long as my humanness can bear, and even if it is just for a month, week or day the experience is priceless. Much love to you and your family."

John: "I accepted a job offer and start working on June 2nd. Life is good, very good! Did you hear the song Joe played on Sunday? "Sure as the sunrise, pure as a prayer—You fashioned hope right out of thin air—Every dream I abandoned, seems it could come true—I believe in miracles, there's no one like you." Well, it sounds like a nice fantasy but it is happening as I write! Every dream I had abandoned about how a relationship could work, how close two people could be, how closely their spirits dance . . . now it seems like those dreams could come true . . . I am, we are so in love . . . this is so much better than I had ever dreamed. Thank you everybody for all the energy you have sent me during and since our Inner Vegas Adventure!"

Our Stardust years ended abruptly, when we had a participant complain about her room on one of those satisfaction survey cards. The card went up to highest management. As best I can tell, they pulled the record of our group and found that everyone had won every session for that trip. My casino host called me and said that the casino no longer felt that we deserved executive hosting as our play was too low. We then moved over to Palace Station which has been our gracious host for many workshops since.

At the time this book is going to the publisher, we have just completed our fifty-seventh Inner Vegas Adventure. Nine women and nine men came to Palace Station. We experienced stellar psychokinesis and healings, with everyone winning every group session at the dice tables. We raised $927 for the blessing bucket going to Doctors without Borders and the Monroe Institute scholarship fund.

There were several unique features of this workshop including all participants attending Paul Elder's Remote Viewing (RV) workshop immediately beforehand. We visualized long rolls during patterning, carefully practiced the energy arch before going to the tables, and encouraged more hugging and playfulness at the tables. Most of the group worked with the SyncCreation course at home before attending. All these factors helped create the magic of abundant PK and healings.

Healing: After three months of partial facial paralysis, Karen was able to blink and see much better. We did a healing circle for Crystal, who had experienced two back surgeries and she felt immediate and continuing relief from pain. Jean's cold rapidly improved. Several other group members reported healing of physical and emotional issues, including stances toward abundance.

Gaming Sessions: We played four dice sessions as a group, totaling over five hours of play. Everyone won every session. We had visualized long rolls as our goal and having the targets of 5, 9, and hardways. We consistently hit our target numbers with precision and had lengthy rolls, including one roll of fifty minutes, two rolls of forty-five minutes, one of thirty-five minutes, and two of twenty-five minutes. We also experienced many substantial wins at the slot machines.

I would like to end this section by presenting with his kind permission a short article written by Richard Madaus, Ph.D. He is the author of a wonderful book called *Think Logically, Live Intuitively*. A brilliant and incisive man, he has just retired from a high-level government position and has spent the last decade exploring the mystical and practical aspect of the game of craps. I thank him for allowing me to include this article. My dad enjoyed a twenty-eight year retirement filled with wonderful experiences. I wish my friend Richard the same good fortune.

Richard wrote this article after experiencing several Inner Vegas Adventures. He felt one could look at what happens during these programs as a microcosm of what happens when we come into a physical incarnation. To me this is a fascinating way to look at what we are doing in the programs.

The Yoga of Dice
By J. Richard Madaus, Ph.D.

Souls seek experience and knowledge as they traverse the quantum universe of physical probabilities. Classes are taught and lessons practiced through life incarnations in the three-dimensional earth plane. Learning is not done in isolation, however, as guidance and support from non-physical realms is always available. One needs only to open one's eyes, ears, and heart to perceive it. The clues are everywhere, and profound insight can always be found in unexpected places. For example, one might think that casinos could never be considered cosmic learning centers. Yet, as in all things metaphysical, information about the true nature of the universe is most available where you are least likely to seek it.

Considering Las Vegas as a model of the physical universe can create an illustrative mini-adventure. In this example, the craps table becomes a small slice of three-dimensional reality where finite lifetimes can be explored. A timeline and culture for incarnational choice is selected by picking from one of the various casino decoration themes. One can visit the earth plane in ancient Rome at Caesar's, Egypt at the Luxor, Italy at the Venetian, and the American Wild West at the Frontier and so on.

We begin the experiment as a small group of intrepid souls gather around a chosen craps table to watch and play within the infinite potentials created there. A "shooter" (Higher Self) takes the dice and an incarnation is scheduled to occur. A life choice is immediately presented. Will this be a long life with manifested joy and abundance? Will this be a short life with only a few lessons learned? Only the roll of the dice will tell.

The "shooter" shifts focus momentarily to align body, mind, and spirit. The "right" instant is felt and dice are thrown. The cubed incarnation tumbles in a dance of energy, focus and intent. A seven appears. The entire group of Spiritual Beings rejoices. Pass line wagers are paid, and abundant energy flows. It is a perfect demonstration of instant grace and harmony in life.

The "shooter" pauses briefly to reflect on the joy of the game and then picks up the dice to roll again. On-looking spirits cajole and provide guidance from the non-physical realm around the table. They, too, seek new insights on each roll of the dice. Experience and knowledge are available to all as they wager and invest energy on the events of each particular lifetime. It is, after all, an incarnation from their soul group and learning can be at many levels when supported by others.

The dice are thrown a second time. On this roll a point is established and a goal is set on the wheel of Karma. The experience of each lifetime, each target point, is unique. How to live and experience each incarnation? How aligned are the body, mind, and spirit? In the craps table lifetime, the feedback is instantaneous. Energy can ebb and flow. Each Higher Self must balance the Yin of Intuition and the Yang of focused PK as the game of life progresses by the choices made in each moment. The harmony of body, mind, and spirit reflect the power to create joy and manifest abundance in a particular lifetime.

Challenges and lessons are always available. The money can become too "real." Desire for financial success can block potential lessons. If one is too attached to the outcome, the resulting mind chatter will break the connection to the dice. Conversely, blind trust in magical powers from the non-physical realm can separate one from the real game at the table. Without balance the death knell seven may appear earlier than could have been. The dance of the physical and nonphysical must be harmonious to keep the energy going for wisdom and abundance to flow.

However, as in a human lifetime, death is a certainty. When the incarnation-ending seven is eventually thrown, the shooter will reunite with the on-looking spirit world. Rejoining the soul group after death is met with cheering and applause. All have learned. All have experienced. Manifested joy and abundance is available for those open enough to receive it. All are interconnected in so many ways, at all times, whether experiencing incarnation as a shooter or providing energy and support from the spirit realm. As the soul group journeys together, the dice will pass from one to another so each can experience the magic of an incarnational lifetime as a shooter.

More than a metaphor for life, the Yoga of Dice is a microcosm of reality itself—both physical and non-physical. Life is a game and the money is merely one of many ways of keeping score. But in the craps table version of life you *can* take it with you! Ultimately however, you cannot lose because money is only energy and the Yoga of Dice helps you identify your ebb and flow within it. And just like in "real" life, the messages are always there, the only question is whether you are sensitive enough to listen and balanced enough to take action on what is heard. With an open heart and a clear mind the dance of the universe is all seen in the Yoga of Dice.

The Yoga of Dice offers us a chance to experience ourselves as our Total Selves see us. It is cosmic joy and humor at its finest, so Enjoy, In Joy.

(This narrative is drawn from notes of material experienced in meditation while attending Inner Vegas Adventure, October 7, 2002.— J.R.M.)

PART 4

CHAPTER 17

Manifestation and Creation Squared

After doing Inner Vegas Adventure workshops for two years, and seeing the highly positive results in terms of PK, healing, and manifestation, I was thrilled about what we were learning about human potential.
I began to wonder about just how far we could go in this exploration. It
was obvious to me that the Inner Vegas Adventures were a powerful way
for people to explore experientially their potentials as creators. For this
reason I felt strongly that the Vegas programs should continue. The introductory programs plus the graduate programs, as they were now designed,
seemed to be working exceptionally well and were likely to require only
fine-tuning going forward. These programs, because they took place in
the casino environment and involved money, were uniquely positioned
to help individuals face important issues that influenced abundance creation. These issues included attitudes toward money, such as money as an
energy, and feelings and beliefs about money, risk, and deservingness. The
lessons learned about financial abundance in Vegas were clear and quan-
tifiable. And these lessons were directly applicable to other ways in which
people desired abundance. But I wanted to explore these other important
abundance areas such as relationships, career, and health in a more direct
manner.

The next step was to create the opportunity for people to explore these
areas in a way that had potential to be broader and deeper than what could
be experienced in a three-day workshop in a casino environment. I decided
that I wanted to double the length of the program. This would provide time
to present more content and to be able to meditate at an even deeper level,

to raise even higher energy. I wanted the seminar environment to feel safe and sheltered, with all needs for food and shelter taken care of in an elegant way, so that people could really concentrate on their learning. I wanted the seminar to occur in a retreat setting where the group would be free of other people's energy that might be at a much different vibrational level. It would be ideal if they could disconnect from media, cell phones, and email if they chose to do so. This type of protected environment might allow the energy to build to a much higher and cleaner level. And I felt that higher energy might be the key to experiencing even more powerful miracles of PK, healing, and manifestation. I also wanted a place where there would be no dogma that anyone had to accept in order to participate. Finding a place where all these conditions could be met was a tall order.

Fortunately I was familiar with such an enhanced environment already, having been a trainer at the Monroe Institute for many years. TMI has a unique brain wave technology which allows the person by wearing headphones, to hear exercises that shift brain-waves and therefore consciousness, to ever-deepening levels of awareness. As discussed back in Chapter Six of this book, these deepening levels of awareness are designated in the Monroe system as "Focus" levels. I had been using Focus 1, 10, 12 and a bit of Focus 15 in the Inner Vegas Adventures meditations, combined with exercises that contained beautiful music designed to help with opening the heart.

I decided to approach Laurie Monroe about allowing me to develop a six-day residential program for TMI on exploring the limits of human potential, using the topics of PK, healing, and manifestation. As you remember she had been to the first Inner Vegas Adventures and was very excited about my work there. She thought such a program would be an excellent idea. I decided to call the program MC² for Manifestation and Creation Squared. This was a play on Einstein's formula $E = MC^2$, where E is energy, M is mass, and C is the speed of light in a vacuum. I liked the name because it implied that MC^2 would involve tremendous energy and be playing with the relationship between energy and matter.

Laurie and I set up an agreement where I would develop the program and TMI would produce the Hemi-Sync® exercises we would use in the program, following my scripts for these exercises. It would be an official TMI program, open to graduates of TMI's premier program, Gateway. At the time, people were coming to the Inner Vegas Adventures who had never heard of TMI, and having experienced the marvels of Hemi-Sync and experiencing the wonderful group interactions in Vegas, were attracted to going to TMI to learn more about consciousness using this Hemi-Sync technology. We also expected that at least some people, after experiencing PK and manifestation in MC² would want to try out and expand their new skills by participating in an Inner Vegas Adventure. Plus, we would be able to take what was learned in the two different programs and use it to cross-enhance the other program.

As in Inner Vegas Adventure, I wanted the fact that a group met in MC², to tangibly benefit other people around the world. A critical component of MC² would be to teach about the energy of generosity as a key to bringing good energy into your life. By then we had raised about $20,000 in the blessing bucket in Vegas. So the concept of a blessing bucket became part of MC² as well. In MC² contributions to the blessing bucket would also be completely anonymous and voluntary. This has turned out to be a powerful concept. As I have mentioned before, between the two programs we have raised nearly $100,000 for charity at the time I am writing this book.

The MC² program would work with clearing and raising energy, forming and focusing intention, and then letting go and trusting that what was desired or something better would be created. To raise energy further and to utilize even deeper levels of awareness, I decided to use Focus 11, 21 and 27, in addition to Focus 1, 3, 10, 12, and 15 that I had been using in Vegas. Focus 11 is an interesting state of consciousness where one can be in greater conscious communication with all the facets of who you are, including your conscious mind, subconscious, higher self, emotional self, and physical body. We would use Focus 11 in MC² to learn skills in creating reality, dissolving anything that you no longer desired in your life, and for enhancing intuition and wisdom. Lastly we would use Focus 11 to facilitate having "all of who you are" have clearer and more conscious access to "All That IS."

We would use Focus 15 in MC² quite extensively. Focus 15 is defined as a state of consciousness where we are free of the construct of time. Such a state of consciousness is often the called the Void, a place of everything and no thing, and of infinite potentiality. In my opinion, this state is similar to what other systems might call the causal plane. Focus 15 consciousness may also relate to what other's call the zero point field, or the eternal timeless now. It is a place of no-form wherein one can inject an intention and have it come quite easily into form or physical reality. This would be particularly helpful in manifestation work.

Focus 21 is defined as the bridge between the physical world and the spiritual or non-physical world. It is a great place for clear communication with spirit and guidance. Focus 27 seems to be a nonphysical dimension where there is still human thought and energy. It seems to be a place that simple but world-altering ideas can come from. We spontaneously receive information about ideas and inventions from this level of consciousness in our dreams. In MC^2 we would be able to access this state of consciousness for wisdom and manifestation power.

Even an idea as simple as the "Life is Good" slogan that is on coffee mugs, is a powerful reminder in these stressful and fear-filled times that there is an alternative view to this fear. There would be many exercises in MC^2 that would verbally guide participants into these highly altered states. But I had found from Vegas how important and powerful the energy of the heart is, in creating positive PK, healing, and manifestation. To engage the heart in MC^2, we would use what is called Metamusic, which is beautiful music with the binaural beat signal embedded within. Metamusic is for sale to the general public mostly with a Focus 10 signal. We would custom-make Metamusic for MC^2 with Focus 12, 15, 21 and 27 signals embedded within it, to achieve both an open-hearted flow of energy and at the same time as very deep levels of awareness in the body, emotions, and mind.

A week of high meditation is fine, but we learned in Vegas that for powerful and rapid manifestation, PK, and healing, we need to have all that high energy very strongly grounded. The trick was to be highly energized and spiritually connected and at the same time strongly linked to the present moment and to the sacred energies of the Earth. Several grounding activities were added to MC^2. The blessing bucket was one of these activities that would continually remind participants that they were earth beings connected to the entire earth community.

I wanted group members to have direct experience with PK tasks, so that they could transform their beliefs into a strong knowing that PK was real and that they themselves could accomplish it. The immediate feedback from personal success at PK was essential for this. I felt that having a variety of PK tasks would be an ideal way to do this, in that different things might appeal to different peoples' interests and talents. Each PK activity, while essentially using the same process, requires a slightly different energy, intent, and release pattern.

We would keep the dice-rolling that we found so helpful in the Inner Vegas Adventures. It has the unique qualities of giving immediate feedback and of bringing in the issue of money, which is a key energy in peoples' ability to thrive on this planet. I decided that we would build a dice table and have people roll for points instead of directly for money. We would have them each roll the dice ten times and they would get twenty-five points for the number that they chose as their target, ten points for hitting any double (similar to the hardways in Vegas), and one point for any other number. These points would then be totaled for each person. We would designate three charities in each MC², and then people could donate their points earned by how they threw the dice to their favorite of the three charities. At the end of the program the blessing bucket would be divided by how many points each charity received. For example, if one of the charities was an animal shelter and it received forty percent of the points donated, then the animal shelter would receive forty percent of the money in the blessing bucket. I felt that this was a good way to put some motivation behind the dice throwing, because we already knew that PK tends to be results driven. It works better when there is a reason that is important to the person attempting PK for it to work. So the favorite charity rather than individual financial gain became the incentive. I was curious to see how this would work because in Vegas even a small amount of money on the table encouraged people to pay very close attention to the instructions on how to develop PK and then see the principles implemented at the dice table.

The next PK task that I decided to include in MC² was metal bending using only your mind or energy. When I first heard of spoon bending, it was way back when Uri Geller came over from Israel at seventeen years old. Uri caused a sensation with his metal bending skill. He was reported to have been successful at several major university laboratories, in front of multiple cameras recording him from different angles, and in front of master magicians watching for tricks, in experiments designed to eliminate fraud. He also did this PK on live TV in the United States. I was intrigued by Uri but then discouraged by reading many peoples' protests that this had to be sleight-of-hand or a magician's trick. My attention turned toward metal bending again when a fellow Monroe trainer who I trusted deeply after working with her closely for ten years, told me that yes, PK metal bending was real and that she could do it. Plus, she had seen Uri work at close-range and was convinced that he was, at least most of the time, legitimate.

That said, I had tried metal bending with a few groups in Vegas. Some people could indeed bend very heavy metal forks or spoons during the Vegas groups. I had provided the flatware, knew it to be hard stainless steel and knew it had not been tampered with. But try as I might I had no success myself. Finally one time while I was trying my damndest, my friend George who was good at metal bending, came behind me and put his hand on the middle of my back. He sent energy through his hand into my back. Immediately the metal softened in my own hands and my spoon bent as easily as if it were rubber. It was quite a rush—to know that this really was possible and that I could do it! I still could not do it on my own for what seemed like a long time. Laurie Monroe was good at it so she would lead the spoon bending exercise in MC².

I also decided to have the participants in MC² attempt to grow seeds in their own hands within five minutes, and then to send energy to their seeds for a few days. Then we would compare the growth of their seeds to control seeds and see if there was a difference in growth. I had heard that this was possible including stories in books such as *The Secret Life of Plants,* which suggested that living things such as plants respond positively to human intention and energy. I felt that this exercise would appeal to folks who like nature and plants and might involve a similar energy as we were using for healing in Vegas.

Lastly I added the task of lighting fluorescent light bulbs with one's energy as another MC² exercise in PK. Bob Monroe had come down one evening at dinner when I was training the program called LifeSpan 2000 and took me and the other trainer aside. He had two fluorescent ring light bulbs in his hand. He said, "Have the group light these with their minds tonight." He turned and left, as we called after him, "Ah, Bob, have you ever seen this done, do you know how to do it?" Well, that ruined dinner for us. We found a dark place and began to try this. My co-trainer and I tried everything we could think of short of plugging the things into a wall circuit and darkness prevailed. Finally we gave up, saying, "This will never work." As we put the lights down on the table in surrender, they lit up. So fluorescent bulbs would be great for having the group take themselves lightly (couldn't resist) and learning to let go, for energy to flow.

MC², as it was being structured, included the aforementioned specialized Hemi-Sync meditation exercises, the PK tasks, and lecture segments on psychokinesis, healing, and manifestation. The meditation exercises and lectures also focused on how to remove the most significant and common blocks to manifestation, including fear, lack, guilt, and shame. Fear tends to freeze our energy and set us up for manifesting negative circumstances. Because thought coupled with strong emotion tends to create results, negative thoughts and emotions such as fear tend to create negative results. There is a saying, "Fear is prayer for what you do not want." Feelings of lack (not having what we want or need) tend to create more lack in our lives. As Seasick Steve said, "He started out with nothing and still has most of it left!"

Feelings of guilt say to us, "We do not deserve good, in fact we deserve to be punished." Feelings of shame can be brought to awareness by asking questions such as: What would you rather your mother not know about you? What do you want to keep hidden from others? Feelings of shame are perhaps the deepest drags on manifesting a great life. Shame suggests that we don't have a right to exist as we really are. Shame creates self-hate.

I felt strongly that while MC² would be a very high energy and joyful program, we needed to look at these negative emotions and limiting beliefs and give people effective tools to deal with them. This shadow work would be very important to do. If people raised their energy high and yet still were carrying around a lot of negativity, they indeed would probably manifest things into their lives much more quickly. But there was high potential that at least some of these manifestations would be negative. From my point of view, this is where most manifestation systems and movies such as *The Secret* fall down by being incomplete.

It is a disservice to tell people that all they need to do is to think of something, perhaps by using visualization, and it will become reality. In some circumstances this may work, but very often for the things that we want most and have not been able to create, it is the shadow that is holding us back. There is tremendous power for good in the shadow, but if the shadow is denied its power it usually sabotages our every attempt at better health, relationships, and abundance. I saw this clearly in Vegas for myself and for participants. The Universe does really give us what we are thinking, particularly when there is strong emotion attached. I remember one participant coming to Vegas with a strong fear of loss but with high hopes and a good heart. She did indeed lose money at the tables but then a kind and generous fellow participant covered all her losses and took her out to a fine dinner on her way back to the airport. She arrived home and unpacked to discover that she had left her favorite shirt in Vegas. No one could find it. She literally "lost her shirt" in Vegas, as she had feared.

A critical component that I added to MC² was formal healing and manifesting circles. In MC² each person would have the opportunity to be in the center of a circle while the whole group sent them energy, first for healing and then for what they would like to manifest. We have six circles scattered during the week for this purpose, with four people in the middle, one at a time. We draw lots for each person's healing position, asking them to trust that their higher self will select the perfect time for them. Some would have healing very early in the program, some at the middle, and some at the end. My hope was that these healing circles would help with all issues of body, mind, and spirit. The circles would also serve to balance and integrate new energies and shifts in perceptions. At the end of the week we add three additional circles. We have one circle for people invited from outside the group who would like healing. There is a circle for healing planet Earth and all her inhabitants, including the mineral kingdom, plant kingdom, animal kingdom, and the human communities that live on Earth. And our final circle for the week is for any loved ones and friends of the group members that are not present who would like healing.

I felt that it would be important for the trainers to do all the exercises with the participants. This would help build a coherent "all is one" energy, as opposed to "we are the trainers and you are the students." I wanted to be sure that we would not ask the participants to be putting themselves on the line by doing anything that the trainers were unwilling to do. After the first few workshops Patty Ray Avalon became my co-trainer and has done all the programs with me at TMI since. Patty is an experienced TMI trainer. She is an excellent manifester in her own right, and a very well-trained healer. She was previously on the teaching staff at the Brennan School of Healing. Patty is also an accomplished artist. She has been to Vegas with me several times and had some excellent PK rolls there herself. She is very curious and creative by nature and loves to explore new applications for PK. Patty has been an ideal training partner over the course of MC² and I appreciate her contributions to the program immensely.

Much of what we do in the program softly, gently, and continuously encourages people to feel safe and respected and to risk opening their hearts more fully than perhaps they have ever experienced before. People are encouraged to love themselves and one another unconditionally. This reflects my strong belief that heart energy is the best, purest, and strongest energy available to help with healing and positive manifestation. And that learning to live from actively flowing heart energy is the best thing you can do for yourself, the people around you, and the whole planet.

MC² starts on Saturday afternoon and is designed to generate higher energy each day through deeper meditations and exercises to reach an energy crescendo by Wednesday, and then have a big celebration on Thursday, before ending Friday morning with breakfast and return home. It is designed to be a catalyst for the rest of one's life-work in manifesting. Many of the exercises are designed to help the person access pure unlimited energy directly from Source.

I believe that we are energy beings and designed to have complete access to energy from Source at all times. In life we usually cut ourselves off or become cut off from this energy. We can become cut off when our survival and ego programs are activated, generating fear and stress. When this happens we become energy starved. This starvation is a threat to expressing who we are and can even be fatal. Infants sometimes die from failure to thrive where all their physical needs are met but they are not being nurtured with energy and love. Older people die more often from heart attacks if they do not have loving community support. When we are not getting all the energy we need from Source, we look to other people to fulfill this need. We can get energy from them by getting their attention. We can do this by being the good girl or boy, or if that doesn't work, being the bad girl or boy. We can receive attention by becoming powerful and accumulating more wealth than we can use. We can be the rescuer or the mess that needs to be rescued. All these ways to relating to others are manipulative as we try to get the energy we need. But the energy from other people, particularly when based upon some rigid role we are playing out, is of poor quality compared to energy from Source. And being energy starved and seeking energy from others allows others to manipulate us. If we need to be liked, someone will come along, sense this and infer that they will not like us unless we perform to their specifications.

It is very difficult to heal and manifest from a low energy place. So MC² addresses this aggressively with continual opportunities to receive energy from Source. This can come from contact with God and all his or her facets. It can come through beauty expressed in nature, music, dance, pets, children, etc. It can come through deep prayer. It can come through very high and clean relationships with others where both you and they are seen in the highest light. Such high energy is a true joy to receive.

MC² was first offered in November of 2000. We have a maximum of twenty-four participants in each program. It filled with a waiting list, and we were on our way. At the time that I am writing this book, MC² has been given at TMI and also in Canada and Europe over thirty times with great success. I want to give you an idea of what an MC² is like. But rather than talk about what has happened program by program, I think it will be smoother if I hit some of the highlights of the components I have mentioned such as the PK tasks and the healing circles. In each area, as the program continues to be offered, there has been an interesting evolution and sometimes revolution in what people have been capable of achieving.

CHAPTER 18

Bending Metal and Growing Seeds

I would like to start our story of what happens in MC² by talking about the PK dice exercise since it is the first PK task that people encounter in MC². One of the interesting things that happens with the dice in MC² is that they bring up many of the same issues as we found in Vegas. People were faced with performance anxiety—how would they do with the whole group watching? What if they were they only ones who didn't do well? Many people were obviously tense before this task. Some hated games and saw this as a competition. Some associated it with gambling and hated that idea. The Monroe Institute for them had always been a place of sacred space. What were we doing by introducing something as profane as dice into such an environment? Many people who would have never considered going to Vegas for these reasons found themselves confronted with similar issues in MC². I thought that this was excellent because it brought up issues that needed to be addressed both for PK and manifesting abundance.

We immediately had to talk about these issues. We noted that they indeed could make the dice game into a initiation gauntlet that they had to pass through, or they could relax into inner child, magician, healer, or any other role that allowed them to be genuine and roll comfortably. We employed the idea of an energy arch as we do in Vegas for their support. And the rest of the group sent the healing energy of unconditional love to them as they rolled. As each person rolled we cheered them. We encouraged them to get loose and be grounded, moving to the music that we had playing: songs such as: Paul Simon's *Graceland*, Clearance Clearwater

Revival's *Proud Mary*, etc. Songs were chosen to have a beat and positive words to help energy flow.

In Vegas we focus on dice for three days. In MC² we focus on dice for about three hours. I was interested to see what we would get in terms of PK performance. The charity points were designed so that people were motivated to roll well for something larger than their own ego, and for the benefit of others. We have had some great results in MC² with this PK task, with considerable variation between groups and between people. Because of the way we set up the points, it is fairly easy to assess PK strength. We know that doubles should come up by chance one time in every six rolls. In a typical group of 24 people plus the two trainers, we have a total of 10 rolls each, times 26 people, equals 260 rolls. We can divide this number by six and know that by chance doubles should come up about 43 times in such a group. We analyzed several of the early groups and found that the groups were rolling doubles at a rate that one would expect by chance only once in 3,000 times.

The way we had structured the PK task also involved each person picking the number of their choice as their primary target. This was intentional because we wanted to introduce them to the challenge and power of choice in manifestation. It would seem that choosing should be easy but it is not. Human beings are naturally fairly ambivalent creatures, being pulled by many desires and fears at once. For example if you are graduating high school, you might be happy to be leaving the school but sad to leave your friends. Excited about going to college yet scared about how you will do away from home. You might be looking forward to your independence and worried about making new friends. And you might have no clear idea what you want to major in that will lead to a viable occupation. So there would be this complex interweaving of factors and you are not 100 percent happy and not 100 percent sure of what you want. Yet for rapid manifestation, clear intention and motivation are essential.

The dice target selection became the first place in MC² where this idea of choice and intention is introduced. The task was deceptively simple; pick a number and put all your energy behind rolling that number. The numbers present a spectrum of difficulty. Rolling a twelve or two, for example, would happen only once in thirty-six times by chance, so if you wanted strong PK proof you could pick such a number for your ten rolls.

Conversely if you wanted to make it easier for yourself statistically you could pick a number such as seven that should come up once in every six rolls by chance. We wanted people to keep the same number for the entire ten rolls because commitment is part of intention. Sounds simple, right?

Well, you might even try this yourself now at home. If you were going to roll dice for points for charity with of a bunch of people watching, what number would you pick? Often for people a number jumps immediately into their head. This number is likely by intuition to be the best number for them today. But they are likely to then assess this number by logic and ego. Is it an easy or hard number to roll and how will this look to the group if I pick too easy a number? Is it my favorite number? People often then pick another number that for some reason seems more logical or acceptable. When they get to the table often they roll the number that came by intuition more than their second choice.

During the dice sessions we ask people to be very aware of their choice process. What number? Do they choose to take their turn first, last, or in the middle of the group? Can other people pressure them into changing their mind? The dice session goes on for about ninety minutes, which gives the whole group a chance to experience holding a lot of energy for a long time, while being grounded and connected to spirit, as they support each other. We found out some interesting things. In most groups the roller would be nervous within their energy arch. If they stop and receive a hug from one of the people forming their arch, their next throw will be a target or a double. In one group we kept track and eight-five percent of the time after a hug, the next roll was successful. But the hug had to be a genuine heart-felt connection with the other person. It did not work to think manipulatively: "Give me a hug so that I can roll a double."

We found also that by carefully assessing a person's roll we could often find evidence of PK that was not readily apparent. For example a woman selected the challenging target of twelve for her rolls which should only occur by chance once in 36 rolls and can only be obtained by rolling 6-6. She hit no twelve's and was disappointed. But we noticed that she had rolled a six on one of the two dice every time she rolled. This would occur only once in 125,000 times by chance. Hearing how unlikely this pattern was by chance, she walked away thinking that perhaps she had affected the dice more than she thought.

One of the best PK evidence stories that we have is also a funny one. We had a group where most people were from France. Their English was way better than my French but still there was a bit of struggle to be understood when we were talking about complex concepts. All this proceeded in a very good-natured fashion. When we got to the dice portion of the program I explained the rules carefully. The first person did quite poorly but seemed happy about it. The next person did the same. And the group continued to roll in this pattern. Patty and I were confused. We were doing all the cheering and encouraging that we usually do. When we ended we found that as a group their results were highly statistically significant but in the wrong direction. They had rolled much fewer targets and doubles than you would expect by chance. It turned out that they had misinterpreted the directions and thought that for every point they accumulated that they would owe a dollar to the blessing bucket! This was great proof that PK is results driven!

In MC² we have our group dice session fairly early in the week. Then we leave the dice table available for people to play on during breaks in the program. Often people report (with witnesses) that they do better and better as they relax and practice, and the whole group is not watching them. Many times people are able to accomplish rolling up to five targets and four doubles in their ten rolls. In the thirty MC² programs with 600 participants about seventy percent of people were able to roll dice at an above chance level, showing PK was operating, either in group or on their own with witnesses. We take this as an excellent PK result. Further, with all the laughter and fun we have playing with dice in MC² many participants have thought of going to Vegas who would have never considered it seriously before.

The next PK task that people approach in MC² is enhancing the growing of seeds with their energy. We use winter wheat berry seeds for this in most programs. Before the exercise we soak them overnight to soften the outer covering. I expect that most any seed that can be sprouted for eating, such as you might find at a health food store, will work. After doing a Hemi-Sync meditation to raise energy, we give people a handful of seeds and ask them to inspect them carefully and memorize what they look like at this point. Then we guide them through a meditation while they are standing, that goes something like this: "Get into relationship with them and ask permission of your seeds to accelerate their growth. With your eyes closed get in touch with the earth, extend gratitude to the earth for supporting life, including your own life. Pull earth energy into your heart. Now pull in the highest energies of spirit and bring that energy into your heart. Send this energy from your heart to your seeds. Send the energies of sun, warmth, air, water, all things necessary for life. Feel your seeds growing. Welcome your seeds into this world and into their new form as green plants with roots and leaves. You can even sing to your seeds, 'Happy Birthday to you' (everyone usually sings gently the Happy Birthday song and laughs). Take a few more minutes now to send energy and visualize growth."

After about five minutes we have people open their eyes and look carefully once again at their seeds. Often a few people will see that their seeds now have small roots extending from ½ to 1 inch long, and are thinner than a human hair. These roots have grown during the five-minute meditation where no roots were present before. About half the group usually has an increase in the swelling of the white ends of the seeds or other signs of growth. Folks are usually impressed with these results occurring in just five minutes of energy sending. They run up to one another to look at what happened for the other people in the group.

We then have each person put the seeds wrapped in damp paper into bowls and put their name on the bowls. They are instructed to send their seeds energy in any way they wish over the next few days but to keep the seeds moist, at room temperature, and away from direct sunlight. We

then treat several bowls of control seeds to the same conditions but with no energy sent to them. On the last day of the program we compare participant's seeds to controls. When we do this comparison, we usually see that about sixty percent of the group has had dramatic results compared to controls. The control seeds show some root growth beginning. The PK seeds often show dense mats of roots. At times leaves are beginning to form whereas the controls have none. The difference between the two groups is very clear. People gather round and cameras click to show the folks back home.

Within this experiment we see several interesting things. Over many groups we find that the growth will be different depending upon the type of energy sent. Often people who already know that they are powerful energy healers, as well as people who experience a natural affinity for gardening and plants have strong results. People who know Reiki healing methods and send Reiki energy usually have a distinct pattern of dense, fat root growth. Other energies produce long, thin roots. Some types of energy tend to produce more leaf growth. And participants who have a specific vision such as to create green leaves, often have just the result they envisioned.

Most people really enjoy this exercise and some report that they liked linking with life energy better than playing with the dice. We point out that asking permission when working with PK, with anything from dice to plants, is important because it is respectful. It acknowledges that everything has consciousness and that we are moving to a place in PK where we work with other things cooperatively rather than forcing our will on the thing. You need to move into relationship with whatever you are going to work with, or else there is no connection through which energy can flow. In working with the seeds or in healing circles, the connection is often more natural. We may see the seeds as little babies that need our care, and when sending healing to pets or people we may easily be compassionate and want to enhance their wellness and happiness. For dice, spoons, appliances, etc., we may have to stretch a bit to find the connection. But it can be done. People often name their favorite car something affectionate and may even talk to their car. We have had reports that when people do this, sometimes very strange things happen such as driving for hundreds of miles and using almost no gas.

I like to tell a story about this that involves intuition, manifestation, and PK. A long while back, I think it was around 1986, I was walking through a casino and saw a bank of slot machines over which was suspended a beautiful car under shining lights that really caught my eye. The idea was to play the slots and win the car as the grand prize. It was a 1985 BMW L-7, which at the time was the ultimate BMW with all leather interior including the dash board, headliner, side panels, and seats—plus six other fancy features compared to the normal BMW 735. When I saw the car, which I never before even knew existed, I fell in love (or lust) with it and felt strongly that I would win that car. I sat down and played twenty dollars through the slots and nothing happened. Oh, well. I have learned that sometimes strong feelings are "just gas." But usually such feelings are not just random. And for those few minutes sitting there I had been fully in the present moment and had visualized strongly owning that car while looking at it gleaming in the lights. I decided to see what would happen.

When I returned home, a person told me about stock options and gave me a tip on a certain stock. I put some money on the tip as a stock option and quickly made ten times my money, enough to buy the L-7, that I had seen in Vegas. I found a used L-7 in perfect shape at a great price in Charlotte, North Carolina, which is about two hours from my home. I purchased it and had my dream car. I kept the L-7 until it was fifteen years old and never had even a scratch on it. Due to its wonderful emergency handling, the car also saved me from a few potential accidents along the way. In the last few years of owning it, the fancy six-speed electronic transmission began to slip badly and would have been very expensive to repair. Instead, I would put my hand over the gear shift and send loving, appreciative energy and said, "Come on baby, heal. Become smooth and strong." All the slippage would cease and for about six months it would operate perfectly again. I would repeat the process and get another six months out of it. I did this several times and when I finally sold the car, I told the new owner about the issues and, hoping that he would not think that I was too crazy, told him what I had been doing to "fix" it. He was surprised but agreed to do the same. I talked to the new owner recently. He is still very happy with the car. The car, now twenty-seven years old, is still running today with no transmission job as far as I know.

In MC², after more energy preparation we approach the PK task of lighting light bulbs with our energy. We use 12-inch diameter fluorescent rings because they are easy to hold. But I have seen other size rings, and long fluorescent bulbs work just as well and I have received reports of incandescent bulbs lighting as well. This PK task is one I am least sure of in terms of what is going on. I cannot rule out entirely that there may be a possible physical cause for the bulb to light, rather than PK energy. These fluorescent bulbs contain an excitable gas that in normal operation is excited by the electricity passing through the circuit, causing the bulb to shine. When we attempt PK with them, they may be responding to some physical energy. Static electricity can also cause the bulb to light. But we have ruled out static electricity by having them light when a person is standing in the shower with water cascading over themselves and the bulb. Also they will light when held motionless and the person is motionless, and for static electricity one needs to rub them, or one's feet on the carpet, etc. I have asked a few electrical engineers to see if they can come up with a physical explanation of why the bulbs light the way they do during the exercise and so far they have not been able to offer any viable electronic or physical explanation.

There are other things that suggest that PK is operating in the way we approach the task. I find that if I am tired, the bulbs will not light or only weakly. When I start off in front of a group and haven't done this lighting for a few months, usually it takes me about ten to fifteen minutes before the bulb lights. Once I do one light this way, I can pick up a cold bulb which has not been touched and it lights immediately. What I think is happening here is that initially I am self-conscious in front of the group and trying too hard, with a little bit of fear in terms of, "What will I do if it doesn't work?" Usually my first flickers are when someone asks me a question and my attention is diverted from the struggle to light the bulb for just a few seconds.

We wait until nightfall, explain the exercise, and have the group sit in a circle. We demonstrate with the lights on how to hold the bulb and instruct them that they can play with another person. In that case, one needs to be sure that one knows who agrees to always have at least one hand on the bulb. So far we have never dropped one, which is good, because there is a noxious gas inside the glass! The usual way to start is to keep one hand on the bulb and while grasping the bulb with that hand, send energy down through your other hand and into the bulb, holding the intent that you want it to light up. Then you release your second hand from the bulb and let go of your intent. One can also hold on with one hand and take a few fingers of the other hand and gently move them in a circle around the bulb sending energy for it to light. As mentioned you can also hold the bulb still with both hands, in front of your energy centers and the bulb will often glow.

Then we turn off all the lights and demonstrate. Once the trainers are successful, we turn on the lights again and ask for questions, and give them further encouragement. Then we distribute a light bulb to each person and ask them to stay seated so that they don't crash into one another in the dark. We turn off the lights for the second time and let them have at it. The trainers stay in the middle of the circle and use their lit bulbs to navigate around and help others get started. Standing in the middle we begin to see little glimmers and then bright flashes with people exclaiming in amazement in the dark. It is a really fun exercise that raises the group energy very high. We remind them not to try too hard. "Angels can fly because they take themselves lightly."

Participants are free to take the bulbs with them to their own rooms and experiment further with them or to play with them in small groups. We usually get about sixty percent lighting the bulbs during group and another twenty percent reporting good results on their own. Some people really are attracted to this PK task and continue to expand their skill at home. The best report that I have received was from a massage therapist who practiced for months and then told me excitedly that he was able to light a six pack of bulbs from across the room and that they stayed lit for a few hours. I have no way to verify this account but he seemed to be a very trustworthy and sincere person.

On the same night once everyone is excited from the light bulb lighting, we prepare them to attempt the PK task that for many people is the most anticipated exercise on the program: using nonphysical energy to bend metal. We save this task until we feel that there will be a good chance of success for most people due to the work that they have done up to this point. When we interview each person at the beginning of the program they often share anxiety that they will not be able to bend their spoon.

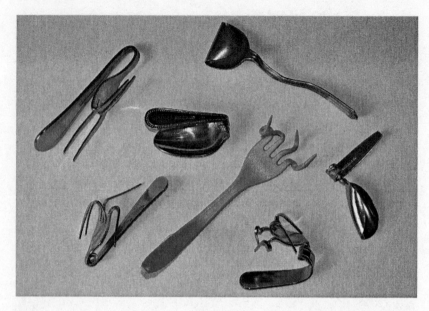

If we ask deeper questions it often becomes apparent that they are also afraid that they *will* be able to bend the spoon! Why would this be? Well, if the spoon does indeed bend, it means that their belief systems will be challenged. They will have to consider that the world works differently than they might have thought. And that they may have considerably more power (and therefore responsibility) in creating reality than they have thought previously. Metal bending can be a paradigm-shifting experience!

Before the exercise we show them examples of metal that had been bent in other groups. We have an assortment of silverware from quite light to the heaviest of stainless steel. We have examples including handles being bent four or five times around, handles being twisted like a corkscrew, like the shape of the candy, Twizzlers. We also have examples of the tines of forks being twisted and interwoven with each other and the bowl of spoons being folded over on themselves. Some of these items have been closely examined by experts in metal working and pronounced impossible. As it has been explained to me by these experts, the molecule chains in the metal are too long to bend this tightly without breaking. The steel is too hard for physical strength to account for the bend, and in the case of the bent bowls of the spoons, there is no way to get enough physical purchase to have the leverage to bend it by physical force (trust me I've tried it!).

Indeed, in the book, *The Metal-Benders* by physicist John Hasted, the author finds that under an electron microscope the molecular structure of metal bent by PK looks different compared to metal bent by force or a combination of heat and force. Hasted also has many photos of children bending straight metal paper clip wire into animal shapes inside glass balls where they cannot touch the metal. All-in-all Hasted has written a very interesting book for those who would like to examine this phenomenon in detail from a scientific perspective.

We also show examples of bent plastic forks, the kind of forks that you might take on a picnic. These are made of fairly brittle plastic and will snap if you try to use physical force to bend them. We have examples of plastic forks with each tine twisted around in a corkscrew shape. A plastic fork is included in the photo of the bent silverware.

Jack Houck is probably the most famous host for spoon-bending parties. Jack worked as an engineer for McDonnell Douglas. He would bring several hundred people together in a room, making sure that there were children present. He would lead the group to all yell "BEND!" together. Often the children's spoons would bend first. Children usually have not dampened their natural PK abilities with the "I can't—it's impossible" beliefs that adults have adopted. In Jack's large group, much energy is generated and much inspiration is provided by seeing others bend their spoons. In MC² we work with a much smaller group but have spent days building energy and learning how to focus intent for this exercise.

There is a great clatter as we dump about eighty pieces of silverware into the middle of the circle. We first use a yang or masculine approach of yelling "bend" and sending our intent with great force, then letting go of the intent. I demonstrate the strong yell and bend my spoon in front of the group. I must tell you that this was something that I dreaded, given I was initially not very good at it. Laurie Monroe was supposed to lead this part of MC² since she was an expert bender. She did for the first few programs. Then one program in the afternoon before the spoon bending part, she came to me and said, "I can't be there tonight, you do it." Surprisingly, after spending the remainder of the day worrying about it, when the time came and it was critical that I do it, it was easy to do in front of the group. PK is very results driven and I felt it was important to do it right then. This same type of criticality to an even more crucial extent may be operating when we hear of the miracle of a small woman lifting a car off a child to save the child's life.

After setting this strong intent, we will sit down, relax, and work with the metal in a more yin or feminine energy way, allowing the energy to continuously flow. We acknowledge that the participants may have a strong preference for either the yang or the yin way, but that we want them to try both ways because both energies are necessary in life, and both can accomplish powerful PK and manifestation. We remind people that they should approach the pile of silver and ask the silver, "Who would like to bend for me?" This may sound silly, but it helps establish a relationship with the object intended for PK.

People start with holding their selected spoon or fork with two hands on the handle and testing the strength of the metal, so that they can get an idea what would be needed to bend it by physical force, or if that would even be possible. We tell them not to worry too much at the beginning whether they are using some physical force combined with PK. They can start that way and work up to heavier items that will not bend by human force regardless of how much pressure they apply. Usually, right before the metal is ready to bend by PK, it begins to feel warm, perhaps oily, and then softer, much like a pasta noodle boiling in water begins to soften. When they feel that softness, they are to bend the metal quickly. Usually at first the metal stays soft only for a second or two. When they gain more confidence and experience, the metal will stay soft up to about fifteen seconds at a time. That is when they can make the fancier designs, such as triple loops in the handle.

Women, perhaps due to their cultural training, are often able to let go and surrender more easily and their items may bend first. But sometimes women have more trouble with strong intent. They may feel that it is not right to yell loudly or to destroy perfectly good silverware. We suggest that they might view this as if they were creating sculptures or Christmas tree ornaments out of the silverware. Men by their cultural training are often good at the strong intent but sometimes have trouble letting go of that intent and relaxing so that the energy can flow. They may also be very left-brained and sit there with their mind asking every second, "Is it bending, is it bending?" So the men need to accent the surrender and trust part.

From this description you can see that we have intentionally talked a lot to the group about what is to occur, both to help with their belief that they can do it and how, and also to build energy to a very high peak of eagerness and readiness. By now most groups are salivating to get started and just wish we would shut up so they can do it! That is when we say, "Okay, grab your spoon or fork, stand in a circle and get ready. Relax and get grounded by planting your feet firmly on the floor. Bring in the highest energies of earth and spirit. Follow me now in setting your strong intent. Let's do it together now, One . . . two . . . three . . . BEND!"

Usually with that initial cry, BEND, a few people get immediate results. We encourage them to circle around the group showing off their successes as it inspires others. We then get into a rhythm of shouting "bend" and letting go of intent. We put on rock music and encourage people to dance around as they are attempting their metal bending. By the time we are done with this method at least half the group has managed to bend their forks or spoons and some have done the more difficult twists described previously.

We then switch to the yin part, put on some soft heart-opening music and verbally guide people through sending energy in a continuous flow through their arms and into the metal. After about ten minutes a few more people are able to bend their forks and spoons. After we break for the evening we encourage people to take a spoon or fork with them and continue to play with it in small groups or on their own. There has been considerable evolution over the years in MC^2 with this PK task. In early groups we were lucky to get about half the participants to be able to bend metal over the program, and the bends were mostly of the simpler kind. As the years have progressed we have had groups where 100 percent of participants have bent their metal and the bends have become more chal-lenging and complex. Note that many of the participants attending are scientists, engineers, and physicians who are quite skeptical of this being legitimate. When they see it with their own eyes and feel the metal becom-ing soft, they often have transformative changes in their beliefs about how spirit and energy works in the physical world.

An early 2002 MC^2 group filmed interviews with each other of how they accomplished the bending. An amazing variety of creative ways are presented in the film. One person talked to the fork about how much they loved their lover and how they wanted to bring home the bent fork as a symbol of that love. Another person talked to the molecules within the spoon and patiently held still until they felt the molecules shifting. Several people took their spoons into deep meditation and had success. A woman tried for hours with no success and then fell asleep, only to wake up at three in the morning feeling strong vibrations in her body, and holding the spoon in her hand. Barely awake, she felt the metal bend and re-harden the moment she became more fully awake.

No matter how they accomplished their bends, many people are amazed and proud of their accomplishment. Because they are eager to practice, we provide each person with at least four pieces to play with. But we have to plead with the group not to use TMI's house silverware for practice! One can work with the same piece for many days, gradually adding new bends to the piece until it does resemble a sculpture. Taking them home, if they get through airport security without creating a scene, they will often put the bent spoon on their desk at home to remind themselves of what they capable of. We have had funny stories of people, when they are talking excitedly about the experience to their family, have the spoon that they are eating their soup with just bend over by itself while they are in mid-sentence!

At home I find that I do not have much interest or success with bending, unless there is a reason. One time my teenage daughter was dating a new boy that I did not like very much. I took a fork in front of him and twisted it into a knot while saying to him, "Have her back home by ten o'clock." He stared at me and stammered, "Yes sir." My kids hope I will not bring out my bent metal collection and show it to their friends because they don't want our family to appear too weird. When my youngest daughter was about twelve years old, having seen bent pieces scattered around, pronounced that it was not real. I told her that she never even let me show her how to do this. She rolled her eyes and said, "Okay, how do you do it?" I wound up into my long lecture about how to do it. After a few sentences, the phone rang and I turned away to pick it up. When I turned around my daughter's spoon was bent. I gasped, "What did you do?" She replied, "I got tired of listening to you and just shot fire out of my eyes at it and it bent."

All these PK tasks of dice rolling, seed growing, light bulb lighting, and bending metal and plastic, taken together, give MC² participants a heavy dose of mind expanding experience with non-physical energy. Metal bending and other things such as fire walking are used in empowerment seminars and corporate retreats around the world to show people about how much potential they have. James Twyman taught spoon-bending over the internet to 100,000 people and when they were inspired with their success, he asked them to apply their energy all on the same day to pray for peace. We have had reports of groups clearing lakes of pollution using energy and intent. One fellow I know, coming from a farming background, reports being able to measurably raise the level of nitrogen in the soil on farms, reducing the need for fertilizer and its subsequent pollution of the water table. It will be interesting to see what human beings accomplish, once it is accepted that we have the power to affect the physical world with our own energy.

We find that as energy is raised for PK, people's intuition, telepathy, and clairvoyant abilities also increase. It may be that finding out that one can do one type of psychic skill empowers the belief that one can do other skills as well. But I think that the energy itself, when high enough, and our suggestion that "all is one" and to connect with the heart, serve to make these varieties of intuition much clearer and stronger.

In the first MC² we tested intuition by putting three objects in a box. These objects were unknown to participants and could have been anything that would fit into the large box. We placed a soft cat-in-the-hat doll with a red, white, and black hat, a stapler, and a green bowl with four crystals in it into the box. Within minutes one participant guessed "a cat-in-the-hat doll with a red, white, and black hat," two guessed stapler, and approximately six guessed a bowl, with two specifying rocks or crystals in the bowl. One person got both the stapler and the bowl correct. On another intuition task involving guessing playing cards, a participant first asked if there were any jokers in the deck to which I replied, "No"—having (I thought) removed them all from the deck. On the fifth card, two participants said, "Black Joker"—indeed it was that very card!

CHAPTER 19

Spectacular Healings

The healing and manifesting circles that occur in MC² are for many participants one of the most profound parts of the week. The circles are definitely satisfying for the trainers as well. They are a chance for people to demonstrate their caring for each other in a very tangible way. Much like we found in Vegas, for many people, just the act of opening up to receive help from others and being the center of undivided attention is a scary leap of faith. This deep trust is necessary for a person to be able to connect with all the goodness that the universe would like to lovingly provide us. Yet it is a free choice universe, where our freedom even to reject goodness is respected. When sending energy to the person in the middle you can actually feel that for some people the energy is joyfully received and taken in with great appreciation, much like a thirsty person is grateful for a glass of water. With other people in the middle, the energy seems to meet resistance or even bounce off of them. Often these people voice a great deal of difficulty receiving.

The healing circles start early in the workshop on Sunday and finish by Tuesday evening. Wednesday we bring in people from outside the group who have requested healing. And Thursday we have a circle for the earth and then finish with our last circle which is for friends and loved ones. We give the person the option to share with the group where they would like the energy to be focused for healing and also what they would like help with in manifesting in their lives. The person in the middle has the option of silence or gentle healing music, and we usually do a group Om for them to start the process. We ask the person after the healing to return to the rim of the circle in silence. After we send all four people healing we go back to the first person and ask if there is anything they would like to share about their experience. The people in the rim of the circle hold their comments overnight to give the recipients a chance to integrate the energy before talking about it. This process has worked very well with truly sacred space created within the circles. It is a wonderful, joyous, and loving experience for most people, both in the middle and on the rim. Such energy given freely and fully for highest purpose is a marvelous use of PK energy.

We have regularly witnessed dramatic miracles of healing of the physical body, such as the healing of arthritic joints, the instant disappearance of cysts and tumors, help with pain in all parts of the body, help with hearing and eyesight, curing of migraines, insomnia, and digestive issues, etc. We also have seen excellent healing in the emotional and belief areas with people reporting elimination of anxiety, depression, and phobias, clearing past anger, guilt, resentments, releasing feelings of victimization and trauma, and experiencing expanded happiness, ability to love and trust, forgiveness, etc. In follow up emails we receive reports that the healing effects can even deepen over time and appear in many cases to be long lasting.

Each healing is special and important to the individual, to their loved ones, and to everyone participating in the circle. Because I have done many workshops over more than a decade, the healings do begin to blur for me. But a few will always be remembered. One beautiful woman in her nineties with very angelic energy stands out. Upon entering the circle she initially said that her life was wonderful and that she was so grateful for everything that she could not think of one request. When the group pressed her, she finally mentioned that she really missed being able to hear well. It was a real strain for her to follow conversations. The group really loved and appreciated this woman's presence in the group, she had added so much to the week's experiences for everyone. We built a gentle and powerful energy. Within minutes of the group starting to send energy, tears came to her eyes. She whispered in wonder that she that she could now hear the birds outside our closed windows.

Another story is just as dramatic but a bit gross. My apologies are extended, but I just love the story and so I have to tell it! A fellow came to MC² and when it was time for him to be in the center of the circle he seemed hesitant to share what he wanted help with. With encouragement from the group he told us that he had a severe case of foot fungus that had discolored all his toenails. He had been to many specialists over three decades with no relief. He then went into great detail about what they looked and smelled like, providing the group with an overly-vivid picture in their highly sensitive state of consciousness. I could feel the group shrinking back energetically from him. Remember that we ask the group to see the person being healed in their highest and finest health. I felt that the group was having difficulty doing this with him after such a colorful description of the disease. As the group started to Om, I had a strong feeling that someone here had to behave as Christ might have done. He was lying down in the middle of the circle. I went up and grasped his sock-covered feet with my hands. I could feel much energy from the group around us and I tried to channel this energy to his feet. He reported that while in the middle of the circle he felt like his feet were on fire. The next morning he was almost jumping for joy. He reported that all his nails were completely clear of fungus and looked entirely normal.

We also have had excellent success sending energy to people who came into MC² not as participants but as guests invited to participate in the healing circles. We had a person with numbness in their leg, hip to toes. They had been to many specialists that week to seek an answer to the sudden symptom and to rule out blood clots, etc. Within a few minutes in the circle, the person reported feeling returning to the leg completely except for a few toes. Another person received healing and then reported back to us the next week that her MRI was cancer free for the first time during her long illness. We had two dogs join us for healing. They were in bad shape and were facing a long trip across the country by car, as their owners were moving coast to coast. The dogs went around to each person while we sent them energy and they had an effortless trip to their new home.

Sometimes it is not possible for the person requesting healing to physically join us in the circle. The healing can often be just as effective at a distance. Here I would like to tell the story of sending remote healing to a dear friend of the Institute. She has given me permission to tell this story. Her name is Rosalind McKnight, author of *Cosmic Journeys*. Rosie, as we called her, had worked with Bob Monroe since 1972 and was one of his most avid explorers of consciousness from the beginning of his work. Rosie talked to the participants during the TMI program called Guidelines about her many OBE adventures. I liked to embarrass her in a friendly way by introducing her to the Guidelines groups as the person closest to a living saint that I knew. I introduced her in this fashion because I meant it. When I visited her on her Virginia homestead, comprised of a mobile home on a few acres, I was overwhelmed by the number of stray dogs and cats that she had taken in and given a home. I would guess at least twenty dogs and thirty cats, all getting along famously. She always shone with gratitude for her life and celebrated her modest financial resources. She liked to lead the group at the end of her talk in chanting, "I am light, manifested in love and living in joy, joy, joy!"

At the time of the remote healing Rosie was in her mid-seventies. She had suffered from congestive heart failure for several weeks and a severe case of the flu that had left her very weak and mostly bedridden. She was depressed and discouraged. We asked if she would like us to send healing. Her response was, "Would I ever! I would be so grateful." The cool thing was that Rosie was one of the most psychic people that I knew, and it would be interesting to see what she could perceive and experience.

We did not tell her exactly when we would be doing this healing because we did not know when we would get to it. At 11:45 a.m. we began to send her healing to her while she was home in Lynchburg Virginia, approximately sixty miles from the Institute. We continued for about ten minutes. Several of us felt during the healing that Rosie was very weary and might even leave the physical, if it was not for her sense of responsibility for the animals in her care. Rosie reported afterward that at exactly 11:45 a.m. she heard a voice say, "Welcome." She immediately lay down and began to feel as if many angels had entered her room and began lovingly to work on her, focusing particularly in her heart area. After about fifteen minutes of this she fell into a deep and restful sleep. When she woke up, coincidently (we had no knowledge that this was planned) a big fruit basket had been delivered to her living room from the staff at TMI with a card saying, "Get well, Rosie." She woke up feeling charged with energy and happiness. She went to the basket, removed the pink cellophane covering it, removed her clothes, wrapped herself in the pink plastic, and began to dance around the house in joyful celebration of how good she felt.

Next Rosie asked her angels what she should do with all this energy.

She felt that they said back to her, "You can use PK to clean your house, all you need do is relax and trust." She began to clean her house from top to bottom from all the mess of that many animals, food dishes, and litter boxes. She finished at midnight with the house sparkling and still having energy. She watched a bit of TV and then fell asleep for the night. The next morning she woke filled with a renewed joy of life and started her second book, *Soul Journeys*. She then drove all the way up to TMI to thank us in person and to report her experience. When she arrived at TMI it seemed to me that her energy field was huge and glowing. We celebrated with her and there were many hugs all around.

As with the PK tasks, the healing circle experiences at MC² evolved over time. In the beginning when we would send energy often the person in the center would jump up after just a few minutes and say, "Thank you, that is enough for me." They would experience the energy as a very intense, almost an electric type vibration, or as blazing heat. As we began to emphasize using heart energy, people would stay in the middle for the whole time allotted, basking in the energy, and be reluctant to leave the middle, saying that they could stay there forever. They would use descriptions such as: "I felt that I was floating on a cloud of warm light"; "I felt surrounded by the most exquisite peace and love"; "I felt beautiful warmth."

We have our healing circle for the earth on Thursday after a silent morning. The day starts with a high-level extended meditation in Focus 21 to help the participants contact new energies for healing and manifestation and to integrate these energies back into physical reality. This is followed by a silent walk in the beautiful natural surroundings at the Institute. People are encouraged to further ground what they have learned, and in their high energy state to perceive the earth in a new way. Often magic happens on these silent walks. For example, on one walk I was called by intuition to gently put my hand deep into a privet bush. When I pulled my hand out it was covered with about twenty baby praying mantises, each tiny quarter-inch creature holding its hands in what looked like prayer. After communing with them for a long time, I put my hand gently back into the bush and did not shake my hand. I just left it there perfectly still. When I removed my hand all the babies had returned back into the bush.

When the bell rings signaling the end of the silent walk, participants go back to their rooms for a high-level meditation in Focus 27 and then come in silence into the group meeting room for the healing circle for the earth. We have prepared a tableau in the center of the circle with many of the good things of earth: flowers, leaves, crystals, fruit, and representations of dolphins and other animals. The group sits in a circle while we play the beautiful song, *This Island Earth.* Then we lead them in a meditation, having each person connect with the earth, giving thanks and seeing the planet at its finest. We encourage the participants to connect with the highest of spirit energies and to let their own energy be met and increased 10,000-fold by all the high beings of light that love the earth. We suggest that they can send this energy to the great oceans, mountains, deserts, and forests of the earth. And to all the kingdoms: the great mineral kingdom, the vast kingdom of plants, and the majestic kingdom of animals. And then we suggest that they send this beautiful energy to all the peoples of the earth for peace and health. This circle often moves people very deeply and you can feel the room glowing with light.

Continuing the silence we then put out a basket where participants can place the names of loved ones and friends they would like us to send healing to. We put these names in the center of the circle and affirm that energy is infinite and free of time-space. And seeing ourselves of great light and great love, we send energy to our loved ones, with people softly calling out the names of those they would like to have remembered. And thus we conclude our healing circles in MC².

Energy healing seems effective in about sixty percent of cases, which is well above what is expected by placebo. I do not claim that it is a substitute for traditional medical diagnosis and treatment, but it can be a powerful addition. I think this natural healing ability is our birthright as humans. We do not know with our ego mind what is best in any given situation. People may be having illness to learn something important, such as to have the experience that they are loved and cared for even if they can't perform their usual functions. They may be ill to teach others around them important lessons in empathy, or to give those people the opportunity to give back to them. When we send energy to someone who is critically ill, they may use the energy to exit, if it is their time, instead of staying in the physical body. These are just some possibilities of illness used for sacred purposes, though not often consciously. My co-trainer in MC², trained as a healer, likes to say that we tend to think that the purpose of prayer is to terminate illness, when illness' purpose may be to initiate prayer.

When my mother was ill with dementia and in a rest home for two years, to my ego it seemed to be a grisly scenario. She had been vehement that she never wanted to be a burden nor go to a rest home. But it became necessary. Once she was in the rest home, my dad, then in his eighties, was getting exhausted from the twice daily drives to be with her. It was costing an obscene amount of money. She was unhappy there. When she finally died and I communicated with her on the other side, she was happy and light. She explained: "Forgetting everything was the best way for me to release all my Catholic guilt to be free from it over here. The slowness of the process gave your dad time to adjust, to learn to cook and clean, make new friends, and to be ready for my absence after sixty-four years of marriage." These thoughts helped me reframe what had happened to her. Now it looked like an elegant and loving plan by higher self.

What we find in terms of manifestation results in MC² is very similar to what we have experienced in the Inner Vegas Adventure groups. Participants report all kinds of positive manifestations in their lives. These include personal victories in the areas of finances, relationships, career, health, increased synchronicities, and improvements in emotional and psychological functioning. There have been new cars, houses, jobs, promotions, dramatic changes in work, from that which no longer was satisfying to new career paths that are filled with passion. Some have found soul mates, achieved peace and resolution with divorced partners, been accepted to prestigious schools with scholarships, while others report soaring achievements and recognition in the arts. One woman who was severely phobic about public speaking, ended up being invited to Dubai to speak on TED in front of hundreds and being filmed to be watched by thousands of people; and she did so beautifully. I watched the video and she spoke eloquently from the heart with great impact about her subject.

My co-trainer Patty Ray in addition to bringing her own amazing energy and full dedication and excitement with her, has added many wonderful components to MC². She added a treasure map or manifestation board exercise. The participants enter the group room after a meditation exercise, to find the tables set up with magazines, brightly colored paper, glitter, glue, etc, looking very much like an early grade school classroom.

We greet them with a "welcome to Hogwarts manifestation school!" We encourage the participants to be very creative in pasting together pictures and drawings to depict what their hearts would like to bring into their lives. They approach this task with great energy and intensity and in a few hours, beautiful creations emerge that through pictures tell the story of their hopes and dreams.

We take these manifestation boards into our closing circle the last night and everyone goes around the circle admiring them and blessing them with highest energy. The participants are encouraged to take their boards home with them and to put them in a prominent place where they can see them every day and to give gratitude when items on their boards manifest. We have had many people report that all the items on their boards manifested within weeks of returning home.

As MC² evolves, we continue to explore new PK challenges. For example, in the last MC² we experimented with flowers that were in tight bud, seeing if we could, through PK, get them to open within a fifteen-minute exercise. We had some success. But even more dramatic was that the flower buds arrived looking quite ashen and dull, and by the end of the exercise many of them looked much more vibrant and alive. I got the idea for this exercise after reading an interesting book called *China's Super Psychics* by Paul Dong. In this book Dong relates that for many years China has been researching, selecting, and training many of their children to do PK tasks with great power and effectiveness. Often the martial art of Chi Gong is used to generate and control the energy necessary to do these tasks. PK in China is called EHF, for Exceptional Human Function. Studies of EHF have included breaking sticks at a distance, moving objects at a distance, dematerializing objects, and moving objects through walls. There is also study of telepathy and remote sensing of hidden objects. The Chinese find that pre-pubescent children tend to be the best and only a percentage of these children keep or expand their skills into adulthood. There is also a film of several Chinese healers sending energy to a tumor in the bladder that is being imaged in real time on a sonogram. One can see the tumor shrinking and disappearing over about ten minutes during the film. If the Chinese reports are to be believed, then the United States may be far behind in the exploration and cultivation of these human skills.

Just as with Inner Vegas Adventure, people have taken MC² repeatedly

and found benefit from doing so. We now have a major university beginning a relationship with MC² to assess the phenomena experienced there
in a more scientific manner. The more adventurous have called for an
MC³, Manifestation and Creation Cubed, where we might explore levita-
tion, dematerialization, teleportation, and other more advanced PK skills.
We have heard reports of and sometimes directly witnessed success at all
the things mentioned for an MC³, but I would not attempt such a program unless I was convinced that it was also a highly positive psychological and spiritual path. And that we could find a way to teach these skills
that would allow a significant portion of the class to experience success.
This direct exploration of the limits of PK is more personally interesting
to me than the painstakingly slow study of PK in the science lab context.
While I admire scientists who are willing to do this important work and
have the courage to risk their reputations in doing so, I just do not have
the patience or the funding to engage in it myself.

One of the things that MC² graduates express the most satisfaction
with is being able to help heal their own pets and loved ones. They are
also delighted with the dramatic increase in fortuitous synchronicities in
their lives, and report a substantial increase in personal happiness and
fulfillment.

When people come to MC², most are interested in psychokinesis,
healing, and manifestation. What they are often surprised about is how
transformative the program can be. They are unprepared for how the content encourages an opening of the heart and an expansion of belief systems, to include a much greater appreciation of the power that we have
as human beings to create and shape our reality both individually and
collectively. What MC² does for me as a trainer as well as for the participants is to create a tremendous sense of renewal of faith in the beauty and
power of being human. No matter how dire and fear-filled the news has
been concerning the state of the world, I always leave TMI after doing an
MC² with a much more light-filled sense of hope. I think that this renewal
is a gift that most programs which focus on enhancement of human consciousness can provide.

After training MC² programs for two years at the Monroe Institute, it
was apparent that it was a transformational program with a high degree

of benefit for its participants. MC² fulfilled its promises in the areas of teaching psychokinesis, healing, and manifestation. This inspired me to create a home study version of this course which I called, *SyncCreation: A Course in Manifestation*, which is described in Appendix 1 of this book. SyncCreation has been greatly successful in helping many hundreds of people learn these skills at home, and has generated a series of workshops under the SyncCreation name that have been given around the world.

CHAPTER 20

Belief, Intention, and Knowing

At this point I want to take some time to look at the intention side of the creation equation. Intention is an interaction between belief and will. One can have the belief that one can create something, but without the will to do so, little or no manifestation energy is present and it does not come into reality. Conversely one can have the will that something happen but without the belief that it can, it is not likely to be created into reality. We have talked early in the book about the principle that the stronger the belief, the more impact, and that this impact increases exponentially as beliefs become knowns. Since beliefs are so important to our creation of reality I think it makes sense to focus on just what we mean by the word "belief" and the strongly related word "concept."

A belief system is a pattern of thought that filters, organizes, and ultimately defines reality for us. Our perception of reality is strongly colored by our beliefs, so much so that we might not even see something that is clearly there, if it does not coincide with our beliefs. We also will usually not act unless we believe that our actions will produce a benefit. So if we think that we are powerless to help with the pain in our own lives, or the larger world, we will usually do very little or nothing to improve it. If we don't have the belief or concept necessary for a creation, the creation will not occur.

Joe McMoneagle, one the worlds' best remote viewers, talks during The Monroe Institute's Gateway program. One of the reasons that TMI invites Joe to talk is that his first-hand account about what is possible through Remote Viewing is a fascinating belief-expanding subject. He is a terrific speaker, keeping the audience spellbound for hours. Joe emphasizes the importance of belief and concept. Joe likes to use the example that mankind had all the material available to construct a laser back in the 1800s but did not have the concept or belief, and therefore no laser was created. When at first the laser was created, the rest of us, when hearing about it reacted as if it was akin to a miracle, coming out of the blue. As the new original concept "laser" disseminated through the culture, it stimulated much new thought. I would hazard a guess that the creator of the laser would now be awed by all the creative uses generated for lasers since the original creation.

If we don't believe in something, it is unlikely to happen. Conversely if we deeply believe something, then we can arrange our reality to manifest it. For example, I knew a fellow who wanted to change jobs and was having no luck. In fact, he was showing little enthusiasm for the search, thinking in traditional terms about the concept "job" which basically involves hard work for pay. When asked what he really wanted as a work, he said a job that involved working about three months a year, with pretty women, outdoors in a nice climate. Most people laugh at that point and believe that his hedonistic description does not constitute a possible job.

He was encouraged to hold the thought of what he really wanted for awhile and send energy to it, using Focus 12 meditation energy. He was asked to have faith in his dream. Within weeks a high school classmate called him and took him to lunch. The classmate then sold him his business which was an advertising boat on the North Eastern shore. The season was ten weeks long. A major advertiser such as Coke had one side of the boat and local restaurants the other. Pretty girls in bathing suits drove the boat to attract attention. Within about a year the fellow had three boats, a Lexus, and worked only three months a year at an income greater than he had previously experienced. You can see in this example that most people would be blocked from this kind of job because their concept of job includes hard work and long hours. Their concept does not include pleasure, being outside, great freedom of time, etc. So when they look for a job they find what they conceive to be the reality of "job."

To exist in the physical we have to have beliefs. We are not trying to eliminate all beliefs. What we are attempting to do is be flexible enough in belief to allow for new and more expanded perceptions. We often have a choice to believe something that will empower versus constrict our energy. Beliefs can be rigid or flexible, confining or constructive. They come from family, friends, and culture. They can and do change over time, for example—first it was high status to wear a mink coat, and then a few years later it was not chic to wear mink.

At this time in our culture with many crises including economic and environmental converging at once, it is very important that we expand our beliefs to allow for new constructive solutions. We have been taught survival of the fittest, but Bruce Lipton in *The Biology of Belief: Unleashing the Power of Consciousness, Matter, and Miracles*, makes it clear that current DNA studies show that nature's prime directive is really, "For the good of all." This has very different implications than what we have been taught. It is a more empowering belief that suggests very different strategies with which to meet our challenges. Gregg Braden in his books such as *Deep Truth: Igniting the Memory of Our Origin, History, Destiny, and Fate* provides solid science data that counters many of the limiting beliefs currently taught to us about who we are. Lipton, Braden, and many others point to a different scientifically-backed version of truth, where our brotherhood with all of life and the power of our hearts is acknowledged.

Here is an analogy that illustrates how we come to be filled with beliefs. The Martians deliver the most sophisticated computer in the universe to earth with no programming and no manual. Earthlings program it and some things work beautifully, yet there is also much "garbage in-garbage out" causing weird answers, unreliability, and malfunctions. The computer is still awesome. The programmers did the best they could without skilled directions. The human being (you) is similar to (but much more than) this awesome computer. Your parents and others programmed you as best they could. Some of what you think works beautifully; some of what you believe creates restriction, fear, and inability to easily create what you desire. No one is at fault (they relied on their programming to program you). There is no need to waste your energy blaming others. But you can, as an adult, go inside and re-program that which needs tweaking for greater creation ability.

First it is important to understand just how out of touch with reality we truly are, because when we believe we already know reality, we will not be inspired to widen our view and perhaps will discount data that reality is different than our perceptions. Being in touch with reality is essential for creation. The paradox is that one needs to be able to see and accept "what is" before being able to adjust or initiate change. Many folks of my parents' generation believed that a good corporate job held the best chance for security and success. If fact, at this time with downsizing, mergers, pension and benefit cuts, pay inequities, rapidly changing markets, out-sourcing, and shrinking of middle management, linking one's future to a corporation is not the haven of security it used to be. One needs to see this and accept this change if one is to enhance their security.

We often rely on "seeing is believing" as evidence that we are in touch with reality. Let's go back to our discussion about how the brain sees and expand it a bit. This is what actually happens in an act of visual percep-tion. Our eyes receive two pictures, one to each eye; both pictures are upside down and reversed. Both pictures have holes in them at their cen-ters where the retinal nerve attaches to the eye. The pictures are sent to the back of the brain for processing. There the hole is filled in from previ-ous pictures taken as the eyes rapidly jump around. The pictures are then compared to many other memories, the data is filtered, with anything unacceptable eliminated, and sometimes things that are expected, but not really there, are added. And we then see what we expect to see. The best we can do is to see the immediate past. We never see the actual present because of the time it takes to do all this processing.

There is a short film that shows people in white shirts passing a bas-ketball. They are intermingling with people in black shirts also passing a basketball among themselves. If you ask an audience to focus in and count the number of times the ball is passed between the people in white shirts, an interesting thing happens. Usually no one, no matter how large the group, sees a man in a gorilla suit that walks out, center stage in the middle of the film, looks at the audience, beats his chest and then walks off stage. You can show the film again, asking them to note anything unusual and only a few will see the gorilla. This is a great example of how strongly our seeing is colored by our expectations. And we never know it. We go through our day missing much and feeling as if we are catching everything important.

We continually and consistently create a story and we perceive through this story. We usually consider the physical universe to be very concrete, solid, and objective compared to the universe of self-perception that most people would acknowledge is rife with distortion. Here are some examples of how we filter the reality of the physical universe to be more comfortable. In our story of the physical universe, we are of fairly good size. In fact, the universe is vastly huge. The Hubble telescope has measured one hydrogen cloud that is 12.5 trillion light years across. So compared to the universe, we are in fact quite tiny. It is even difficult for many of us to enlarge our reality story enough to acknowledge that we may be but one of trillions of other civilizations on planets similar to Earth.

We like to feel that physical objects are solid when in fact they are mostly (ninety-nine percent plus) empty space. In our story, most of what we interact with is matter, when in fact it is energy in various forms. We feel our lives take up a good bit of time when in fact we live but a moment in the vast stretches of time. We like to ignore that we have bugs that live on our eyelashes and eat dead organic matter, and bacteria swarming through our bodies, and dust mites in our beds. We like to feel fairly separate from nature when in fact we are interwoven into the fabric of life. In fact our genetic code is nearly identical to other mammals.

Current physics theory suggests that we actually live in a hologram of information or consciousness. And that almost all of what we perceive is both real and an illusion at the same time. The book, *Stalking the Wild Pendulum*, suggests that we wink in and out of this time-based reality into being infinite many thousand times a second. I mentioned earlier that this type of thought is ancient. *The Kybalion* from Middle-Egyptian times posits man's most important wisdoms. It starts by saying that the physical world is both real and illusion and the least wise thing one can do is to treat either side of this equation as not being true.

This is the magical Alice in Wonderland universe that consciousness has created. A vivid appreciation of this magic is the elixir of creation. The more things seem very solid and unchanging to you, the harder it is to muster belief in the power to create your own reality and to have the will to do so. To further reinforce this concept I want to give you several thoughts from the book, *The Tipping Point,* by Malcolm Gladwell. This is a great book on how change occurs in the interpersonal world. He demonstrates how massive cultural change occurs basically like an epidemic, where a few key people (some who serve the role of connectors with other people, some who assemble information, and some who sell the idea) facilitate an idea's spread throughout the culture. Once a critical mass is reached the idea reaches its tipping point and grows explosively.

We feel that we form our beliefs based upon rational facts. In actuality we are strongly influenced by many subtle and non-rational things. Gladwell notes one experiment where subjects were told they were testing new headphones for comfort and told to shake their head side to side, or up and down while listening to a proposal to raise tuition. The folks shaking their heads "no" became significantly more against the proposal upon exit interview than the ones shaking their heads "yes." At times the influence produces odd effects. Suicide stories in newspapers produce a rise in the single-car accident rate for up to ten days following the story. If the story is about a teen suicide then teen accidents go up; if about an elderly person then elderly accidents go up. If it is a suicide-murder story then multi-car accidents go up.

Gladwell feels that one very strong perception error that we continually make concerns false attribution. We tend to attribute to character things that are really changeable behavior, caused by environmental and social context. We do this because much like in the physical universe, we want things stable and predictable in our interpersonal universe. So we see a person as lazy or hostile because of the context in which we have met them, perhaps doing a boring job which they hate. And we would be surprised if we saw them in another context such as home where they are energetic, loving, and cheerful. Studies have shown that within twelve hours, normal healthy peoples' behavior becomes savage when they are put into another context, for example being asked to simulate prisoners and prison guards. Also folks we would consider thugs and criminals act destructively at a much lower rate if the context is ordered versus suggestive of disorder. New York City caused crime rates to plunge by cleaning up the graffiti and petty infractions of the social code, more than by attempting to crack down directly on major crime.

The ultimate in strong beliefs are what we can call knowns. Knowns are different. Our individual knowns come from our direct experience rather than what someone else has told us. Once we touch a hot stove we know that it is hot. The same goes for internal truth: If we bend a spoon with our mind, then we know that matter can be affected by using only the force of the mind, that spoons can be bent using the mind, and that we can bend spoons with our mind. Until we do it ourselves, we may believe it is possible or impossible, depending on who we have been listening to. But we will not have the same strength of conviction.

I invite you to explore as much direct knowing as possible for yourself. Several paths, including casinos, workshops, and home study are offered as examples of how to experience these things directly. Knowing is much more powerful than belief when it comes to manifesting what we desire. Once you have manifested many miracles, your belief that "I can do so" begins to move toward being a known, and you take a quantum step into a new reality where you can consistently create what you desire. That reality will then be rapidly confirmed by experience.

To choose your own beliefs consciously, you first have to understand and overcome the trance of current culture-created reality. There is a hypnosis of lack in our society. Without your conscious intervention, or without direct contrary experience, what we are programmed to believe when we are young, usually remains quite stable for our whole lives. To paraphrase from Sy Safransky's *Notebook,* The Sun Magazine: "They handed me a suit of beliefs and told me to try it on, it didn't fit very well, but it was better than being naked. Years went by—a lifetime."

We can use money as an example. For many of us money is a challenging energy to master. We don't have the money we desire, or we have to work in unpleasant ways to get it. The culture has many myths about money that can be disempowering. Some of these myths are: Hard, unpleasant work equals money. It is not right to enjoy your job and get paid handsomely for it. Education is needed to earn good money. There is not enough money to go around. Rich people tend to be greedy and obsessed with money (Midas).

The truth is that money is not real in the same way that a rock is real. There is no gold standard backing it up. It is basically real like a promise is real. And as we know promises vary in their realness and involve faith by at least one party to exist. The faith we all have in the promise of money can shift rapidly at anytime. Money was invented for people's convenience—the only thing constructive that you can do with it is to share it with other people for mutual benefit. Even if you save your money in a bank, you have given it to the banker to use. Monetary wealth is created by the human mind and is limitless. Your imagination and the imagination of your culture are the wellspring of your financial abundance. The faith of your culture is all that keeps in existence the concept of money as having value.

What is the predominant cultural programming concerning abundance and the ethics of manifestation? *That life is suffering and heaven is someplace else.* No! Heaven is within. The myth is that abundance and spirituality don't mix. In reality, while fear, greed, and attachment challenge spirituality, abundance handled properly, can be a great source of spiritual development. The whole universe is of and from Source—you can't get away from Source by being materialistic!

Some common beliefs, which may be unconscious for many of us and cause poverty consciousness are:

> "I will get even with my parents who blocked my
> desires and wanted me to be successful, by not reaching
> my potential."

> "When others help me financially I know that I am
> loved."

> "Money is a man's thing, not a woman's."

> "I'd have to take insane risks or spend all my time
> working to have lots of money."

So, just using the area of money, we can see that there are many beliefs that block an easy flow of energy. This blockage of energy (or energy that goes in conflicting directions) is true in all important human concerns. We are ambivalent creatures and our culture reflects this. When we announce our engagement to marry, the first person we meet may congratulate us, the second may kid us about our loss of freedom, and the third may warn us to get a pre-nuptial agreement. We have to find our way out of these mixed messages and beliefs if we are to muster the clear energy and focus we need to manifest easily. So let's look more closely at what is happening.

From my point of view the physical and non-physical universes are both abundant beyond measure. Some examples are:

Physical numbers—We would be challenged by the task of counting the blades of grass in a single lawn, let alone stars or galaxies. The latest estimates from Hubble data is that there are 400 billion galaxies each containing billions of stars. Just eighty years ago we thought there was just one galaxy.

Time—Each of us has 1,440 minutes—moments to be in the present, given to us freely each day. If the time from now back to when life first appeared on this planet is compared to the height of the tallest skyscraper on earth, then all of recorded history is but a millimeter of paint on top of the tallest building, and we have no way of comprehending the vast stretches of time to come.

Energy—The sun, oceans, and wind contain energy in uncountable measure. Atomic energy is awesome in quantity—all is in motion, all is in change. Science has begun exploring zero-point energy that exists in incomprehensible quantity even in the near vacuum of outer space.

Love—Each of us seven billion humans has the opportunity to love each of the other billions of humans on earth, plus each animal, insect, and plant, sunset, mountain, grain of sand on the beach, music, warmth, rain, and sun.

With reality being indisputably and grandly abundant, how can we possibly be plagued with a feeling of poverty in any area of life? We feel lack because the general culture has created stories that distort abundant reality and sicken our souls. Promoting feelings of lack allows those in power to sell us something. Those in power, be they religious, scientific, educational, economic, or political want us to believe that it is dangerous, hostile, and scarce out there. And only they have the one true way out of lack, and into control, pleasure, and peace. If we believe them, then we will comply with their demands in order to be safe and happy.

Religion says that we are sinful creatures who need salvation or we will burn in some type of hell. Science says that religion is wrong, that there is no god and that if we don't rely on what we can prove by its method, we will burn each other at the stake of superstition. The education system requires that school be compulsory, for without such formal training we will be ignorant, unskilled, and unable to compete for scarce resources. The political system says that without their leadership we would be in chaos and ruin, and so on.

We want to fit in, be good people, do right, and to be successful, so it's difficult not to listen to these messages, and we usually end up with a fear of lack and a life-pattern of struggle. We struggle to have enough money, take enough workshops, take enough vitamins, get enough exercise, read enough books, have enough friends, meditate enough—and then we are surprised when we find ourselves tired, and say that we don't have enough time or energy to keep up! *This is not resonant with who we truly are!* We can instead choose to be aware of the reality of abundance and empower ourselves to great joy and creativity in everyday life.

It can be very rewarding to spend some time becoming aware of your own feelings and beliefs about the nature of reality in general and abundance in particular. Consider how you feel about money, risk, and deservingness. Replace negative and restricting beliefs such as, "Nothing good comes easy" with positive, empowering beliefs—that you can be trusted with and will benefit from the power of abundance. For example, if you see the material world as dark, affirm that you are willing to light a candle in the darkness. If you see risking money as a danger, remember that it is only money and that you regularly take much bigger risks such as getting married, having children, and selecting an occupation.

We risk in order to learn, grow, and live. Risk is good. Since risk is unavoidable, and is such an important dynamic in life, wouldn't it be nice if schools, parents, or someone helped us learn how to be skilled and confident risk takers? Given that they usually didn't, you now have the opportunity to teach yourself.

An interesting example from my own life would be insurance. Upon recommendation of my elders, as I went along I accumulated insurance for life, health, disability, malpractice, car, house, rental cottage, mortgage, and an umbrella policy to cover other liabilities. I passed on long-term care, veterinary, legal, and a few other types of insurance. I have since pared this list down quite a bit. These expensive products do not prevent these calamities from happening, they just promise to mitigate, after many loopholes and exclusions, the financial consequences of them. They are also incomplete and still leave us financially vulnerable to many challenges such as raising a special needs child, and losing a job, etc. Basically they are bought to enhance financial security and yet when added together the premiums threaten middle class financial well being by taking a substantial percentage of after-tax income.

Additionally they present a challenge to the clear energy and focus needed for manifestation, as they only yield a return if something you don't want to manifest happens. This causes mixed motivation. You are spending money and focusing upon something you don't want. From a manifestation point of view, insurance may actually tend to bring to you what you are insured against. This is because part of you may want to realize a return on your premium investment, which only pays when something undesired happens!

Some manifesters who I know have become so confident (the culture would say foolish) that they have dropped all their insurance except what is mandated by law. They report feeling much freer and lighter. Some folks simply feel they cannot afford the insurance in the first place. And with health insurance premiums increasing at about fifteen percent a year, affordability will be impossible for most individuals and businesses very soon. Each adult needs to make their own decision about this—I am not recommending either way, just looking at this interesting problem. Is insurance the best way of dealing with risk? What I would say is that as long as there is significant fear about something, such as being in a rest home, then having insurance to cover rest home expenses probably serves to reduce that fear and that is a good thing.

Ironically the general public does not insure themselves at times when they are at great risk, such as in the stock market, even if they have most of their retirement assets in stocks. Professional investors consider this foolish and insure their investment though hedges. They consider the hedge as part of the cost of investing. Some people refuse to risk money at all and then lose money to inflation and taxes by putting it in the bank.

Our example in this discussion has been money. In our society money is often used to attempt to fill a lack in the heart. Fill the heart and the pockets will follow may be a wise axiom. But first one needs to soften all the cultural and family programming about how much money is enough, about what money can do for you, and about what having money means about you, and then see what you would really like to manifest in terms of money, in harmony with all the other important qualities you would like in your life.

Understand that there are many layers of beliefs, so ever-present and subtle that they are often difficult to perceive, yet they influence our ability to create the reality we desire. In groups I often ask how many people would consider themselves seekers of peace, wisdom, etc. Most everyone's hand goes up. Then I ask, wouldn't you rather be a finder? That is a different energy than seeking. So many us of have been seeking for such a long time, that we unconsciously hold that pattern rather than the energetic pattern and expectation of finding what we desire. We end up manifesting seeking instead of finding.

What we now believe will tend to be confirmed, strengthening that belief further, until it seems like fact. If we believe differently, that will also tend to be confirmed. If early in my school career I receive a C, then I will begin to view my academic possibilities to be in the C range. That will produce C effort and behavior, making C's a more likely reality for me, confirming my view. My friends, teachers, and family will likely reinforce this. But things can change if my own thinking changes, perhaps through the inspiration of someone who sees greater potential within me.

Be aware of what you believe as well as what you want. My hope is that reading *Inner Vegas* inspires you to focus and practice what you already know, adds to your empowering beliefs, and helps bring your dreams into reality.

Let's elaborate further on this idea of the power of knowing, since it is so important to our being able to create this magic. As I mentioned early in the book, one way to look at what I have been doing all these years is that I have been exploring the idea that we create our own reality—and moving this idea from a belief to a known for me. As you move from believing to knowing, authority and energy are increased. You may believe that bee stings hurt. But you do not truly know it until you are stung yourself. If you are stung, you will then know the unique combination of surprise and fire that such a little insect can deliver. You will probably change your thoughts and behavior around bees. A bee sting is very concrete. It is much more challenging to know the dynamic concepts that govern our reality.

The astronaut Edgar Mitchell was a scientist who believed before going into space that the Earth was an interdependent, unified ecosystem. Yet upon seeing the Earth from space as a beautiful, miraculous sphere, his belief instantly took a quantum leap into knowing. This inspired him to found the Institute for Noetic Sciences (IONS). The Institute explores the importance of human consciousness and has created a bridge between the fields of science and philosophy. The Institute for Noetic Sciences has become a pivotal organization in our world, with thousands of members worldwide. According to IONS, the word "noetic" comes from the ancient Greek *nous*, for which there is no exact equivalent in English. It refers to "inner knowing," a kind of intuitive consciousness—direct and immediate access to knowledge beyond what is available to our normal senses and the power of reason.

Edgar Mitchell's experience illustrates the power of a true known versus weak belief to create a new reality, in this instance literally changing Mr. Mitchell's world view, his life's work, and impacting global consciousness through the IONS organization. One of their projects is to study our ability to send energy without regard to distance to effect healing in another person. Their studies are carried out under rigorous scientific protocol and their findings are inspiring. Their results support what has been presented in this book about our amazing abilities to heal with energy. You can learn more about this fine organization by going to *www.noetic.org*.

We may believe that it would be amazing to see the Grand Canyon. This belief may or may not be strong enough to trigger us into going to see for ourselves. Suppose we give ourselves the gift of acting on our belief. We are then privileged to stand on the rim of the canyon. Its complex wonder then touches the depth of our being and we begin to know the Grand Canyon. We each will have our own experiential symphony of the Canyon. Our symphony will perhaps include apprehension about heights, anticipation, awe, an opening of our heart, and a connection with the wisdom, order, and beauty of nature. We may experience how we are so physically small and yet our consciousness can expand to take in such a vast presence. Our experience of the canyon is unique. We are truly the composer and conductor of this reality symphony. Our knowing of the Canyon will have things in common with other people's knowing. I would hazard to guess that all who have stood on the rim know the canyon to be big. Its magnificent, breath-taking bigness is a surprise for those who have previously experienced it through a post card, or flying high over it on their way across country, or have just heard someone else say that it is big.

Most visitors arrive at the canyon at midday; given it is a few hour's drive from nearby tourist points. Some visitors to the canyon will stay ten minutes and be preoccupied with their kids or cameras. Many will linger— their canyon symphony will be richer. A few will stay on to see the canyon at sunrise or sunset when it becomes a cathedral of spectacular light. Even fewer people witness the canyon's majesty during a thunderstorm.

The direct knowing of a visit to the rim of the canyon often has a profound effect on people. Yet even this can be enhanced. Our knowing can be deepened by going down into the canyon itself, or deeper still by living a year there as its rangers may do, joining with its ever-changing rhythms through bitter cold to blazing hot.

The best way to make the idea that we are continual creators completely solid and real to you, is to actually experience the process of creating and manifesting your reality yourself. There is no substitute for this direct experience. There is no other way for something to become a genuine known in your life. If I have been successful, reading *Inner Vegas* will at least bring you to the rim of the canyon at sunrise, rather just seeing the Canyon in a picture book. The movement of a thought from a possibility, through belief, to a known is a marvelous adventure. And to journey all the way from belief to known you will have to experiment with this directly yourself and see the results in your own life.

As I mentioned at the beginning of this chapter, intention drives creation. And the first step is to have the belief that we can consciously create our reality any way we wish. Once we believe this strongly, then the next step is having the will to do so. Another thing that Joe McMoneagle often mentions in his Gateway talk is that when scientists use the most advanced Cray computers, they can measure every neuron that fires during the act of picking up a pencil. But then something magical happens. When the subject is asked to pick up the pencil sometime in the next few minutes, no neuron fires in the brain to indicate the act of will, or decision of when to pick up the pencil. From this data scientists conjecture that the mind's act of will may not occur in the brain, that our minds may actually be non-physical or non-local.

It is challenging to develop the will unless your beliefs tell you that your desire is feasible. Will activates when we can conceive of something and believe it to be possible and desirable. We can reinforce this will by a conscious decision to exert our energy in that direction. The clearer we can see our goal and its benefits, and the clearer we can be from opposing or distracting thoughts, the stronger and more constant is our will power, and therefore intent.

We may naturally be monitoring for signs of progress toward our goal. But paradox enters here. We need to first have the will to do something for it to happen, but for many things we also have to *let go* of that will for it to happen. What we are really looking for, as a process, is to form will strongly, and then let go or ease up into more of a willingness for it to happen. If we constantly monitor and strive, we can get in our own way. This is true even with very concrete tasks. When I build a new addition to my home, I need to see it as possible, desirable and then at some point after hiring the right contractor or subcontractors, I need to let go and let them do the work with me monitoring and fine-tuning as I go. If I push too hard I will get resistance and create struggle towards my goal. Some might talk about this as being smooth, loving, elegant, and less of a focus on the results, while traveling from intent formation, though execution to completion. So for manifestation, healing and PK, it is good to understand the dance from strong intention (comprised of strong belief or knowingness plus will) through letting go, into a trusting willingness for this or something better to happen.

Why might it be important to learn how to influence matter with your mind? What good is a bent spoon—they do indeed work better in their original form! Working with dice and spoons gives immediate and certain feedback of results and also trains one into the thinking and energy required to achieve manifestation and healing results. PK gives confidence and empowers you to create what you desire in your life. This will help you reach your full human potential for authentic and enduring happiness. By fulfilling more of your potential, in a way that balances power with wisdom, you will help the world become a better place for all.

In my opinion, there is a battle of ideas now on this planet, for the *soul* of the planet, if you will. Materialism in the form of traditional science and economics yields dramatic and immediate practical results compared to superstition. Yet materialism alone leaves us hollow, and eventually with more problems and less happiness and meaning. Witness the tremendous imbalances today in wealth distribution, environmental crises, and profit motivation versus healing in the medical profession. Materialism without heart energy has led to a grave imbalance toward consumerism that threatens the planet through pollution, over-population, and political unrest. This is the dominant reality we are currently co-creating. We are all responsible for it and swept up in its currents.

Living from spirit and heart feels good but also needs to be practical. To gain widespread acceptance as a better way to live, it has to have clear survival value to compete with, compare with, and balance the materialistic view. Strong manifesters can teach, by example, just how effective and life-affirming creating our reality from the heart can be.

When people hear that I can affect dice and slot machines in Vegas or help heal an illness, I have their attention. Everything in this book reflects my opinions or the thoughts of others. You, of course, are encouraged to accept or disagree with any part of it based upon your own truth. I do ask that you just temporarily suspend strong disbelief in what is possible, long enough to consider new thoughts and see for yourself what miracles are possible. Through this book I am offering you an invitation to try new ways of thinking and being, and an opportunity to practice lighter, more conscious living. This can result in greater personal power, joy, healing, and positive manifestation. Remember, in the grand freedom of this world, you are in charge of your own attitudes and outcomes.

CHAPTER 21

Quieting the Left Brain
to Glimpse Infinity

For the Inner Vegas Adventure, MC², and SyncCreation programs to be successful at teaching people to the level of a deep knowing, they needed to be highly experiential, so that people could actually feel what these PK events are like and to know that they could do these things themselves. To do this, the person has to be able to raise and focus energy in a very advanced way. Hemi-Sync is terrific at enabling a person with no meditation experience to rapidly access the energy and states of consciousness needed for PK. Without such a rapidly acting, non-dogmatic tool for changing consciousness, progress in PK would be much more daunting. It might take years to learn the meditation techniques that would result in being able to do PK with some consistency.

This is so because our ordinary state of consciousness has several features that block our PK abilities. Most of us live from a very linear consciousness where much of our thinking and awareness involves focus on the past and the future. Yet PK magic occurs in the present and is supported by a consciousness focused strongly in the present. There is no magic in the past or future. Each present moment is the eternal now. By that I mean that the present is not really part of linear time, it is not on a line between past and future as we usually view it. Rather the present just is. Time, as we linearly experience it, is an illusion of the time-space consciousness. When we are out of that illusion by being in the present moment, we are also out of the illusions of limits that linear time-space supports. This allows the opportunity for miracles to happen from the perspective of time-space. People often report a sense of no time when in the zone in sports or other activities, if they are fully engaged in the present. Also they can experience an elasticity of time. People moving toward a car accident often report that everything slowed down so much that they had ample time to see everything and easily choreograph their movements to avoid the collision. In other situations a person might give a two-hour speech and if in the flow, it may seem that it has occurred over a few minutes.

This variation in how we experience time can be quite dramatic. A book that I read about thirty years ago described people having experiences where they thought that they would be dead in just a moment. For example, if they fell off a cliff, in the few seconds before they hit ground, they reported reviewing their entire life, experience by experience in just those few seconds. I apologize for not being able to remember the title of this book; I read it so long ago. We can have dreams that seem to go on for a long time and then discover that in clock time it has been seconds or just a few minutes. In near-death experiences people report that while being clinically dead for a few minutes that they have what seems like hours or days of experience.

There seems to be an interesting relationship between time or time perception and PK. Once, when I was in very high energy at the dice table, as I threw the dice they seemed to just hang over the table at the top of their arch and just kept spinning there. It felt that I could have gone to the restroom and come back and they still would be rotating slowly in mid-air. I was fascinated by this for what seemed to be a long time. Finally it got boring and I willed them to land on hardway six (3-3). They obliged by renewing their journey downward, hit the table and landed as a hardway six.

Many meditators have identified this melting of our usual time sense when one enters altered states of consciousness, and that this often produces deep bliss, feelings of connection with All That Is, and access to the eternal present. Eckhart Tolle wrote the popular book, *The Power of Now,* exploring the exquisiteness and impact of such a timeless state. A physicist who took MC² and saw all the PK activity that seemed to violate Newtonian physics, went home and after carefully analyzing the mathematical formula that underpin phenomena such as gravity, felt that the only way PK is able to happen was by being able to affect time.

Richard Bartlett, in *The Physics of Miracles*, tries to explain how practitioners of Matrix Energetics, an energy healing modality, accomplish their healings. He feels that to create miracle healing we move out of linear time and into the quantum field of infinite possibilities and select another reality in which the person is fully healed and then bring that reality back to the linear time line. In his book he tells a story of a person who accidently slammed their dog's leg in a car door and fractured it, so that it was just dangling at an awkward angle. As he rushed his beloved pet to the vet he applied Matrix Energetics principles, and by the time he arrived at the doctors, the vet asked, "What are you here for?" The dog's leg was fine on physical exam and x-ray!

EMDR *(Eye Movement Desensitization and Reprocessing)* is a respected psychological treatment technique which is very useful for trauma relief. Here, rapid eye movement is used to alter consciousness and then re-program the person's psychology. In EFT (Emotional Freedom Technique) tapping is used to break the linear time focus and allow a new reality to form. All these methods to me have something in common. They induce a momentary shift away from normal time consciousness, and in that gap, alter reality.

Albert Einstein said, "We can't solve problems by using the same kind of thinking we used when we created them." This could be translated as we cannot solve problems from the same level of consciousness that created them. There is an interesting book called *Stalking the Wild Pendulum*, written by physicist Itzhak Bentov. By the laws of physics, when a pendulum changes the direction of its swing it has infinite velocity and occupies infinite space; then as it continues its arc in the opposite direction it returns to normal time space. He relates that we have pendulum motion in each cell in our bodies, suggesting that we also wink out of normal time-space into the infinite possibilities of the quantum universe, and then come back to linear time-space. And we do so several thousand times a second.

Dean Radin's book, *The Conscious Universe*, is a wonderful exploration of the scientific data supporting PSI functioning including telepathy, remote sensing, and PK. His follow-up book, *Entangled Minds:*

Extrasensory Experiences in a Quantum Reality, explores how consciousness and the quantum universe interact to explain PK and other PSI. Lynne McTaggart also explores this area in her book, *The Field: The Quest for the Secret Force in the Universe.*

It has been said that those who claim to understand quantum physics really do not understand it. I surely don't claim to understand it. But it looks like within quantum physics is where we will find a scientific explanation of what regularly occurs in Inner Vegas Adventure, MC², and SyncCreation. And part of what is happening in these programs is that Hemi-Sync is particularly good at shifting consciousness in a way that allows us to move beyond normal time-space consciousness to perform what look like miracles. This translates all the complexities of physics down to the practical level of application without needing to know fully how it works. In fact we are in that situation with many things including electricity. We do not have to fully understand electricity to have it work for us. Some understanding is very helpful, however, so that we know to plug things into the grid and also to avoid electrocution.

Serge King, in his book, *Urban Shaman*, approaches the phenomenon of instant healing from a Hawaiian healer/shaman tradition. He feels that our emotional body is where we tend to store the memory of past reality and carry it forward to the next moment. This is what makes it possible for us to have an injured leg for decades, when all the original cells involved in that injury have long since been replaced by the body with new cells. He tells the story of a doctor who was preparing a salad for a party and cut his hand deeply with a knife. To rewrite this event into a new reality, the doctor then made a similar motion over and over but without cutting his hand, to reprogram his emotional body with a different memory of what had happened. Then he went about his business and looked down in a few minutes and his hand was completely healed.

Having read this I soon had an occasion to try this technique. I burned my thumb severely enough to char the flesh when picking up something hot. Remembering what I had recently read, I immediately repeated the motion several times as if I had avoided the hot object. Then I turned my attention elsewhere for a few minutes and when I looked again at my thumb there was no sign of the burn and no pain.

Given this shift of our attention out of its usual linear time illusion works so well for changing reality, how come we don't use it routinely? The answer is that it is difficult to do without years of meditation practice, or extensive training in some other consciousness altering technique. That is, unless you have a technology such as Hemi-Sync that works quickly. Why is shifting our consciousness so difficult to do? The answer lies partly in the way our brains work. Permit me to take a journey into brain science that greatly simplifies what we know and honors that fact that we really don't know much with certainty in terms of how the brain relates to consciousness.

At the level of the cerebral cortex (the outer part of the brain and the part that is most evolved in humans) we have two separate brains in our head, called the right and the left hemispheres, that are completely separate from each other physically (you can literally hold them apart, as each is a complete unit). These two hemispheres are connected through a massive information transfer point comprised of hundreds of millions of fibers like telephone wires that carry messages from one hemisphere to the other in an area called the Corpus Callosum. These connections and the communication between hemispheres allow us to operate smoothly, acting and feeling as if we had one brain.

We are very good at this. For example our two eyes see different pictures of the world. Each picture has a significant dark hole in the middle of the picture because there are no light receptors where the optic nerve exits the eye. But through active brain processing we have the experience of one three-dimensional picture, and therefore see one visual world not two. We think that we are seeing reality at that moment but we are not. We are creating a story from visual data a short while ago. In order to feel comfortable we must also feel that there are no significant errors in the story we assemble and label as reality, but we make errors all of the time. We can take the situation where there is car accident witnessed by many people, a situation where we can expect that people gave it their full attention for a few moments. What we find is that the various witnesses create very different stories of those few moments of reality. They may disagree on the colors of the cars, how many people were present and what they looked like, who collided into whom, speed, sounds, etc. My point is that our experience of a seamless sequential series of moments, always moving from the past into the future, and a seamless point of consciousness that we label as "I," accurately perceiving this movement, are illusions that allow us to operate in time-space which itself is proving to be an illusion.

Our two brain hemispheres have very different things that they specialize in and very different types of consciousnesses associated with them. I want to state from the start that I am not prejudiced against one brain or the other—I am extremely happy to have both! Activities such as word recognition, selecting the right word to say, and organizing it into a sentence is a left brain function. Yet the rhythm, pace, and intonation of speech involves right brain processing. Facial recognition and other pattern recognition is a right brain activity. Putting a name to that face is a left brain function.

For our purposes we can greatly simplify and say that our usual consciousness of time as linear with a past, present, and future strung out in sequential order, is a function of how our left brain processes information, which is sequentially. The left brain does the comparing and contrasting of one thing to another, so it is the seat of "better than and worse than" judgments. Because the left brain is so involved with language it is the part that says, "I exist." It determines where we stop and the outside world starts. Our sense of ourselves as individuals separate from everything else is a function of how our left brain works.

Our right brain processes information very differently. It takes in vast amounts of information through the senses and other parts of the brain and forms a mosaic of the present moment. For our right brains there is just an eternal now. Right brain consciousness is non-linear and non-contrasting, everything just is. Appreciation of music and beauty is mostly a right brain function. For the right brain there is no "I" because all is one. And its view of reality is just as accurate and compelling as the left brain's view, as we are learning from modern physics.

As we develop in the womb there is actually a contest between these two brains for dominance. This contest continues during maturation, and the left brain usually becomes the one we hear from and identify with the most. The left brain as the winner has mostly constructed our modern culture, and the culture in return strongly reinforces the left brain's dominance to the extent that many people are not even aware of any other consciousness within them. From our left-brained point of view, we label some civilizations as primitive. Yet these societies know how to tap into the right brain consciousness better than we do, and therefore often have a very different world view. That view accepts magic because it has direct experience with magic. In *Chinese Super Psychics*, Paul Dong relates that when the Chinese government goes out to find people that have psychic ability, the rate of people found to be psychic is much higher in rural areas than in the sophisticated left brain dominant cities. As we have mentioned children have a much easier time learning PK tasks. This is partly because their brains have not yet become fully left brain dominant and their view of reality is not yet so tightly determined by enculturation. They have an easier time being in the now and accessing right brain function.

Jill Bolte Taylor is a neuroanatomist and named one of *Time Magazine's* 100 Most Influential People in the World for 2008. This Harvard-trained brain scientist, when she was thirty-seven years old in 1996, experienced a massive stroke or cerebral hemorrhage. She had the misfortune and opportunity to observe what happens in stroke from the inside of the experience. She gave a filmed talk of her experience that has gone viral because of its power and impact. Since then she has written a beautiful book with the same title as the talk, called *My Stroke of Insight*. I recommend strongly that you see the film (accessible on the web) and read her book. What Jill found as the stroke shut down her left brain function was that she entered the world of right brain consciousness where she felt that "all is one" in an eternal now. In this consciousness she felt total peace and great bliss. Then her left brain would kick in and say to her, "We are in trouble here" and try to plan her response to the emergency. She alternated between these two realities for many hours until finally losing consciousness. In her right-brain mind the world was oceanic and infinitely vast with no boundary between her own skin and the world. In this state she was overwhelmed with love. Yet with her left brain severely impaired she could not recognize numbers to dial the phone for help, and when she finally reached someone their speech and her own voice sounded like nonsense. She now wonders if we can somehow integrate the wisdom of the right hemisphere consciousness with that of the left. The good news is that we can integrate these consciousnesses and we do not have to have a stroke to experience it!

I think that Hemi-Sync works so elegantly in Inner Vegas Adventure, MC² and SyncCreation because it is excellent at facilitating the two hemispheres of the brain to synchronize and communicate more fully with each other. This results in less left brain dominance and more whole brain co-dominion over the person's consciousness. Hemi-Sync, when coupled with the correct intention, can accomplish this in a few minutes, versus years of meditating. This allows clearer perception of oneness, freedom from linear time-space illusion, knowing the reality of the eternal now moment, appreciation of connection, experiencing of beauty, and feeling deep love. All these things facilitate powerful PK, healing, and manifestation when combined with the left-brain intention of doing these activities.

Another way to look at this is that most all of the dragons that I mentioned in the Vegas section of this book that impair PK show themselves when the left brain is being too dominant. They include harsh judgment of self or others, impatience, worry about the past or future, egotistical traps, etc. The solution to this is to incorporate more right brain functioning. Bringing in a more balanced whole brain state, where the right brain is allowed input, sings these dragons to sleep so that the treasure can be found. The right brain's ability to feel oneness, to have instant knowing in the form of intuition, to recognize patterns, to move out of linear time and into the sacred gap where we can choose a more desirable reality, all make PK, healing, and manifestation much more likely. Once the right brain breaks the hammerlock of over-verbal and over-ideational consciousness, then it is much easier for the person to access the energy field of their heart—the higher feeling center. We can then perpetuate and deepen the heart energy through beautiful music, remembering loved ones and blessings, experiencing gratitude and praise for life, speaking our truth and helping other people. And as I have said repeatedly in this book I feel that heart energy is the key place from which to live a miracle-filled life where intuition and positive manifestation abound.

There may be even more effective consciousness-changing technologies in the future. It would be tremendously helpful to have additional technologies, which can cater to diverse personalities and learning styles, to facilitate the shift out of the overly left-brain consciousness that currently is so prominent in developed nations.

CHAPTER 22

Viewing the Tapestry

Thank you for following me on my journey across two decades of PK experience. I would now like you to look back with me and see what I have learned along the way. Some of the things have been very surprising to me; others were more a confirmation of what I had already guessed was true. Let's turn the tapestry over to the picture side and see what the overview looks like.

The first thing that I am struck with is that while I initially thought that I would do this alone, it is clear now to me that the journey happened within a community of many wonderful explorers, helpers, and guides. I was helped by many other beings who interacted with me along the way. I say beings and not just people, because even the dogs that we did a successful healing with provided invaluable feedback, delivered with love expressed in wagging tails and doggy kisses. I also was graced many times with a strong connection with beautiful spirits from the other side, and even a wonderful communion with what I take to be God. The parade of people is legion who have given me ideas, supported me in my projects, and trusted me to be their guide, as they were at the same time teaching me. Very important to me were those who arranged the practicalities that supported my quest, from serving me meals, through helping to design my website. And lastly I want to express deep joy and gratitude for all who supported me energetically, including many who I am sure that I will never consciously know. I am going into a bit of detail here because one thing that I have learned through experience is that consciousness is really a community and that much of our feeling of being an individual is a very limited way of looking at who we are.

When I look out my window right now I can see my dog curled asleep at the edge of the woods. We usually perceive this way—the dog is the figure and the rest is background. Yet in reality my dog is part of a huge context that we can look at in many different ways. From the hawk's eye soaring above, there is dog interwoven with trees and other small animals. We can make the dog the center point of a sphere which can extend for miles or out to infinity. Our usual way of perceiving with us as the figure, is a very isolating view. There was a fashion model who was discovered as a young woman in a tribe in Africa. She became a huge success. The first night in a large hotel suite in a big city she trembled in fear throughout the night. In an interview about how she was enjoying success she commented that she could not believe how lonely people in the developed world were. She had always eaten, slept, and lived with her community within sight and touching distance at all times.

One time when I was being guided into a past-life regression, my guide asked me where I wanted to go. I said, "Lets try ancient Egypt," figuring it would be cool to have a memory of being some big-shot there. I found myself on a chain-gang of slaves helping to build some project. I remembered being ripped from my tribe and kidnapped for this purpose. Going back earlier in that life I remembered being with my nomadic tribe as a young child. The interesting thing was that my consciousness was so different than it is now. It was much simpler and more present-focused. It was one big "Group I" consciousness. This Group I included all the people in the tribe, plus all ancestors and natural elements such as vegetation, sky, and sand—all feeling as present, real, and intelligent as my individual self. During the regression I could feel the whole tribe's consciousness shift moment to moment, like one ocean, and I was a drop in that ocean connected to all, important to all, and no more important than any. It felt amazingly supportive and bigger than any individual can feel. There was a thought, "Always know where your water is" that felt similar to our, "Remember to look both ways before crossing the street." But this thought was held by the whole tribe at the same time, not just by me. And as the tribe moved along, its entire consciousness subtly shifted with the distance away from water.

When we do PK healing and manifestation work I have learned that it is good to soften the strong sense of being an isolated "I" consciousness and allow our awareness to extend to and appreciate that we are really a huge "we" consciousness. The resulting awareness of connection is what allows us to dance with greater energies that can help us with our intent. David Spangler, in his book, *Everyday Miracles*, suggests that our consciousness is similar to light—both particle and wave at the same time. Physicists have found that light can behave as a particle in some circumstance and as a wave in other circumstances. In manifestation we become aware of something that we want as an individual (particle). We can then go to our nature as unity consciousness (wave) to link with all creating forces, and then bring the manifestation into reality to be enjoyed personally.

I have also learned that anywhere and anyone can be our classroom, if we turn our awareness to what is going on in the present moment in whatever environment we find ourselves. Casinos and cabbies can guide us to greater growth and insight as easily as the great cathedrals and sages. Our complex relationships with objects as simple as dice, to huge systems such as world culture, all interact with us to teach. Why I picked cabbies in my example was because as I was writing this I remembered a time when I was in Vegas about a month after the 9-11 attacks. The country (and Vegas) was in a terrible mood. Our group consciousness was filled with fear, anger, and grieving. The casinos were nearly empty and there had been massive lay-offs. All my energy techniques felt like trying to shine a light into a black hole and I did poorly at the tables for days. I found that without some energetic support from the community around me in Vegas that I could not PK my way out of a paper bag!

After giving it one last try at the Vegas Hilton and losing once again, I was truly beaten down and very tired. I went outside and hailed a cab for a ride that was only about two blocks long, but I was too drained to walk. When the cabbie heard where I was going he did not protest about the short ride. When I got to the Sahara where I was staying, I handed him a $100 and said, "Please keep the change, I'd rather give it to you than the casino." The cabbie locked eyes with me with tears shining in his eyes and smiled happily. He told me that I was the first fare that he had picked up in two days. He thanked me from his heart. I do not even know his name but he taught me that even when we feel most powerless, we have choices that can have tremendous impact. So, I need to thank him and I do.

I have learned that we can make everyone either our lover or our teacher. And that even people and events that are teaching us through frustration and pain are part of one consciousness that is lovingly attempting to facilitate our movement forward into the best of who we are. We are part of facilitating everyone else to remember their own grand beauty. As they say, there is a hard way and an easy way. And it is much more fun and fulfilling to be part of the easy way for other people by being positive and encouraging of their dreams and dignity.

As much as we feel that we are separate, we are actually part of a grand unity consciousness that embraces the entire human family throughout history and relates to all living things. And we are constantly learning from and teaching one another by example and word. When we put these two things together, it calls us to be more aware that every choice we make has impact wider than our self. When we stay home and play computer games, we enjoy ourselves and help support the computer industry. When we go on social media sites and do something as simple as wish someone a Happy Birthday we begin to impact others in a more personal way. When we find a need, such as helping a child learn to read, that exists in our community, and fulfill it, we can enjoy our impact even more personally as we receive smiles and hugs from the child and gratitude from the child's parents. The entrepreneur risks his or her time, energy, and money, and may produce great abundance for themselves as well as jobs and wealth for thousands of other people.

In these stressful times we might feel powerless against bureaucracies or political conditions, but the truth is that there had never been a time where it has been easier for one person to have a huge impact. A person gets the idea to use a social networking site to find kidney donors. Via the internet, the idea goes viral and many lives are saved and connections are made. In this time in which we live, we can have an idea, and if we express it, the idea can stretch around the world within days. My experiences related in this book have taught me to reach out more readily to individuals and to the world. It is an amazing experience to be given a standing ovation, followed by the warmest of hugs in another country after speaking your truth. I am deeply proud that one of my daughters worked hundred-hour weeks in puppy rescue. She helped build an organization spanning many states that has saved hundred of dogs and cats from suffering and death, and provided treasured pets for hundreds of families.

Because it is so deeply satisfying and helpful, I am entreating you to reach out more into the community of consciousness of which we are all a part.

My brother John, once a high powered executive, has suffered for a decade from an insidious disease called Inclusion Body Myositis. This disease slowly and inexorably wastes away all one's voluntary muscles. The large muscles in his arms and legs went first so that he could not walk nor pick up objects such as a carton of milk. The muscles in his forehead that keep his eyebrows from drooping weakened. The muscles in his eyelids weakened making it difficult to close his eyes. He is now in a motor-ized wheelchair with a feeding tube, and needs help with basic bodily functions. The disease itself is not fatal because the involuntary muscles that beat one's heart and handle digestion keep working. But he faces the prospect of literally not being able to move a muscle. He lives next door to me. I just talked to him today and he was filled with affection, humor, and interest in my life's activities. To me John is a hero. He teaches me that regardless of our circumstances and resources we can have a positive impact.

I come from a family of helpers and so I know it comes more easily for me than for many that have not been raised to see that they can have impact. My sister is a nurse. My mother volunteered her time freely even while raising our family of seven. Depression and anxiety can distort our view of ourselves so greatly that the thought that the world really thirsts for our help and presence may be quite inconceivable. But even milder forms of distorted perception such as feeling not good enough, or that we have nothing important to contribute, can impair our ability to see our value to the world. One of the ways that many Americans feel lack right now is feeling lack of enough time to do even the things necessary to earn a living and take care of our homes. We can feel that we are in survival mode and all this talk that we are meant to thrive can be discouraging instead of inspiring. As I have mentioned, feelings of lack manifest more lack. So please consider releasing yourself from any of the tension and discouragement that feeling that you do not have enough time produces. You do have enough time and energy to thrive for your own benefit and the good of the world around you.

There is a place for you to contribute and to be nurtured both by your contributions and the contributions of all those around you. This is true regardless of your circumstances and personality. I am an introverted person, and I also tend to extend myself into many projects at once. It can feel like I have ten balls in the air at once and am not always a graceful juggler. Yet I can work with this. My introversion makes it easy for me to be on my mountain, writing for many hours per day by myself, for the months that it is taking to write this book. My introversion nurtures my soul and is a wellspring of ideas. But my extension out to teach and engage the world also nurtures me in essential ways and brings much joy. I just need to balance things in a way that works for me. This is true for each one of us, regardless of our interests, talents, personality, and resources. The world awaits you.

The next thing that I learned is that following your passion can take you to amazing experiences well beyond what you first might envision as your goal. When I first started out, all I wanted to do was to see if PK was real. Once this was confirmed and I saw that it related to healing and manifestation, then I developed a burning desire to learn more about it. This led to Vegas, without any idea of teaching others about this topic. Once I discovered how useful and transformative learning about PK could be, my passion to share it was activated. At first this idea was limited to the initial Inner Vegas Adventure group. Once that proved to be so interesting, fun, and expanding, then I really put energy into having ongoing groups. Once this was experienced, I had a curiosity and passion for exploring how much further this could go, resulting in the desire to develop a program for TMI. Once MC² was developed and we began to see what happened there, there was a passion to spread the word further and SyncCreation was born. With the feedback pouring to me about how beneficial this home study program was, the desire to write this book was born. And of course I do not know how much further the journey will take me, but I will continue to follow my passion.

All along the way there have been amazing people and miraculous experiences that were much richer and fulfilling than I could have anticipated. And each level of experience pulled me to look deeper into myself and the nature of this wonderful time-space illusion that we create, and the greater realities that we inhabit. At each level there were fears that manifested about failure, rejection, causing unintended damage, raising false hopes, etc. I started this journey meeting fear with courage. I now melt fear with love.

Perhaps the most significant thing that I have learned in these two decades is to gather a much deeper understanding of the power of the heart. When people ask me what I know, not just what I might 99.9 percent believe, I come up with just one thing—that love is real. I am 100 percent sure that love is real. Much of what we might think, perceive, and experience might be part of the time-space illusion. This includes even things we hold dearly such as who we think we are. But I know that love is real.

We need illusion to have experience. Without experience there is just beingness in an eternal present without differentiation. There is the ONE that is all time and all consciousness and all that is, period. In order to have experience the first illusion that we need to adopt is that we are separate from the ONE. Even science shows us how much illusion we adopt to be able to function in time-space and have experience. I know that the desk that I am working at and the floor that my chair is resting upon are not solid. Science says that at an atomic level they are composed of 99.9 percent nothing, with that other tiny percent being matter in the form of atoms, which if broken down, are made of energy, which broken down appear to only be packets of information.

We feel that we live a relatively long time in our physical life. Yet remember that all of recorded history would be like a millimeter of paint on top of the world's tallest skyscraper, if all of time past was represented by that skyscraper. And we have no idea of the amount of time to come. So on a realistic time-scale, our existence is an infinitesimal micro flash. In terms of size we feel of a fairly good size. Yet remember that just one hydrogen cloud in space can be 12.5 trillion light years across. On any real scale of size we are unimaginably small. So science suggests that we are a micro speck that exists for an infinitesimal micro flash in time, operating in a world comprised of information packs with no real solidity. How amazing that we can create illusions so that we can have such rich experiences within our parameters of existence!

Even knowing that we live in a world of illusion, I have declared that I am 100 percent certain that love is real. I am not sure that I can explain how I know love is real. It is mostly that I just know it to be true and that this knowing has become the compass of my existence. I can point to some parts of this knowing. No matter how dark and depressed I have been, no matter how horrific outside circumstances have been, and no matter how much events have torn my heart, love has been there. Love was present within my body cast, my brother Pete's suicide, my mother's Alzheimer's, and my brother John's illness.

What I strongly suspect is that the energy and information which make up this physical world is really consciousness and that consciousness and love are the same thing. The ONE and love are identical. As differentiation from the ONE occurs there is the exciting possibility of many flavors of consciousness, but it is still all really love, all present and eternal, playing games within the world of experience. And the main game is for love to love itself, through a giant game of hide and seek. How exciting it is to hide and how marvelous to be found by love!

Within this knowing there has been much learning about how powerful and positive the force of love is. Just being more loving toward one's self and all of creation, creates miracles of healing and manifestation. Coming from a place of deep love also allows us to enter into a new relationship with the physical world that allows PK to be easy. I often say with PK that it is impossible until it is easy. By that I mean until we are in the right heart-based relationship with the physical world and ourselves, the PK door remains firmly shut except for extraordinary circumstances. When we enter into a deep heart space, PK is just one of the natural flowings that occur in that space.

I have found that all decisions made from love are the right decisions, even when the consequences have not been what I consciously intended or predicted. Some say that hate is the opposite of love. I think that everything is love and therefore love has no opposite. I do think that fear in its many forms can cloud our perception of ever-present love. And when fear is strong enough, it can create very unpleasant experiences for us within the free will granted by love.

Saint Augustine, the highly influential third century theologian and philosopher living in Africa said, "Our whole business therefore in life is to restore to health the eye of the heart whereby God may be seen." Writing in the United States in the twenty-first century, Elizabeth Gilbert in *Eat Pray Love* asks a Balinese Shaman how to balance the good and the beautiful, pleasure and devotion. She relates that the shaman drew a picture of a beast with a human head, with four feet on the ground and a head-full of foliage, looking at the world through the heart. The shaman said, "A balanced person may live in the world and enjoy its delights and also be devoted to spirit. To do this you must keep your feet grounded firmly in the earth, as if you had four legs instead of two. That way you can stay in the world. But you must stop looking at the world through your head; you must look through your heart. That way you will know God."

One of the best ways to open our perception to the presence of love is to open our hearts. This can be difficult to do. We feel strongly within our current culture that living from the left brain's analytical, logical, sequential consciousness is the best way to survive and thrive on this planet at this time. Living from an open heart can feel vulnerable and foolish. Opening our heart can threaten us with emotions so strong that our logic and composure might be washed away. We are right to feel this as a threat to the extent that we are choosing to live from ego. The open heart is indeed much stronger than the ego and if we open our heart, the ego will no longer be able to be the dictator of our lives. When faced with powerful heart energy ascending within us, the ego can feel as if it will die. In fact what will usually happen is that if heart energy is allowed to emerge, the ego will still have an important place within the symphony of our selves. It just does not get to be the conductor all of the time.

So, if you want to do PK, healing, or positive manifestation, your open heart energy will empower this beyond expectations. If you want to have wisdom, and clear signs and intuitions about how to live and what to do, your flowing heart will provide this. If you want to help make the world a better place, your heart will provide all the inspiration, energy, and feedback that you need to accomplish this. If you want to be happy and experience a rich and impactful life, your heart is your best friend. I have found that it is worth every effort and price to open your heart full-wide. This may include activities such as psychotherapy, experiencing therapeutic touch through massage, learning how to meditate to quiet the left brain, becoming closer with open-hearted people, taking courses such as SyncCreation and many others, and surrounding yourself with beauty and goodness in nature, pets, art, and music. The Institute of Heart Math[6]

---

6 www.heartmath.org

has biofeedback devices that you can use to practice opening your heart, and see your increased heart energy coherence on a monitoring device or computer. But mostly opening your heart will require trusting yourself to survive the journey and the universe to support your quest.

CHAPTER 23

Psychokinesis, Healing, and Manifestation

Since this book has focused extensively on PK, healing, and manifestation, I think it would be good to summarize some of my thoughts here about these topics. Again, I now know that these three areas are all part of the same process or energy. Applying the same principles of intent, energy, and an open heart, works for all three phenomena. Each has a bit different set of characteristics, advantages, and challenges.

Psychokinesis: One of the characteristics of PK is that results tend to be seen immediately and this can provide an excellent advantage for feedback purposes. This is particularly useful when consciously attempting a PK task. It is also very useful if one is attempting to quantify or measure results. For many PK tasks we can get a statistical read out of how the results compare to chance. One of the challenges of PK is that even considering that it is possible to do PK can be against conventional belief systems, both that it is all nonsense, and then if it is possible, that you have to be extra-talented (or extra-weird) in order to be able to do it. The next challenge is that many PK tasks involve working with inanimate objects which we usually don't have much affinity for and relationship with, such as dice, spoons, and light bulbs. So for PK to occur, we need to be careful to cultivate a feeling of relationship and respect in order to get into a resonant relationship with these objects. And this resonance with "things" may not be easy to achieve. Some of us might feel funny talking to a slot machine or car transmission, particularly in public, but I swear I have seen this work countless times for many different people. Another challenge is that PK can be negative (broken appliances from the thought of broken home). And finally PK can often be the result of unconscious thought and emotion and at times have unnoticed results. I may not be aware of harboring negative thoughts and emotions and when negative events start to happen, may attribute them to bad luck, bad karma, or to the universe picking on me. Also, if I have been in a great mood and thinking constructive thoughts, and good things happen, I might just think of this as good luck. By ascribing PK results to good or bad luck, in either case I miss the opportunity to learn that what I am doing is creating my reality.

I would like to address some of the findings in the PK literature to add to our exploration. From the literature we see that pinning down the true nature of PK is tough because what we discover will be based upon our belief systems. For example, the Russian literature suggests that the PK field extends to a distance of about five feet from the person doing PK. But the United States literature suggests that the PK field is unlimited by space and can extend across the world and perhaps further. These dramatically different findings are likely to be caused by the experimenters' belief systems. If we ask the research question, "How many feet does PK extend?" and feel that the answer lies somewhere between one and five feet, then we are likely to get an answer in feet. If we ask the question, "How far can PK extend?" and feel the answer may be a great distance, then our answer is likely to be across the world.

Here is another mind-bender about PK. It appears from the Princeton studies and others, that PK is not only independent of space but also independent of time. You can affect the experimental results in a PK study just as easily in the past or future as in the present. So if you tell a person to affect data that was collected by a random event generator a year ago, they can do this with as much impact as if they were influencing the data as it was being recorded. The key limitation here is that for this to work (influencing past events from the present) it has to be that no human being has seen the data yet. Once one human being has observed the data then no further influence appears possible. They have shown this by having a computer run the experiment and then storing the results for a year unobserved by anyone. Then after the year has past, they have a person attempt to affect the data into a non-random pattern via PK. After the person finishes their effort, then the data are pulled from the computer and observed.

I want to mention the topic of using PK to win the lottery. I have not won the lottery . . . yet. I think that using PK to purposely win a mega prize in the lottery is a very challenging PK task for anyone. It is not only difficult because there are so many possible number combinations and the odds of any one combination being the winning one are astronomical, but also because millions of people are sending thoughts to the same drawing for different number combinations to be selected. This establishes a very confused PK field. It is much like in Vegas groups when we had different people attempting to PK different numbers. We began to have much better results when the whole group focused upon the same numbers. I would love to see an experiment where a million people agree to focus on the same lottery number on a given week and we would see what would happen. I would not be surprised if that number came up as the winning number!

If you desire more information about PK, in addition to the books that I have already mentioned, *Conscious Universe* and *The Metal Benders,* there is a book that is an excellent summary of the field. It is called *The PK Zone: a Cross-cultural Review of Psychokinesis (PK)* by Pamela Rae Heath M.D., Psy.D.

You may be puzzled by the question, "If PK is real, why do most scientists ignore or disparage it?" The fact is that most scientists feel that PK is possible. But there is a highly vocal minority that insists, despite overwhelming data, that PK is not possible. They claim to be skeptics but they are not, in fact, open to objectively looking at the data, as a true skeptic would be. The most cogent and clarifying book that I have found that describes this often hostile debate between parapsychology researchers and the naysayers is *Science and Psychic Phenomena: The Fall of the House of Skeptics*, by Chris Carter.

I would like to finish this section on PK with my special guidelines, in case you would like to experience PK yourself.

Joe's PK Tips

I have found these steps to be very useful in
generating reliable and positive psychokinesis:

- Raise a very high and open-hearted energy by getting in touch with gratitude and praising yourself, all
others, and the universe. Appreciating the beauty of
nature and music can help take you there.

- Focus that energy by putting out a crystal clear intent
and then let the energy flow by letting go and surrendering to highest purpose.

- As you raise energy, focus, and let go, you may need
to clear any limiting beliefs and blocking emotions
that surface for you, such as fear, and lack of confidence.

- PK is results driven, so have an important purpose in
mind such as to demonstrate to yourself the power of
spirit expressing in the physical.

- Don't try to kill your ego but soften it by being playful and relaxed.

- There is a PK zone that is similar to the zone in
sports where one is energized, graceful, focused,
unselfconscious, and unaware of time. With practice
entering the zone becomes more and more natural.
Once you know how to get into the zone easily, then
PK becomes much more reliable.

- Find workshops, books, and friends that support
you in melting emotional and energetic blocks and
affirming your power and goodness. Inner Vegas
Adventure, MC², and SyncCreation are great ways to
be guided into direct experience with PK. The movie,
Phenomenon, with John Travolta and Kyra Sedgwick
portrays what it might be like to have advanced PK

skills, and the changes and challenges that might
result from possessing this power.

- To motivate yourself to progress, see the benefits
of becoming skilled in PK extend beyond bending
spoons, toward healing self and others, and powerful
manifestation.

- Best wishes on your journey—it is truly a celebratory
one.

Energy Healing: From my experience, applying energy for healing
can have instant results about twenty percent of the time, results within
a day or two about thirty percent of the time, a bit longer perhaps ten
percent of the time, and no apparent result about forty percent of the
time. Under the "no apparent result" I would include that the identified
problem remains at least in the short term, but that the person's attitude
toward it becomes more positive, or other positive changes occur including insights into what might be the cause or what might need to change
in lifestyle for the problem to be resolved. One of the advantages of energy
healing is that is tends to be much easier to enter into relationship with a
plant, animal, or person, than in the PK examples with objects mentioned
previously. We can more readily use the natural compassion we have, and
our natural desire to alleviate suffering. This makes the open-heart part of
the equation much easier to generate. Perhaps the most difficult person to
apply the open-hearted compassion to is to ourselves. We may feel guilty
about having the illness, or because of the pain involved have rejected part
of our own body that has pain, as evidenced by using phrases such as "my
bad knee." We may have much fear that will need to be transcended, such
as doing healing while waiting for a biopsy report.

With dice and spoons it may be a challenge to have a strong desire
or the will to create the PK effect. With healing we may have too much
desire and find it hard to move from willfulness to willingness. Just as
with PK we have the challenge here of being unaware that our thoughts
and emotions are creating either a positive or negative effect, and we may
attribute what is happening to luck, or to "God is punishing us" or "God

is rewarding our prayers." I am not saying here that in either PK or energy healing that we are doing it all by ourselves. As you know, my view is that "All is One" and that we are in communication with essential forces when doing PK of any variety, including healing. And the essential forces that we may be in communion with, in my opinion, include God, grace, and spirits. In fact I actively affirm the presence of these forces and extend my gratitude for their assistance when doing healing.

Finally there is something about using energy healing for others that I am reluctant to call a challenge but it is definitely an issue. We are working with another being that has consciousness and free will. As we have mentioned, illness can have unconscious sacred purposes. When we enter into agreement to offer and accept healing energy, we enter into a sacred dance where it is best to send energy for highest purpose and to acknowledge that neither person in the contract can be absolutely certain what the best outcome will look like. Just as I did when finishing the section on PK, I would like to end this section by giving you some energy healing guidelines that you may find useful if you choose to engage in energy healing.

Joe's Energy Healing Tips

Energy occurs in the context of the entire person—body, mind, and spirit. The diagnostic and treatment tools of traditional and complementary medicine, high quality nutrition, positive environment, exercise, and psychological and spiritual guidance all may be powerful healing avenues. Please obtain medical attention if needed.

- Approach healing with unconditional love, defined as love-unbounded by the personality of the sender or receiver. This opens the heart, unleashing the most powerful energy from which to do healing, and softens the ego which can restrict full energy flow.

- Healing can transcend time/space if one believes this is possible. There is no need to be in the same physical place as the recipient for healing to be effective.

- It is helpful for both the sender and receiver to affirm that healing can be instant and complete, or can unfold in the best way.

- Rituals such as a healing space and doing healing according to a methodology can be helpful in focusing intent and creating confidence, but are not essential.

- It is respectful to have consent. If this is not possible then I ask permission from my higher self to the receiver's higher self.

- While you may focus on a desired outcome, also affirm that the energy will result in this outcome or something better, as we do not know what is best for the person.

- Illness can be present for many sacred purposes including as a teacher, or as an imbalance that is being rebalanced. It has been said that the purpose of prayer is to cure illness but at times the purpose of illness might be to initiate prayer.

- In its essence, to do healing pull in strong earth energy into your heart and highest of spirit energy into your heart, so that you are grounded and expanded at the same time. Then ask permission, and affirm that you are willing to be a pure conduit for the highest healing energies for the person's greatest good. See the person in their finest health right now, then send loving energy by any means that seems right to you, such as through your heart or hands, and continue this sending for as long as it seems appropriate. There may be a sense of completion when the healing energy is sufficient to accomplish the amount of change possible at that time. Think of the energy as a catalyst for positive change in the person's life, and that it can trigger a continuing healing process for them.

- Another way to do healing is to be in the powerful balanced loving state described above and just think of the person in their highest, forming a resonance connection with them that can raise their energy into resonance with yours.

- For directing healing towards yourself the same principles apply, including surrender to highest purpose, asking for assistance, seeing yourself in ideal health, and being in loving relationship with yourself.

- The meditation materials and exercises in SyncCreation home study and workshops will greatly help you raise and focus energy. SyncCreation will also melt blocks to being a powerful agent for healing.

Manifestation: Using PK energy for manifestation can also have the characteristic of seeing results occur instantly. But in the case of manifestation versus PK or healing, it often does take a bit more time. Achieving a manifestation where you are dissolving a previous painful pattern and substituting a new positive pattern can take weeks or years. It can also take months or years for some dramatically life-changing patterns to manifest, particularly when they involve other people. For example, if you have been in a painful relationship and now want to manifest the ideal soul mate, many things might have to change within your personality and circumstances, including the healing of your previous relationship experience, so that fear and anger are melted. Then the timing needs to be orchestrated ideally by the universe for you both to meet.

An advantage of manifestation work is that for things that are important to you, the motivation to succeed is high. Another advantage is that often the universe cooperates with you strongly, if what you desire will be something that expands your growth and has positive impact on others. There is also the advantage that it is often easier to visualize just what success can look and feel like, particularly if it is something as concrete as a new car. As mentioned in MC² we do treasure maps that put in pictorial form just what we want to manifest. Often we receive reports that everything on the map has been manifested in a few months.

Manifestation work has its own unique challenges. First, you must have the concept of what you desire and that it is possible to achieve it. Remember the story of the fellow visualizing and then getting a lucrative job working just three months a year. First he had to expand his idea of work to include such a possibility. Another challenge can be to feel deserving of the positive manifestation. Here, think of becoming famous or wealthy, well beyond our past experience or the experience of our family and friends. Fear of change in any form is also a challenge because it presents us with the unknown and a divergence from our comfortable (or not so comfortable, but at least familiar) status quo. For manifestation to occur your desire has to be greater than your fear, and often the speed of manifestation relates to just how much higher your desire is than your fear. The issue of other people's agenda tends to be present more in manifestation work than healing work. When we become different or have an obvious run of great fortune, other people around may be more uncomfortable with the change, than if we have headaches and use energy healing to alleviate them.

Popularized by the movie, *The Bucket List*, people are making a list of things that they want to experience before finishing this incarnation. Being a teacher of manifestation skills, it is interesting to see these lists because they suggest what people would most like to create. While people often say in casual conversation that they would like to manifest a new car, house, etc., on their bucket lists, usually there are no such things. Rather, bucket lists include experiences such as running a marathon, or learning to paint. This indicates to me that experiences are treasured more highly than things. People understand that happiness and feelings of aliveness are more likely to be supported by experience versus possessions.

I wonder if this can be deepened further. How about considering qualities of being for one's bucket list and then making them the direct and clear target of our manifestation practice? Increased happiness, deeper unconditional love toward ourselves and others, greater trust, and many more life-enhancing qualities can be exciting manifestation targets.

For ideas on what to manifest at your bucket list level one can look to inspirational texts. As previously mentioned, Emerson defined a successful life as follows: "To laugh often and much; to win the respect of intelligent people and the affection of children; to earn the appreciation of honest critics and to endure the betrayal of false friends; to appreciate beauty; to find the best in others; to leave the world a bit better whether by a healthy child, a garden patch or a redeemed social condition; to know even one life has breathed easier because you have lived. This is to have succeeded."

The task is to translate this lofty statement into practicality. For example, a business partner shared with me that as a frequent traveler, he transforms his airport experiences from the usual hectic and hassled event by seeing to whom he can be of even small service, raising his own energy by helping others.

There are many sources for ideas for your deeper bucket list, helping you answer the query, "What would I really like to experience in this life?" Here is an example from *The Deserata* (desired things), a 1927 prose poem by American writer Max Erhman.

"Go placidly amid the noise and haste . . .
As far as possible without surrender
be on good terms with all persons . . .
Neither be cynical about love;
for in the face of all aridity and disenchantment
it is as perennial as the grass . . .

Be gentle with yourself.
You are a child of the universe,
no less than the trees and the stars;
you have a right to be here.
And whether or not it is clear to you,
no doubt the universe is unfolding as it should."

You are free in this incarnation to focus upon and create whatever you desire. There is nothing wrong with material things, but making a bucket list might lead you to even more fulfilling creations. You can use the techniques and principles that I have mentioned with a high degree of success for the gamut of blessings available to us during this precious physical life, including the deeper things such as increased personal happiness.

With all this talk about abundance I do not mean to imply that all circumstances of life are meant to be a bed of roses. Even roses have thorns. But we can use the same skills used in abundance creation to flow through the hard parts of life more quickly, consciously, and soulfully. Adversity can be a rich source for deepening our understanding and appreciation of ourselves, our loved ones, and of the world.

Just as I did with PK and healing I would like to end this section by offering some brief manifestation guidelines.

Joe's Manifestation Tips

- Before starting, invite your intentions to have surprisingly positive results. Be open to the delightfully unexpected.

- View the physical world as delicate and changeable— and the spiritual world as solid, strong, real, and constant. Spirit is the foundation from which to change the physical.

- Manifestation power is enhanced by energy. Raise a high energy through open-hearted gratitude, and praise yourself, all others, and the universe.

- Affirm that "I am in brother-sisterhood with all, I release all supplication and victim energy—I now grow up and claim my power."

- Being well-grounded is a key secret to strong creation. Bring your spirit *fully* into your body, suffuse your body with energy and light, encourage your body and emotions to speak to you freely, fully feel your connection with the earth, and receive her sacred energy—so that you are fully spirit and flesh at the same time.

- Form your goal. Visualize what would make your heart sing without being held back by limits. See and feel your dream as real right now, fully experiencing how good this manifestation will make you feel and how it will benefit others.

- Send your energy before you—affirming that synchronicity and intuition will take you toward your goal or something better.

- Detach from results with full trust that goodness will come to you and knowing that you are already are a sacred being to whom all good is available.

- Send positive energy to all others, seeing them in their maximum soul potential. Allow others to help and guide you. Be abundantly generous with yourself and others, and the universe will be generous with you. This includes being joyfully generous with your money, smiles, time, attention, and positive thoughts.

- Make sure that your desire to succeed is greater than your fear of failure. For example, are you are more afraid of being jobless than you desire the best job in the universe for you? Fear truly is a prayer for what you do not want. Remember: Fear is expensive and love is priceless—choose wisely.

- Fear in all its forms, from procrastination, boredom, doubt, cynicism, impatience, self-criticism, laziness, etc. can be very challenging to release especially if it is held in life-long patterns. Use meditation, friends, coaches, and workshops to help you identify and release these limits.

- Refresh your energy and repeat your visualizations organically when it feels right. Obsessing about this through over-repetition implies lack of trust and is counterproductive.

- Happy Manifesting!

I want to share one final story with you because it shows well the dance between our thoughts and outcomes, and illustrates the power of the heart. This story happened fairly early on in my journey when I made a strong request to the universe to help me become more aware of how my thinking affected reality. Be careful what you ask of the universe!

I was booking a trip to Las Vegas where for the first time in my life I was going to fly first class. Because of my previous play at the casino I was being given a free room for the first time. I was very excited about the trip and had just two small niggling worries. They were: "I wonder how they will treat an old hippy like me in first class?" and, "I wonder what kind of hotel room they will give me for free?"

I dressed in nice slacks and sport jacket to go on my journey. My plane was late. When I boarded the plane at my small town airport for the short hop to Charlotte to catch the big jet to Vegas, there was someone in my first class seat. I smiled and showed him my boarding pass which was 1B. I said, "Excuse me sir, I have 1B." He frowned disapprovingly at me and flipped his boarding pass at me, like he was flipping me the bird, and grumbled "I do too," and then quickly looked back at his newspaper. I went to the flight attendant and told her that someone was in my assigned seat. She said testily, "Oh, sit anywhere." I had never been treated as poorly in coach. The only seat available was right next to the grouch in 1B. When I settled in awkwardly next to him, I realized, "Ah, that is my fear-thought, "I wonder how I will be treated in first class" being manifested into reality. The next flight went fine.

I arrived feeling very tired at midnight Vegas time, which was three in the morning my time. I checked into the hotel and went up to my room which was on the twentieth floor. As soon as I put my bag down, I notice a terribly loud hum in my room. I said to myself, "Oh man, I can't sleep with this." I called down to the front desk. They sent up a maintenance man who arrived about a half-hour later. He searched all around then went down to the basement, finally returning to say that he could not track down the source of the noise and that I would have to change rooms. I called down to the desk. By now I was beyond tired. They said that I would have to come down to get a new room assignment and key. I picked up my bag to leave the room and the noise stopped. When I had originally placed my bag down upon entering the room, the electric shaver in my bag had turned on and the bag was pressed against the wall which contained a heating duct that acted like an amplifier for the sound. This was the expression of my fear-thought: "I wonder what kind of room I will get for free."

I had a great trip and was now heading home. Having learned my lesson and having raised good energy during the trip, I was careful in my thinking. I was returning on a red-eye flight getting into my home town at about nine in the morning and going straight to work to see a full day of clients. As I was preparing to leave the hotel I decided to pattern for a great flight, "Universe, how about arranging it so that I sit next to the prettiest girl on the plane?" Yet I knew that I needed sleep and could not help myself from thinking, "I hope there are no screaming babies on the plane, I have to get some sleep." I boarded the plane and took my seat again in first class at the window 1D. No one was sitting next to me. I thought, "This is great, I have the row to myself." At the last minute before the door closed, a ravishingly beautiful woman came in loaded down with bags and with a screaming baby in her arms. She looked with embattled eyes at the seat next to mine. I had a split second to react, much like I did in the story of the Royal Flush in hearts with which I started this book.

On the plane at that moment I opened my heart. I turned to the woman, smiled and said, "Would you like me to hold your little one as you get settled?" Her expression changed to surprise and then softened. She became a bit misty-eyed in appreciation and said, "Would you? My husband said that they would kill me in first class. Our baby girl has colic." I said it would be my pleasure and took her infant gently. The baby stopped crying immediately and gazing into my eyes, she gave me a wonderful hug with her whole body. Perhaps she thought I was her father, I do not know.

After Mom got settled in, I attempted to give her back her baby, and the child immediately started to cry again. I took her back to me. I slept more peacefully than I ever have before or since on a red-eye flight, all the way across the country with the child sleeping comfortably on my chest. It was almost as if the universe, in the form of this innocent child, was loving me unconditionally. As I drifted to sleep I thought of the impact it would have on my life and the lives of others if I would just lead with my heart.

When we landed, the woman gathered her things. I handed her baby back and the infant started crying again, but this time softly.

I continue my journey, knowing that this book will have surprising benefits and send me on unexpected adventures. It has been helpful for me to write this book, for it has allowed me to see more clearly the tapestry that has been the previous two decades of my life. I hope in reading *Inner Vegas* that you have enjoyed hearing about my journey and that it has confirmed your highest thoughts about who we are and what we can do on this planet. If it has encouraged you to play with energy to create a better world for yourself and those you love, then my heart has been successful in expressing my passion for this work.

Epilogue

I started this journey feeling that miracles were rare and wonderful events. I felt mostly that we prayed for them and, if deemed worthy of such grace, a miracle might descend upon us. In this context, energy healing and PK seemed like miracles that might be quite difficult to experience on any regular basis. I now feel that we swim in a sea of constant miracles. They abound with such great frequency that we lose track of them quite easily. Now I am amazed on a daily basis by the common miracles of our bodies, such as the incredible grace of the human hand. I am more aware that we live in a world of technological miracle. Sometimes we get so jaded that we complain when our luggage is thirty minutes late after we have flown several miles high up in the air across the country within hours. Or we complain that our cell phone dropped a call, losing sight of the magic of being able to call nearly anyone on earth and be connected within seconds.

Everyday there are countless miracles of caring from one person to another. My wife likes to take what she calls her "goddess trips" to be with some of her closest female friends. On one trip they were basking on the Outer Banks in North Carolina and noticed a fellow struggling in the rough surf with its strong undertow. They sprang up, and running up and down the beach gathered people and dog leashes and formed a long human chain out to reach the man. The two people deepest into the ocean on the end of the chain closest to the drowning man did not even know how to swim. The man was pulled to safety, and back to his wife and children by strangers acting as one for his welfare. The story never made the news. And stories like this are occurring minute to minute on this planet every day. If you are aware that you are living in a world of constant miracle, then the miracles of PK, energy healing, and manifesting wondrous experiences become a natural part of who you are and what we do.

I found that without a doubt, the Inner Vegas Adventure workshops, MC², and the SyncCreation programs are all dynamic ways to nurture magic. As soon as we think we have a definite pattern for "guaranteed success," the pattern shifts, and always a new pattern emerges. Direct analysis and application (where the ego is awaiting the tried and true formula to produce cookie cutter results) often fails. This constantly reminds us that "we are the magic," not any formula that we come up with. Yet certain things work consistently. Success is bred through high heart energy, openness to intuition, and feelings of gratitude, joy, and abundance. This dynamic interplay between conducive structure and serendipity is what has made this manifestation and healing work so interesting and constructive.

Having been raised in a conservative Catholic family with parents who experienced the Great Depression of the 1930s, I was taught that risk was dangerous and mostly to be avoided. Hearing, "Oh, that is risky" about something was equivalent to "better not do that, you will be hurt." Through my learning in Vegas I have realized that risk is good. Risk is how we learn and grow and how we advance as individuals and society. I have also learned that, pardon my pun, risk is fraught with risk. This is because we were never taught how to risk wisely. And our natural abilities to accurately gauge levels of risk–reward are quite easily distorted by fear, other peoples' opinions and actions, and many other factors. But with better knowledge of the factors involved in the situation and better energy and attitudes applied, most risky situations can reward us very handsomely with something of value, be it money, experience, relationships, or new creativity.

Many natural processes move along in cyclical patterns. There are small up and down movements usually, and large swings occasionally. Relative quiet is followed by bursts of activity. Dice, slots, real estate, stock markets, weather patterns, health, personal growth, interpersonal relationships, creativity, job opportunities, etc., are examples of these cyclical phenomena. Some things occur randomly but very infrequently, such as pulling a royal flush or winning the lottery.

Because the game of dice and other PK activities give immediate feedback on quickly presenting patterns, I found these PK activities to be a highly effective way to learn about this rhythm of activity, rest, and consolidation. One needs to learn how to view short-term loss as part of a larger cycle, have patience, and be open to intuition. Real estate may move slowly for years then have thirty percent gains for two or three years in a row, then become quiet again or retreat. Stock market cycles tend to be a bit shorter. Personal growth also cycles. PK dice throwing can teach you to be content and accepting of the present moment and trusting of the cycle and your energy within it.

In the two decades of playing with PK another thing that surprised me is just how effective dice throwing in Vegas is to train a person toward more enlightened behavior. Classical conditioning in psychology relies on reward to increase desired behavior and punishment to extinguish undesired behavior. We also know that the closer the effect is to the behavior, the faster the conditioning. Conditioning results in very deep, stable, and automatic responses. With money on the table as the reward and the loss of it as the punishment, I paid careful attention. Conscious dice play conditions us very well in qualities and behaviors that are highly useful for an exciting and abundant life, as well as for spiritual advancement.

At the dice table I am instantly rewarded with money for the behaviors and attitudes that I want to manifest in my life. If I am happy, trusting, in high energy, and focused, I usually get paid at once. The useful life skills of intuition, discernment, awareness, emotional balance, letting go, knowing what is enough, and decisive action when appropriate, are often rewarded immediately at the dice table. And I am fined instantly for expressing attitudes that I want to extinguish. If I am greedy, fearful, unfocused, or irritated, the casino gladly takes my chips. Impatience, worrying about the past or future, fear of taking risks, greed, confusion, anger about loss, and many other undesired behaviors are punished swiftly. I am being psychologically conditioned (rewarded and punished) in the direction that I want to go.

I found that for me and most others, playing dice for money brings up real-world issues. And the craps table can be an ideal place to learn how to better handle these issues without having to risk our health, career, relationships, or retirement accounts. We can play with alternative approaches and viewpoints, get immediate feedback as to what feels and works better, and then practice our desired new behaviors and attitudes. Some of these issues are huge existential questions such as:

- What is our true nature and capacities as human beings?

- What is the reason that we are here?

- What will make us happy?

- How do we define what is a great life for us personally?

- What is our proper relationship to other people and to the larger world that includes other creatures and all of nature?

- What is God? How can we approach such an energy, and can we be in communion with God?

Other issues that surface at the dice table also impinge upon us as we try to live well in our greater lives. We can use PK activities to become aware at a deep level as to how we feel and operate with these issues, and also play with alternatives that may enhance our lives because the dice table and other PK challenges will give us clear feedback. These concerns include:

- Having trouble staying in the present moment because of worry about the past or future.

- Fears about the loss of money and concerns about how we generate money. We often don't want to work too hard for money but are suspicious about it coming too easily or being too much, under the cultural beliefs such as, "Nothing good comes easy," "Easy come easy go," and "Filthy rich."

- Most of us have issues with personal power and how much power is okay to have and to use. We may have fear that we will abuse power or harbor wounds from others abusing their power over us. PK represents unknown power and we often fear the unknown.

- We can apply our skills learned with PK to other more important areas of our lives, to financial investments, to relationships and health, and to personal growth for spiritual advancement and joy.

APPENDIX 1

SyncCreation®

After training MC² programs at the Monroe Institute, it was apparent that it was a transformational program with a high degree of benefit for its participants. This inspired me to create a home study version of this course so that people could learn psychokinesis, healing, and manifestation at home. I called this program, *SyncCreation®: A Course in Manifestation.* The reasons for a home study course were two-fold: accessibility and support.

First, I wanted to make the content of MC² accessible to more people. There were some fairly high barriers for many to attend MC². As a TMI graduate residential program, people were first required to attend TMI's Gateway Voyage program. As I have mentioned earlier in this book, I feel that Gateway is an absolutely wonderful experience. And Gateway prepared people well for MC² by teaching them the basic TMI meditation tools and providing them experience with expanding their consciousness. But this meant that people needed to devote two weeks away from family and job to attend MC², including the required Gateway. For many people this amount of time away is a more significant barrier than the expense. It is well worth it, but not everyone could do it. Associated with the two programs also is the cost which is approximately $2,000 per program as of this writing including rooms and meals, plus the cost of airfare. Again, it is well worth the cost but a significant barrier to many people. For someone just starting out in their exploration of consciousness and not used to apportioning significant time and money to the endeavor, I felt we needed a shorter rung on the ladder to step up and get started.

SyncCreation was also designed to be an at-home support for graduates of MC² because I feel strongly that exploring and experiencing more of our human potential is a life-long journey. Free from the limits of how much material could be presented and participants could absorb in a week, home study also allowed the opportunity to add more content. Using home study, people have the opportunity to learn at their own pace and revisit the content that was challenging or particularly helpful to them. I have mentioned, for example, that in MC² we do exercises designed as effective tools to reduce negative aspects of the shadow such as feelings of fear, lack, and guilt. These types of energies often need to be softened and healed over a period of time. These issues may present into awareness like layers of an onion, to be looked at a portion at a time and healed. Then the new insights and energies released through the healing need time to be integrated into the person's personality and consciousness. Then one might be ready to deal with another layer. And as people move forward in their manifesting, new challenges in these areas arise. The new career or relationship, along with excitement and satisfaction brings new issues to deal with.

In designing the SyncCreation home study course I included all the lecture content and significant meditation exercises from MC². Plus I was able to add more material and exercises on important aspects such as grounding, and go into more depth on critical topics than is possible in a week's time in MC². All of the PK tasks from MC² are included: Dice, seed growing, metal bending, and light bulb lighting. Dice, seeds and a heavy spoon and fork come with SyncCreation along with instructions about obtaining the proper light bulb. The focus in SyncCreation on PK, healing, and manifestation is the same as in MC².

One thing that I felt would be an excellent addition to the course would be to offer individual coaching or mentoring sessions for participants. As of this writing SyncCreation comes with three sessions on the phone or by email, with a coach who is well versed in SyncCreation and very skilled at tailoring the course to a person's individual needs, interests, and issues. The coaching component has turned out to be hugely beneficial in several ways. It offers encouragement and emotional support along the journey. Often people are very excited about just having someone to share their victories in manifestation and healing with. Many times family, friends, and co-workers may not be very approachable. The experiences one has when studying these subjects may seem "too far out" to share freely in one's circle. Having a coach really helps break up any road blocks to progress whether external or internal. It is often hard to see our own blind spots and to break things down into smaller but significant steps to reach our goals without being side-tracked by distractions or impasses.

To replace some of the excitement and support of the group that occurs in MC², SyncCreation encourages participants to find an energy buddy to take the course with. As I have mentioned previously the energy buddy is a concept I developed for the Inner Vegas Adventures. I have found that is useful to have a "buddy" to help each person navigate intense energetic waters. A buddy can help you stay focused on your goals, help you process anything that comes up within beliefs or emotions, help you get grounded if needed, and celebrate your victories. Also with SyncCreation we provide the opportunity for web-based interaction with other participants via social media. A SyncCreation student can post that they would like help with selling a house, with healing, or with bending their spoon, and other students reading the post can send energy to them to help with their manifestation.

In SyncCreation I decided to use Hemi-Sync once again as the chief meditation aide because it works so well. In cooperation with Monroe Products and incorporating the things we were learning in the first few years of doing MC², I designed twelve custom Hemi-Sync exercises just for SyncCreation. They are suitable for someone with no meditation or TMI experience and also for people who already have extensive experience with Hemi-Sync. They contain most of the favorite exercises from MC² and add a few new ones, such as one that guides a person in metal bending while in a deep meditative state. If SyncCreation was to be successful at teaching people to the same depth as Inner Vegas Adventure and MC², it needed to be highly experiential, so that people could actually feel what these PK events are like and to know that they could do them themselves. To do this, the person would have to be able to raise and focus energy in a very advanced way. Hemi-Sync is terrific at enabling a person with no meditation experience to rapidly access the energy and states of consciousness needed for PK. Without such a rapidly acting, non-dogmatic tool for changing consciousness, progress in PK would be much more daunting.

It might take years to learn the meditation techniques that would result in being able to do PK with some consistency.

I am happy to say that *SyncCreation: a Course in Manifestation* has fulfilled its mission. Many hundreds of people have taken the course since its inception. We found that people were able to experience everything that we were experiencing in MC², and have used SyncCreation to support their continued growth. I listed some of the wonderful results of SyncCreation in Chapter One of this book, so I will not repeat them here. There is additional information on my website, www.SyncCreation.com, for those interested in learning more.

After the home study course was out for a few years, due to demand, I developed workshop versions of SyncCreation, spanning from a one-day version to give people a taste of the material, to a full length six-day version. The longer version gives people an opportunity to experience much of what we do in MC², without the need to first take TMI's Gateway program. We have offered this program in many countries. In Europe we often offer the program bilingually both in English and the native language, working through a translator. As I am writing this book the SyncCreation materials are being translated into Japanese for workshops to occur there.

I have produced a CD with an exercise called Manifesting with Hemi-Sync based on the principles we have discussed in this book that is currently available both in English and Japanese. Two other CD's are in process to be produced this year. One is called Liquid Luck which is a guided meditation to create wonderfully lucky days whenever one desires. In beta testing, people have just read the script and then immediately won jackpots on slot machines. Another Hemi-Sync CD called Partners is being produced, bringing these principles to bear for enhancing relationships.

"PRINCETON'S PEAR LABORATORY TO CLOSE"

"The Princeton Engineering Anomalies Research (PEAR) program at Princeton University, internationally renowned for its extensive study of the influence of the mind on physical reality, will be completing its agenda of basic research and closing its physical facilities at the end of February (1997).

"The purpose of the program, established in 1979 by Robert G. Jahn, an aerospace scientist who was then dean of the University's School of Engineering and Applied Science, was "to study the potential vulnerability of engineering devices and information processing systems to the anomalous influence of the consciousness of their human operators." The research was funded by gifts from Princeton alumni James S. McDonnell, patriarch of the McDonnell Douglas Aerospace empire, Laurance Rockefeller, Donald C. Webster, and by numerous other philanthropic benefactors.

"Jahn and his colleague, Brenda Dunne, a developmental psychologist from the University of Chicago who has served throughout as PEAR's laboratory manager, together with other members of their interdisciplinary research staff, have focused on two major areas of study: anomalous human/machine interactions, which addresses the effects of consciousness on random physical systems and processes; and remote perception, wherein people attempt to acquire information about distant locations and events. The enormous databases produced by PEAR provide clear evidence that human thought and emotion can produce measurable influences on physical reality. The researchers have also developed several theoretical models that attempt to accommodate the empirical results, which cannot be explained by any currently recognized scientific model.

"'We have accomplished what we originally set out to do 28 years ago, namely to determine whether these effects are real and to identify their major correlates. There are still many important questions to be addressed that will require a coordinated interdisciplinary approach to the topic, but it is time for the next generation of scholars to take over,' Jahn and Dunne said.

"Their future plans involve oversight of the International Consciousness Research Laboratories (ICRL), a non-profit organization established in 1996 to promote quality research, educational initiatives, and practical applications of consciousness-related anomalies *www. icrl.org*. The members of ICRL represent some twenty countries and a broad range of professional backgrounds, and most have had some association with the PEAR program in the past. Jahn and Dunne currently serve as advisers to Psyleron, *www.Psyleron.com*, a Princeton, NJ-based enterprise that produces a line of state-of-the-art technology to enable public exploration of human/machine anomalies. They will both also continue to serve as Officers of the Society for Scientific Exploration: *www. ScientificExploration.org*.

"More than fifty publications are available on the PEAR website, and Jahn and Dunne's textbook, *Margins of Reality: The Role of Consciousness in the Physical World* (Harcourt, 1987) has been in print for nearly twenty years. As part of their extensive archiving efforts, Jahn and Dunne have recently prepared a 150-page anthology of those PEAR publications pertinent to the burgeoning fields of complementary and alternative medicine, for a special issue of *Explore: The Journal of Science and Healing*, edited by Dr. Larry Dossey, which is currently in press. An educational DVD/CD set entitled *The PEAR Proposition*, produced by Strip Mind Media, offers a comprehensive overview history and accomplishments of the laboratory is also available, and can be obtained on-line from the ICRL website at *www.icrl.org*."

Bibliography

Websites

www.heartmath.org. For the Institute of Heart Math.

www.Hemi-Sync.com. For Monroe Products Hemi-Sync exercises by download and on CD.

www.icrl.org. For International Consciousness Research Laboratories, successors to Princeton Engineering Anomalous Research lab (PEAR)

www.InnerVegas.com. For the book, *Inner Vegas: A story of Miracles, Healing and Heart.*

www.MonroeInstitue.org. For the Monroe Institute's residential programs and research activities.

www.noetic.org. For the Institute for Noetic Sciences (IONS).

www.Psyleron.com. For products that explore psychokinesis.

www.scientificexploration.org. For the Society of Scientific Exploration

www.SyncCreation.com. The author Joe Gallenberger's website for information about his products and services including the SyncCreation Home study course, SyncCreation workshops and the Inner Vegas Adventure workshops.

Books

Richard Bartlett, *The Physics of Miracles: Tapping in to the Field of Consciousness Potential* (Hillsboro, OR: Atria Books/Beyond Words, 2010).

Itzhak Bentov, *Stalking the Wild Pendulum: on the Mechanics of Consciousness* (Rochester, VT: Destiny Books, 1988).

Peter L. Bernstein, *Against the Gods: The Remarkable Story of Risk* (New York: John Wiley & Sons, 1996).

Gregg Braden, Ph.D., *Deep Truth: Igniting the Memory of Our Origin, History, Destiny, and Fate* (Carlsbad, CA: Hay House, 2011).

Jack Canfield and Mark Hansen, *Chicken Soup for the Soul* (Deerfield Beach, FL: Health Communication, Inc. 1993).

Chris Carter, *Science and Psychic Phenomena: The Fall of the House of Skeptics* (Rochester, VT: Inner Traditions, 2012).

Carlos Castenda, *The Teachings of Don Juan: A Yaqui way of Knowledge* (Berkeley, CA: University of California Press, 3rd edition, May, 2008).

Paulo Coelho, *The Pilgrimage: A Contemporary Quest of Ancient Wisdom* (San Francisco, CA: HarperCollins Publishers Inc., 1992).

Paul Dong, Thomas Rafill, and Karen Kramer Ph.D., *China's Super Psychics* (Cambridge, MA: Marlowe & Company; October 1997).

Joseph Gallenberger, Ph.D., *Brothers Forever: An Unexpected Journey Beyond Death* (Charlottesville, VA: Hampton Roads Publishing Company, 1996).

Elizabeth Gilbert, *Eat Pray Love: One Woman's Search for Everything Across Italy, India, and Indonesia* (New York: Penguin Books, 2007).

Malcolm Gladwell, *Blink: The Power of Thinking without Thinking* (New York: Back Bay Books, 2007).

Malcolm Gladwell, *The Tipping Point: How Little Things can Make a Big Difference* (New York: Little, Brown and Company, 2000).

John Hasted, *The Metal-Benders* (London: Routledge & Kegan Paul Ltd., 1981).

Pamela Rae Heath M.D., Psy.D., *The PK Zone: A Cross-cultural Review of Psychokinesis (PK)* (New York: iUniverse, Inc., 2003).

Robert G. Jahn and Brenda Dunne, *Margins of Reality: The Role of Consciousness in the Physical World* (New York: Harcourt, 1987).

Serge King, Ph.D., *Urban Shaman: A Handbook for Personal and Planetary Transformation Based upon the Hawaiian Way of the Adventurer* (New York: Simon & Schuster, 1990).

Bruce Lipton, *The Biology of Belief: Unleashing the Power of Consciousness, Matter and Miracles*, (Santa Rosa, CA: Mountain of Love/Elite Books, 2005).

Richard Madaus, *Think Logically, Live Intuitively: Seeking the Balance* (Charlottesville, VA: Hampton Roads Publishing Company, 2005).

Rosalind McKnight, *Cosmic Journeys: My Out-of-Body Explorations with Robert A. Monroe* (Charlottesville, VA: Hampton Roads Publishing Company, 1999).

Joseph McMoneagle, *Mind Trek* (Charlottesville, VA: Hampton Roads Publishing Company, 1994).

Joseph McMoneagle, *Remote Viewing Secrets: A Handbook* (Charlottesville, VA: Hampton Roads Publishing Company, 2000).

Lynne McTaggart, *The Field: The Quest for the Secret Force in the Universe.* (New York: Harper Collins, 2002).

Robert Monroe, *Far Journeys* (New York: Doubleday, 1985).

Caroline Myss, *Energy Anatomy: The Science of Personal Power, Spirituality and Health* (CDs, Sounds True, Inc. 2001).

Dean Radin, Ph.D., *The Conscious Universe: The Scientific Truth of Psychic Phenomena* (San Francisco, CA: HarperCollins Publishers Inc., 1997).

Dean Radin, Ph.D., *Entangled Minds: Extrasensory Experiences in a Quantum Reality* (New York: Paraview Books/Pocket Books, 2006).

David G Schwartz, *Roll the Bones: the History of Gambling* (New York: Gotham Books, 2006).

David Spangler, *Everyday Miracles: The Inner Art of Manifestation* (New York: Bantam Books, 1996)

Jill Bolte Taylor, Ph.D., *My Stroke of Insight: A Brain Scientist's Personal Journey* (New York: Viking, 2008).

Three Initiates, *The Kybalion* (New York: Tarcher/Penguin, 2008)

Eckhart Tolle, *The Power of Now: A Guide to Spiritual Enlightenment* (Navato, CA: New World Library, 2004).

Peter Tomkins and Christopher Bird, *The Secret Life of Plants* (New York: Harper Perennial, 1989).

John Welwood, *Journey of the Heart: Intimate Relationship and the Path of Love* (New York: HarperCollins Publishers Inc., 1990).

About the Author

Dr. Joe Gallenberger is a clinical psychologist with 30 years experience as a therapist. He has a great interest in human potential, especially in how we can manifest our dreams. In 1995 Dr. Gallenberger began exploring psychokinesis, the ability to influence matter through non-physical means. After achieving powerful results at a university laboratory, he began to teach this skill to groups. He has used his discoveries to host over sixty *Inner Vegas Adventures*™, which take participants on a fascinating journey into personal power. His students achieve dramatic physical and psychological healing, strong influence over dice and slot machines, and many desired manifestations in their personal and professional lives.

Dr. Gallenberger offers a variety of programs, described on his web site, *www.SyncCreation.com* to help individuals and businesses become more joyous and productive. A dynamic, heart-driven speaker, Dr. Gallenberger is in demand internationally as a workshop presenter on topics such as psychokinesis, healing, and manifestation. He is also a senior trainer at the Monroe Institute. The Monroe Institute's founder, Robert Monroe was a pioneer in consciousness exploration. Dr. Gallenberger trains a spectrum of Monroe programs and developed the Institute's highly successful *MC²* (Manifestation and Creation Squared) program that teaches psychokinesis, healing, and manifestation. Dr. Gallenberger also developed *SyncCreation®: a Course in Manifestation*, which is the home study version of the MC² program.

He lives with his wife, Elena, in the Blue Ridge Mountains of western North Carolina.

For more information visit Dr. Gallenberger's website: *www. SyncCreation.com.*

Related Titles

If you enjoyed *Inner Vegas*, you may also enjoy other Rainbow Ridge titles. Read more about them at *www.rainbowridgebooks.com*

The Cosmic Internet: Explanations from the Other Side
by Frank DeMarco

Conversations with Jesus: An Intimate Journey
by Alexis Eldridge

Dialogue with the Devil: Enlightenment for the Unwilling
by Yves Patak

The Divine Mother Speaks: The Healing of the Human Heart
by Rashmi Khilnani

Difficult People: A Gateway to Enlightenment
by Lisette Larkins

When Do I See God: Finding the Path to Heaven
by Jeff Ianniello

Dance of the Electric Hummingbird
by Patricia Walker

Coming Full Circle: Ancient Teachings for a Modern World
by Lynn Andrews

Thank Your Wicked Parents
by Richard Bach

Hemingway on Hemingway: Afterlife Conversations on His Life, His Work and His Myth
by Frank DeMarco

The Buddha Speaks: To the Buddha Nature Within
by Rashmi Khilnani

*Consciousness: Bridging the Gap Between Conventional Science
and the New Super Science of Quantum Mechanics*
by Eva Herr

Messiah's Handbook: Reminders for the Advanced Soul
by Richard Bach

Blue Sky, White Clouds
by Eliezer Sobel

Rainbow Ridge Books publishes spiritual and metaphysical titles, and is
distributed by Square One Publishers in Garden City Park, New York.

To contact authors and editors, peruse our titles, and see submission
guidelines, please visit our website at *www.rainbowridgebooks.com.*

For orders and catalogs, please call toll-free: (877) 900-BOOK.